Dismantling the Disabling Environments of Education

Disability Studies in Education

Susan L. Gabel and Scot Danforth
General Editors

Vol. 24

The Disability Studies in Education series is part of the Peter Lang Education list.
Every volume is peer reviewed and meets
the highest quality standards for content and production.

PETER LANG
New York • Bern • Berlin
Brussels • Vienna • Oxford • Warsaw

Dismantling the Disabling Environments of Education

Creating New Cultures and Contexts for Accommodating Difference

edited by
Peter Smagorinsky,
Joseph Tobin,
and Kyunghwa Lee

PETER LANG
New York • Bern • Berlin
Brussels • Vienna • Oxford • Warsaw

Library of Congress Cataloging-in-Publication Data

Names: Smagorinsky, Peter, editor. | Tobin, Joseph Jay, editor. |
Lee, Kyunghwa, editor.
Title: Dismantling the disabling environments of education: creating new cultures and contexts for accommodating difference / edited by Peter Smagorinsky, Joseph Tobin & Kyunghwa Lee.
Description: New York: Peter Lang, 2019.
Series: Disability studies in education; vol. 24 | ISSN 1548-7210
Includes bibliographical references and index.
Identifiers: LCCN 2018058158 | ISBN 978-1-4331-6316-6 (hardback: alk. paper)
ISBN 978-1-4331-6315-9 (paperback: alk. paper)
ISBN 978-1-4331-6361-6 (ebook pdf)
ISBN 978-1-4331-6362-3 (epub) | ISBN 978-1-4331-6363-0 (mobi)
Subjects: LCSH: Children with disabilities—Education.
Special education.
School environment.
Classification: LCC LC4015.D548 2019 | DDC 371.9—dc23
LC record available at https://lccn.loc.gov/2018058158
DOI 10.3726/b14873

Bibliographic information published by **Die Deutsche Nationalbibliothek**.
Die Deutsche Nationalbibliothek lists this publication in the "Deutsche Nationalbibliografie"; detailed bibliographic data are available on the Internet at http://dnb.d-nb.de/.

The paper in this book meets the guidelines for permanence and durability of the Committee on Production Guidelines for Book Longevity of the Council of Library Resources.

29 Broadway, 18th floor, New York, NY 10006
www.peterlang.com

Printed in the United States of America

Table of Contents

Introduction

PETER SMAGORINSKY, JOSEPH TOBIN, AND KYUNGHWA LEE

This volume is situated within the contours of four related fields concerned with human variation. *Disability Studies* (DS) and its companion (and in some conceptions, its successor), *Critical Disability Studies* (CDS), are concerned with contesting the society-wide, debilitating assumptions about people who do not conform to conventional notions of able-bodiedness. *Disability Studies in Education* (DSE) and *Critical Special Education* (CSE) focus this compassionate view of human difference within educational institutions, both in classrooms and in the physical and institutional structure of the environment. Our work resides within what we believe to be a useful niche, that of teachers and teacher educators from diverse content areas who acknowledge the potentially disabling effects of bodily and mental diversity, without taking the pathologizing perspective of human difference prevalent in society and often in schools.

DS and CDS emerged from the humanities and have a discursive emphasis; that is, they tend to view textuality as central, and seek to shift the rhetoric of representation from deficit to asset. Many claiming a DSE or CSE perspective emerged from within the field of mainstream special education (MSE), yet reject its medical model of sickness and cure. Like DS and CDS, they embrace a positive, empathic view of students with special needs as people with potential requiring knowledgeable and deliberate cultivation. We enter this discussion from disparate research programs that have led to concerns for how people of bodily, cognitive, and neurological difference become viewed as lesser in human value.

We next review how we arrived from outside these established fields to find ourselves working within their general outlines. We provide this narrative to establish our own qualifications for contributing to a body of work with which we are not normally associated, yet which has proven compatible for the goals we have developed for making society and schools more humane and attentive to human diversity.

Our Pathways to the Field

Our pathways have been long and perhaps indirect. We began to develop our individual lines of inquiry before we ever knew one another or began to meet to discuss the overlap across our work.

Kyunghwa Lee and Joseph Tobin became colleagues in The University of Georgia's Department of Educational Theory and Practice in 2011, when Joe accepted a position as The Elizabeth Garrard Hall Professor of Early Childhood Education and relocated from Arizona State University. Through different channels, Peter Smagorinsky of the UGA Department of Language and Literacy Education became friends with each and learned that they had developed shared interests that might overlap with his. Our various conversations led us to begin to meet to discuss what we might have in common and how we could work together to advance our individual and collective understandings. We thus began inductively, talking about relationships across our work and that of our colleagues, rather than beginning by reading DS, CDS, DSE, and CSE and forming an affiliation deductively. Although we were aware of these fields in part, we had no intention initially of aligning our work with them. We thus began as outsiders who found common ground with extant work, even as we felt that our precise niche might require some adjustment and refinement.

Kyunghwa, a South Korean native, had been studying attention-deficit hyperactive disorder (ADHD) and had become interested in how behavior classified as ADHD could be defined differently in diverse cultural and historical contexts. She was particularly interested in examining how ADHD might reflect the middle-class, European American value on the individual, as is typical of mainstream special education's general Piagetian approach (Lee, 2008, 2010; Lee & Neuharth-Pritchett, 2008; Lee & Walsh, 2001). She found cultural psychology (Cole, 1996) to be a useful framework for adopting a perspective grounded in understanding cognition by first attending to the social surroundings of individuals, which led her to read Vygotsky and related sociocultural research. Paying attention to culture in general and today's U.S. early schooling in particular, she embraced the notion of social constructivism, which enabled her to articulate how the designation of one as disabled can go from a social construction to a cultural fact.

As a visitor to Joe Tobin's doctoral seminar on poststructuralism, she began to see ways of applying ideas of French sociologists and philosophers (e.g., Marcel Mauss, Michel Foucault) to investigate how ADHD reflects techniques of the body, a perspective known as *biopolitics*. She thus shares much with DS/CDS and DSE/CSE and their poststructural orientation. Her interest in social science applications through the sociocultural tradition and its materialist foundation, and her work as a teacher educator rather than a special education specialist, led her to broaden her interest in classification to classrooms in general, rather than classrooms designated as either special education or enrolling special education students along with unclassified students.

Peter's pathway to our collaborative was less direct. He began as a high school English/Language Arts teacher. His graduate studies were focused on researching ways of teaching writing, informed at the time by cognitive psychology. After graduating in 1989 and beginning his own university career, he gravitated quickly to the cultural-historical psychology developed by Vygotsky (1987) as a way to explain cultural variation in students' differential performances in school. This work sustained him for two decades of research in literacy and teacher education, until a personal and family crisis led to an understanding of his own, along with his daughter's, location on the Asperger's syndrome spectrum, with chronic anxiety, obsessive compulsiveness, and mild Tourette's syndrome also part of their makeup.

Beginning with an autoethnographic exploration of his family life (Smagorinsky, 2011), he read Vygotsky's (1993) volume on *defectology*, a much-neglected work within Vygotsky's oeuvre. This unfortunately-named field was founded to address the cognitively and physically impaired population in Eastern Europe following nearly two decades of revolution and warfare that produced the Soviet Union in 1922 (see Smagorinsky, 2012, this volume; and Smagorinsky, Cole, & Braga, 2017, for more specific attention to the role of human diversity in cultural-historical psychology derived from Vygotsky). These investigations led him to think about neurodiversity (Fenton & Krahn, 2007), an emerging field that seeks to eradicate the shame and stigma associated with neurology-based conditions such as being on the autism spectrum (Cook & Smagorinsky, 2014; Smagorinsky, 2016). His background thus shared Kyunghwa's attention to cultural psychology, yet from a different perspective and in relation to different sorts of educational and societal challenges. Rather than emerging from any "disability" field, he located himself within Vygotsky's cultural-historical approach, with extrapolations from Vygotsky's defectological writing—concerned primarily with blind, deaf, maimed, and cognitively impaired children injured between World War I and the establishment of the Soviet Union—to neurodiversity as presented via autism-spectrum personalities.

Joe came to our collaboration through his long-time immersion in studies of preschools across international contexts (Japan, China, France, the U.S.), grounding his work in the fields of anthropology, sociology, and child development (Hayashi & Tobin, 2014; Tobin & Hayashi, 2015; Tobin, Hsueh, & Karasawa, 2009; Tobin, Wu, & Davidson, 1989). This approach of doing comparative studies in culturally varied national contexts of a single aspect of schooling—preschool socialization and education—led to an appreciation for the ways in which national cultures socialize children and prepare them differentially to participate in both school and society. His work in these settings brought him into contact with a number of deaf children and adults, leading to an interest in how deafness and other types of difference are constructed and addressed in educational settings (Hayashi & Tobin, 2014; Tobin & Hayashi, 2015). With a background in poststructuralism, anthropology, and psychoanalysis, and with experience doing research in varying cultures and national contexts, he approaches people who identify themselves, or are labeled by others, as different with the intention of understanding life from their perspective.

He further locates his understanding of the educational needs of Deaf and other people exhibiting difference within the affordances and constraints of the larger society in which they live. Joe values both the discursive emphasis of DS/CDS and its poststructural foundation, and the educational mission of DSE/CSE, particularly as it expands beyond its differences with MSE proponents and becomes engaged with the broader challenges of preparing teachers to work with a full range of children across the curriculum (see Dudley-Marling & Burns, 2014; Gabel & Connor, 2014). He is especially interested in work on constructions of ability/disability conducted outside the North American/Anglophone cultural/political context, a broadening of focus encouraged by many scholars in DS/CDS and DSE/CSE. He thus saw our work group as a way to conceive of an alternative that incorporated MSE's attention to addressing the needs of learners classified as disabled, without compromising their social status by treating them according to a "pathology paradigm" (Walker, 2012) that assumes their deficiency.

Our conversations led us to set up a seminar series in the 2013–2014 academic year in which we met weekly to discuss shared readings among ourselves and with a group of graduate students, including some who were deaf or had deaf parents. Further, with both Kyunghwa and Peter acknowledging their own experiences with chronic anxiety, and Peter additionally having begun to write about Asperger's syndrome and obsessive-compulsiveness in his family and personal makeup, our meetings were especially attentive to discussing what are considered disabilities in nonpathologizing terms. This value took on an imperative as the group included deaf participants and sign-language interpreters, demanding attention to the diverse needs of those attending the sessions. This book embodies and extends those discussions.

Our approach thus springs from a seminar series, but is rooted in the various interests and experiences that brought our work together. We enter from different research programs and thus see our work as interdisciplinary yet well-integrated. Where we have arrived is consistent with the values of DS/CDS and DSE/CSE, yet informed by research programs not often associated with the established scholarship driving these areas of inquiry. Like these scholars, we challenge assumptions that view people classified as disabled or disordered to be "abnormal," that isolate attention to their difference solely in the individual, that treat areas of difference as matters of deficiency, and that separate people considered disabled or disordered from the mainstream and treat their points of difference pathologically. Each of us brought long disciplinary histories to these meetings that needed to be discussed and negotiated over time. Rather, then, than viewing our seminar series as a distinctive beginning, we see it as the convergence of ideas that were under development long before we entered the conversation, and that we hope to develop through this volume and beyond.

Epistemological and Theoretical Foundations

Within our purview we include attention to differences that are cognitive (e.g., "learning disabilities"), neurodivergent (e.g., Asperger's syndrome and ADHD), and physical (e.g., deafness). Our approach, rather than constructing people in terms of deficits, characterizes people with such classifications in terms of strengths rather than disabilities, and considers the social environments in which they live and learn as potentially either unresponsive and constraining or as supportive and enabling. In some cases, this environment is local, as in the immediate social surroundings of classrooms; in others the environment is more expansive and includes the policy context of overclassification of disability based on such factors as race and ethnicity. In other words, our approach reverses the customary frame of reference and shifts attention from the "disabled" and "disordered" individual to the disabling environment.

Sociocultural Orientation

We view ourselves as working within the sociocultural field that has contributed to the "social turn" that has directed and shaped much scholarship in the last few decades. Rather than promoting the tribalism that institutes a dominant culture's ways and means as ideal, this work seeks to understand how different cultural practices serve to promote different societal ends. From this perspective, societal norms are contested, and the whole spectrum of humanity is viewed as having potential for producing satisfying participation in a culture's practices. We use the term "spectrum" not to denote a linear order, but more as a non-hierarchical swirl of possibilities (see Burgess, 2016). Rather than going from left-to-right from severely affected to normal or ideal, the notion of a spectrum considers how one's makeup follows a complex, multi-faceted organization.

Our approach has roots in a Marxist perspective that is oriented to understanding the social environment of human development, one that is mediated by tools and signs. As school-based researchers and teacher educators, we are concerned with the material conditions of classrooms and other school spaces and seek to construct them to promote more inclusive possibilities than are typically available. This interest is realized in architectural modifications such as those available through Universal Design and its antecedents (e.g., Goldsmith, 1963, 1997), which have produced large and expensive affordances such as accessibility ramps, and small adaptations such as large, flat light switches replacing small toggle switches. Such features allow the greatest number of people to navigate the physical environment. This concept has extended into the Design for All and Barrier-Free movements that push manufactures to create adaptive and assistive technology such as computer options, wireless control devices, Velcro adhesion, electric toothbrushes, and any other products that bring greater agency and autonomy to those for whom conventional environments present challenges. The concept of Universal Design has applications beyond architectural considerations, in the way social spaces including classrooms can be organized to facilitate accessibility and inclusivity.

The goal of constructing material settings that enable greater social value and participation fits well with our approach. Our hope is that the potential of those classified as disabled and disordered may be more fully realized in spite of the problem that conventional schooling has been designed to accommodate the *normate* (Garland-Thomson, 1997)—the idealized able-bodied/minded person—much more than those who depart from its features. We thus share a rejection of the medical model of disability common in the diagnostic world. In that spirit, we avoid to the greatest extent possible terminology that pathologizes children and youth with disorders, disabilities, abnormalities, and other such terms. These terms are problematic and construct an ideological representation of deficit that positions people as socially inferior.

A Situated, Relational Approach

Our perspective emerges from conceptions of personhood that are relational, situated, and subject to development. This research refutes essentialized notions of personality that emerge from a lack of attention to context, and from limited observations of conduct in specialized settings (see Philips, 1983). It instead calls for studies of how people participate in a variety of social situations that may elicit different forms of interaction.

This understanding of personhood applies as well to conditions considered to be handicaps, impairments, disabilities, and disorders. In a pitch-black room, for instance, a blind person has the advantage over the sighted, a point illustrated dramatically by H. G. Wells in his short story "The Country of the Blind" (1904). The conditions associated with Asperger's Syndrome—also known as Asperger's Disorder—might be debilitating in some settings, but may serve as an "Asperger's Advantage" in academia, where meticulous attention to detail, the ability to recognize patterns, and the disposition to engage in sustained focus on seemingly obscure topics are assets (Smagorinsky, 2014). We thus share a concern that classifications such as "disability" and "disorder" are applied too broadly, and in essentializing and static ways. We foreground instead the whole of a person's value, when other relational and situational factors may draw attention to the same factors as strengths on which potential may be cultivated.

Disciplinary Location

We see teacher education as a field that ought to be more concerned with serving the whole student population (cf. Blanton, Pugach, & Florian, 2011). We thus are interested in how teacher education as a field can take cognitive, neurological, and physical differences into account when preparing teachers for diverse classrooms. Although we find MSE's attention to individual needs to be honorable and important, we are just as focused on the whole of the setting such that adaptations are required of all in the environment, rather than being the burden principally of those who are classified as deficiently different (Hall, Meyer, & Rose, 2012; Smagorinsky, 2016; Vygotsky, 1993). We are teacher educators who are concerned with what mainstreamed and inclusive classrooms might look like, not only for those considered disabled but for those who surround them who share the responsibility for establishing a setting of respectful inclusion. We thus are focused on how to address the beliefs and actions of those who surround the children and youth diagnosed as disabled or disordered, so that they become accepted as productive members of social groups and classrooms as they work toward cultural goals.

We take a social and cultural perspective that views the surrounding social environment as at least as problematic as any point of difference in any individual.

Our approach therefore is *contextual* (looking first to social mediation and second at individual makeup) rather than *individual* (looking first to the individual, with environmental factors of lesser importance). The scholars contributing to this volume feel that if the field of education is to address issues of inclusion among populations considered to be different from the mainstream, then studies of difference should be undertaken from multiple perspectives. Schools are typically organized to accommodate a very narrow range of human differences (Smagorinsky, 2017), and therefore unnecessarily produce conditions that position young people who do not fit the mold for failure more than success.

We lack the experience with MSE that most DSE/CSE scholars have, and also lack their first-hand frustrations with ideologies and practices that often accompany it. In a common rhetorical device among writers from DSE/CSE, their experiences in special education classrooms are reviewed to establish their authority in condemning common practices that are not visible to the uninitiated. Danforth (2005), for instance, relates the following:

> For anyone who has not been a student or teacher in an E/BD [Emotional Behavior Disorder] program—specifically, a school or residential center for students labeled E/BD—the feel and texture of such a social environment is difficult to imagine. I worked as a teacher for seven years in two residential schools and two "day" schools for students considered E/BD. I have visited and consulted with countless others over the past two decades. Although there is some degree of variability across setting, they tend to be strikingly similar. (p. 87)

We cannot begin to approach such extensive exposure to MSE classrooms or specialized programs for students designated for specialized instruction in academics or social conduct. We have, however, been part of other educational settings in which modifications for students with special needs would be advisable, not only in terms of wheel-chair accessibility and other high-visibility provisions, but in light of less apparent needs of those whose divergence requires an accommodating social setting. Many contributors to this volume work with future and practicing teachers, all of whom will need to construct their students as having potential rather than deficits to be overcome. University students who are preparing for careers as teachers are typically required to take a course in special education to inform their work in classrooms. This course might dedicate as much attention to "gifted and talented" youth as to those to whom disabilities are ascribed, and is rarely in dialogue with the core of a discipline's teacher education coursework and fieldwork. Rather, it is taught in a separate discipline as a one-off exposure to those considered disabled or disordered, who are often characterized in terms of their deficits in relation to a perceived developmental norm.

Preservice teachers and inservice teachers in graduate programs thus develop understandings about cognitive, neurological, and bodily difference in a discrete course with which disciplinary faculty are not in conversation, even as the celebration of diversity is woven into mission statements of virtually every college of education. Knowledge about educating students of anomalous makeups is thus outsourced to faculty in special education, often in a department out of dialogue with content-area pedagogues. This division of intellectual labor creates a problem for teacher educators who believe that their preservice and inservice teachers need to integrate the perspectives they are introduced to in their coursework.

Conundrums and Uncertainties

The issues addressed in this volume come in the midst of often-antagonistic disagreements over how to address difference in school and society. Frequently the issues are presented as a war of words, ideologies, and practices in a winner-take-all fight to the finish. We approach this work with acknowledged uncertainty, however. We next outline ways in which we approach the question of human diversity, and how to address it educationally, with as open a mind as we can, given the perils of all-or-nothing thinking.

Dousing rhetorical flames

Much of the discussion we find in scholarship from MSE, DS/CDS, and DSE/CSE is framed in confrontational, absolutist terms and inflammatory rhetoric. For example, according to the contributors to Gabel (2005), MSE imposes a hegemony of oppressive practices. In contrast, to MSE stalwart Kauffman (2005), the DS/CDS and DSE/CSE cause is harmful to children and society as a whole:

> As a profession, we seem unaware that we are in grave danger of being torched by public sentiment and that some members of our profession are fueling the fire. Our vulnerability is being worsened by postmodern rejection of scientific evidence. Maybe we are attracted to any kind of claptrap if it seems to be capturing the popular imagination, as postmodernism and deconstructionism are now doing. … The detonation of [Postmodern/Deconstructivist philosophy] in our profession leaves us with profoundly weak defenses against the glossy assertions of charlatans that they have discovered something miraculous. We become easy marks for those peddling junk science and other frauds. … [Postmodern/Deconstructivist philosophy] helps make us sitting ducks for the quack. (pp. 17, 20)

Kaufmann's rhetoric requires the reader to take his side or be considered a fraud and con artist. We have similarly found dismissive, exclusionary discourse in scholarship with which we generally agree. Our hope is that we can promote a sociocultural view without torching the integrity of those who believe something else.

Inclusion and exclusion

We are more conflicted and less sure than are many of our colleagues in MSE, DS/CDS, and DSE/CSE about many issues, at least as articulated in their publications. We are vexed, for instance, over the question of whether inclusion or separate programs provide the most supportive setting for students with Individualized Education Programs (IEPs) written in response to their physical, cognitive, or neurological makeups. Each has advantages and disadvantages, similar to the conundrum of tracking in schools. Viewing either inclusion or exclusion (or tracking vs. untracking) only in terms of its deleterious effects both romanticizes the alternative and obscures the potential of the targeted approach. We can see possibilities of success and failure in each, leaving us only with the unsatisfying conclusion that providing education for the full range of students in public schools is such a great challenge that it will inevitably fall short of idealistic goals and claims.

Theoretically, exclusion is highly problematic. In the teeming world of public schools, however, there will always be some students who require more attention than is possible in ordinary classroom settings. Moreover, as Valente and Boldt (2014) argue, programs created to serve neuro-atypical children sometimes can be more hospitable than mainstreaming. The ethical and educational dilemmas follow from the question of who decides which is best in which circumstance, and whose interests are served by these decisions. When schools are designed to suit the socialization patterns and bodily makeup of a mainstream population to the exclusion of others, however, the assignment of students to segregated environments as a way to preserve the integrity of a particular set of norms in regular academic classrooms becomes both likely and problematic from an equity perspective.

Anti-expertise pitfalls

We are also not anti-expert, as DS/CDS authors often are in declaiming the authority of those in positions to make judgments about those considered disabled, a perspective aligned with a broader rejection of knowledge and expertise in society (Nichols, 2017). We share the view that many "experts" can be insensitive and many lay people can have important insights, but do not see that likelihood as justifying the exclusion of the perspectives of people with formal knowledge and placing all authority in the hands of those who embody the conditions themselves. Rather, we see the need for broad-based collaboration in the work of providing education and other social spaces for the widest range of students and citizens possible. Eliminating points of view based on where they originate from seems to work against, rather than for, informed decision-making.

Who has the right to write?

Relatedly, we further find ourselves caught in the "right to write" conundrum, which is often invoked in writing about racial matters. Does a White author have the right to comment on, or embody in fictional characters, the Black population? In the world of people classified as disabled, this problem is articulated in Charlton's (1998) assertion, *Nothing about us without us*. As outsiders to special education, do we have the right to form opinions of, and then write about, its province in schools? Do we have the right to write about a field that might be considered the domain of others? We do not consider ourselves "experts" opining on the lives of objects of our research, yet might be constructed as claiming such a status by those about whom we write. Whether or not we have this right is surely a contested matter.

Ideals and material realities

We are concerned that some writings in the fields of DS/CDS and DSE/CSE tend to theorize away persistent problems that have material consequences for people classified as disabled and disordered and to be attracted to utopian solutions. We consider ourselves to be pragmatic, an orientation that requires us to set aside ideals and sentimentality to address the real consequences of different discursive and material environments on the process of mediating human development toward positive outcomes.

We are aware of the fact that in the actual conduct of schooling, difficult tradeoffs and choices must be made, especially during an era of continual defunding of public education at all levels (Underwood & Mead, 2012). Ideals are important for creating a vision for what might be possible, but cannot be met in practice in a material world of limited resources. We believe that better funding would benefit just about every aspect of education: teacher salaries, up-to-date technology, art and music programs, extracurricular activities, state-of-the-art science labs, well-stocked book rooms, safe and solid infrastructures, healthy and sanitary facilities, and much else. Doing so when taxpayers consistently vote against educational investment is not possible. This denial of funds and resources has an impact on what is possible in the realms of special education, faculty inservicing for inclusive pedagogies, physical accommodations for students requiring better means of navigation, and other areas of expenditure. We cannot ignore these realities and be taken seriously in the highly practical setting of schools and their administrators and faculty by speaking primarily in terms of ideals.

Related to this issue is the phrasing of "celebrating difference," which is much easier said than done, and ignores the fact that difference is the norm. Widely ranging difference is actually quite challenging to manage in most social groups, which can be tribal and antagonistic toward "the other" and outsiders in general. It's much easier to use celebratory slogans on posters featuring a group of kittens with various coloration and markings than to get a diverse group of people to work toward group ends. We find this romantic conception both deceptive and counterproductive to the difficult work of integrating diverse people into a single social organization.

Labeling

Another area of ambivalence concerns the matter of labeling students. On the one hand, carrying a label of disorder or disablement can be stigmatizing and demoralizing, and can lead others to view one as a lesser being deserving either scorn or charity. On the other hand, it can be helpful, as we can personally attest, to be given a name and a greater understanding of conditions that distinguish one from the majority of the population. Knowing that one is anxious, and what anxiety involves, can be useful in understanding one's response to the environment and in becoming strategic about managing it. But this knowledge can lead others to treat people according to the most negatively stereotypical of these characteristics. We simply do not have a firm sense of which approach leads to a more humane environment, a degree of uncertainty that we often find lacking in the rhetoric of the various "disability" fields.

Special education teachers are not villains

Our final point concerns the view of special education teachers. The rhetoric of critics of MSE often has a take-no-prisoners tone that includes practicing teachers among the hegemonic villains whose corrupt practices harm more than help children. In contrast, we have known and worked with many committed SE teachers who have followed the medical model of pathology, while also caring deeply about the children under their care. They often are far more flexible than the automatons we find characterized in critical scholarship, driven by a dedication to improving the life prospects of their students. Undoubtedly there are bad SE teachers; the news occasionally reports their abusive treatment of students (see, e. g., Eltman, 2016). Just as all teachers in the regular curriculum are not bad because some are incompetent, all special education teachers should not be condemned because of the actions of a few. Nor should they all be caricatured as oppressive because of the model in which they work, and may be required to work. We see those who work in classrooms—both self-contained and inclusive—as the best hope for creating humane environments, and seek to support them rather than assume the worst of them.

Conclusion to the Theoretical Framework

Addressing the diversity of the human condition is a task of such complexity that it should not be the province of any single group with an exclusive perspective. Rather, it is a highly collaborative challenge that benefits from the distributed expertise of its many and varied stakeholders. Ultimately, if we are anti-anything, it is anti-orthodoxy and anti-certainty. We offer our perspective tentatively and as a long conversational turn that invites response. We hope that we offer our vision with respect and sincerity. The task we set for the contributors to this collection is to respond to the conundrums we present in this introduction so that we collectively provide readers with an appreciation for the challenges we face and a reasonably coherent, if not necessarily consistent given the complexity of our undertaking, set of principles, and pathways. We next turn to how the authors respond to this invitation in the work that follows.

Introduction to the Collection

We have organized this collection into three sections: Theoretical and Historical Perspectives, Emic and Autoethnographic Perspectives, and Challenges of Inclusion and Practice.

The first section lays out the ways in which theoretical and historical perspectives guide our understanding of and attention to human difference in educational settings, including teacher education and classrooms across the school curriculum. We next present two autoethnographic accounts provided by scholars writing in relation to their experiences with blindness and multiple sclerosis. We then move to a section on how inclusive schools and classrooms, as alternatives to segregated settings such as those found in many special education programs, are challenging to implement. This section thus provides an understanding of how our conception eschews romanticized discourse of life's possibilities and attends more carefully to the difficult material lives that follow from even thoughtful and well-intended efforts to change the settings of human development and schools attempting to accommodate diversity.

Theoretical and Historical Perspectives

Curt Dudley-Marling opens the volume with an interrogation of learning disabilities (LD) as an institutional construct. The definition of specific learning disabilities (SLD) authored by the Learning Disabilities Roundtable (2002) asserts that "the central concept of SLD involves disorders of learning and cognition that are intrinsic to the individual." Locating learning disabilities in the heads of individuals leads to interventions focused on fixing students with learning disabilities, usually through the remediation of various cognitive deficiencies. An alternative, social constructivist narrative contends that LDs are constructed outside the minds and bodies of students in the complex web of human relations. The performance of a learning disability requires the specific actions of a group of people performing just the right moves at the right time and place, accompanied by institutional frameworks that assign particular meanings to students' behaviors that, in other cultural contexts, do not carry the same significance. That is, the extent to which one is learning disabled is not a function of hard-wiring, but is fundamentally relational and situational. Constructs like learning disabilities function to obscure the ways schools operate as agents of failure, and shift shortcomings of the system and the exclusionary pressures within it to students with little institutional agency. This problem extends to other population types whose potential is not realized in school settings, giving this chapter broad implications for diversity education in general.

Peter Smagorinsky then provides an account of the Soviet field of "defectology" and its antecedent conceptions in Russian special education. Defectology came into being following over a decade of steady, devastating warfare in and around Russia from World War I through the triumph of the Bolsheviks. This period produced a generation of deaf, blind, maimed, and cognitively impaired children whom the new regime hoped to rehabilitate in schools. Their "defects"—an atrocious term that remains both in use and indefensible—rather than being viewed as disablements, were viewed as aspects of their makeup requiring a special form of education, one that employed alternative means of mediating their acculturation to Soviet society. Inclusion and productive cultural participation serve as the goals for their development. The emphasis of this movement was largely social rather than being oriented to individual pathology, with attitudinal change toward human difference, and the elimination of deficit thinking, fundamental to its values. The field of defectology, founded in the 1920s, predates the Frankfurt School's pioneering role in the establishment of what has evolved into Disability Studies, Critical Disability Studies, Disability Studies in Education, and Critical Special Education, and provides an alternative pathway into understanding and acting on issues of human bodily difference. The chapter provides a review of this field's historical contributions and helps both to broaden the international composition of the various "disability" fields and add the dimension afforded by Vygotsky's contributions to the education of people considered disabled in school and society.

Emic and Autoethnographic Perspectives

Gina Marie Applebee opens this section by providing an autoethnographic inquiry into her life as a blind woman, relating how she has lived her life in and out of school. Her goal with this chapter is to challenge common conceptions of "disability," to help shift artificial barriers to integrating diverse abilities, to position blindness among other intersections that complicate any condition, and to bridge some of the rifts between perspectives on human difference. Within the context of her own emerging experience, she describes how apparent limitations can be leveraged to drive growth, resilience, and dynamic coherence both individually and socially, illustrating an emphasis on assets and potential rather than disability and disorder. As incredibly complex, self-organizing creatures, she argues, people carry an enormous capacity for adaptation and growth in response to challenges of any form in their systems and environments. She thus views adaptation from a personal standpoint, revealing through her experiences the sorts of transformations that she found possible while living in a world that she cannot see. Adversities have directly challenged her into developing different ways of perceiving, engaging with, and expressing herself in the world while also forcing her to become adaptable and resilient. Through this meditation, Applebee challenges notions of disablement and contextualizes them in educational settings, in the process enumerating the social and physical challenges presented by blindness that might be mitigated by a more understanding and responsive social environment.

Dottie Bossman shares her autoethnography of her experience as a teacher who developed multiple sclerosis. She uses this narrative to connect her life to those of students of anomalous makeups who are labeled, sorted, and treated as different from their peers in school. This hierarchical categorization often produces an internalized sense of deficit, constructed by others as disabled and disordered. The narrative describes the author's initial diagnosis and subsequent interactions with healthcare facilities and providers, events that highlight the distancing function of the traditional medical response to sickness. Experiencing this distancing function as a mature adult suggests to her the extraordinary challenge of being confronted in this manner by a child or youth. Although she resists her relegation from agentive individual to numbered case, she recognizes that her status offers her new insight into the experiences of students who have difficulty fitting in to conventional social settings. She views this problem as one affecting the whole school, rather than being confined to the special education wing. Contrary to the dominant perception that a chronic illness is a tragic development that must be reversed at all costs, this piece suggests that Bossman gained pedagogical wisdom as a result of her changing health. This wisdom can be of benefit to teacher educators who prepare teacher candidates across the school curriculum who either have made adjustments to their own health, or who teach classes in which students undergoing change or already dealing with change are enrolled. Understanding their emotional needs as well as their physical and cognitive needs contributes to the sort of supportive environment advocated across the chapters of this volume.

Challenges of Inclusion and Practice

Usree Bhattacharya next details her experiences with Rett Syndrome, following her daughter's diagnosis in early childhood. Her chapter explores her own family's confrontation with her daughter's diagnosis and her effort to understand how it would influence both their baby's life and the family's. These investigations led her to this review of the discouraging scholarship on Rett, which she found entirely focused on pathology. As a bilingual education scholar of Indian descent, she discovered a void in research on bilingualism or multilingualism on Rett-diagnosed girls, even though a significant population of these children grow up and experience the world in multilingual ways. Bhattacharya finds that virtually all Rett-diagnosed girls are denied a meaningful education because they are assumed to lack a worthwhile future. Her chapter both reviews the issues of this poorly-understood syndrome and raises questions about possible directions for both research and practice designed to provide more supportive environments for the development of children diagnosed with Rett Syndrome.

Christopher Bass writes from the perspective of a U.S. High School English teacher, the discipline encompassing literature (and other texts), writing (and other forms of composition), and language study (generally of "proper" English language expression). Bass assumes that educators would benefit from shifting attention from the individual to the setting of the classroom as a way to understand social dynamics as they relate to neurodiversity. In his public school teaching, he has focused on the setting of the classroom by including neuro-atypical voices into the narratives of the classroom so that the course material reflects the general diversity of his students. He situates his work as a school practitioner in a field that straddles the humanities and social sciences in the pragmatic setting of the public school, while also extending his theoretical conception through his doctoral studies. His teaching has included poems, essays, blogs, novels, and short stories by authors who identify as neuro-atypical and neuroqueer. This curricular expansion is designed to explore how neurodiversity can enable pedagogy that calls for inclusive attention to both students with IEPs themselves, and the environments, including their classmates, that define their capabilities and potential. Speaking to both teachers and teacher educators, he considers how classroom settings can be adapted to accommodate a greater variety of student makeups. Including neurodiversity in methods courses, he argues, can potentially disrupt assumptions about classroom settings and environments, often in contrast with the norms created in special education classes that are not aligned with Critical Special Education or Disabilities Studies in Education. His arguments thus simultaneously have implications for theory and practice in teacher education and in secondary school classrooms.

Kyunghwa Lee, Jaehee Kwon, and Jooeun Oh investigate young children's resistance to special education assignments in school, with a focus on a preschooler considered at-risk of being identified with ADHD. Behaviors such as having difficulty with transitions and being noncompliant tend to be interpreted as incidences of ADHD, with all of its pathological associations. Lee, Kwon, and Oh consider an alternative explanation: that noncompliant students are manifesting their unhappiness and discomfort with the requirement that they must shift to a special education classroom every day. Drawing on the work of critical theorists, they accept children's resistance as acts that defy teacher-and-school-defined boundaries of acceptable, sanctioned behavior, pitting themselves against powerful adults and their institutions. They argue that children's resistance, rather than indicating a behavioral disorder, contests adults' ability to organize sociopolitical environments that are potentially oppressive, a form of action that gives them agency and empowers them in determining what is best for them. Rather, then, than lacking self-control, these students are exercising agentic control in regulating both their emotions and their environments. The authors thus challenge conventional interpretations of childhood behavior that results in pathologizing assumptions and the school assignments that follow from them, asking: What are the aspects of the daily routines in his pre-K and SPED classrooms experienced by focal student Shantie that might have contributed to his resistance to transitioning to the SPED class? They provide a brief review of the literature on SPED placement from the perspective of children identified with disabilities, then report on their study of Shantie in ways that allow for their consideration of implications for the education of children with diverse needs and abilities.

Melissa Sherfinski and Sera Mathew follow the journeys of seven families that include autism spectrum children as they navigate societal borderlands that suggest a profound discomfort with atypical cognitive and sensory presentations. The authors interrogate how a culture of expertise promotes the idea that the challenges faced by autism-spectrum children are caused only by their points of difference. This assumption allows environments—particularly the mainstream classrooms in the educational system—to be liberated from accountability in promoting their welfare. In this sense, Sherfinski and Mathew locate their work in the perspective that "disability" is a contextual problem that can be addressed by changes in setting, rather than looking solely to the individual as the problem to repair. The authors focus their inquiry on the question, How do contemporary families of children with neuro-atypicalities navigate the culture of expertise in early childhood and elementary schooling? The authors find that intersectionality—the intersection of demographics such as race, class, and gender with neurodivergence—

is absent from much research. To help construct inclusive possibilities, they employ poststructuralist tools that enable them to explore subject positioning as a mechanism that shapes educational journeys. They move beyond the notion of the disabled individual in school and address the broader context of family involvement and school flexibility as sources of difficulty in engaging proactively with the world. The authors identify "constellations" of storylines that help illustrate the need to explore intersectionalities that provide nuance to the educational needs of neuro-atypical children, with special attention to the ways in which the expertise of diagnosticians and bureaucrats often is misapplied to children's and families' particular needs.

Jennifer Hensley, Patrick Graham, and Joseph Tobin report research that enables them to consider what deaf pedagogy can contribute to non-deaf early childhood education. The education of most deaf children begins with them being mainstreamed in general preschool classrooms or in an oral methods program for deaf children designed to transition them into mainstreamed, hearing-based elementary classrooms. A minority of deaf children attend a preschool based on Deaf culture principles, including instruction in a national sign language. In these settings, educators have developed pedagogical approaches and spatial arrangements that support deaf children's social, cognitive, and academic development. This chapter draws on research in signing preschool classrooms in France, Japan, and the U.S. to describe Deaf early childhood educational approaches and to argue that these approaches can inform educational practice in hearing settings, including special education classrooms that have historically relied on knowledge-and-skill and reward-and-punishment classroom management systems. The authors view Deaf signing education as a unique cultural approach to education whose processes are available through anthropological, ethnographic investigations that question conventional wisdom. They argue that key pedagogical and spatial features of Deaf early childhood education can also enrich classrooms serving hearing children, going against the grain of much inclusion research that tries to fit difference into settings established according to social norms. They assert that the concept of "inclusion" focused on educational placement in mainstream settings is challenging for deaf children, whose communicative practices depart from the norms assumed in classrooms and other social locations. This chapter asserts that attending to the whole of communication practices, which is required for the healthy development of deaf children, ought to inform how mainstream classes are taught.

Xiaoying Zhao analyzes the intersection of discourses of difference, children's school experiences, and disabilities. She presents a case study of Julia, a student who attended two schools in the U.S. under a disability diagnosis of

Obsessive-Compulsive Disorder. The second of these schools, she argues, did not attempt to "cure" her disability, instead seeking to reconcile it through the school's discourse of difference. In this manner, the school served as an asylum for her—not the "lunatic asylum" often associated with difference, but a sanctuary from educational practices that prove disabling when people do not follow anticipated norms. Zhao analyzes Julia's accounts of her experience at the two schools, highlighting discourses of difference at the two schools to better understand the intersection of the discourses of difference, school structures and experiences, and disability. Julia attributed her unhappiness at her first school to the way her OCD and distinctive personality were mismatched with the school's structures and her peers' modes of interaction, producing feelings of inferiority. At the second school, set up as an asylum, Julia thrived when she was allowed to learn at her own pace and her differences were acknowledged but not pathologized. She was not constructed according to what was "wrong" with her, but embraced as who she was and afforded tools to accept and cope with individual variation in her daily school life. Zhao argues that educational asylums should not be reserved for people identified with a particular disability, but instead should be open to all students who struggle to thrive in typical classroom settings.

Gail Boldt and Joseph Valente feature their research at L'Ecole Gulliver, one of four preschools overseen by the community-based organization A.P.A.T.E. (Association Pour l'Accueil de Tous le Enfants [Association for the Reception of All Children]) in Paris, France. They interrogate the challenges of providing an inclusive education, including those involving emotional struggles, resistances, difficulties, and aggressions inherent to working across differences. Their focus is on "disability" as difference. The A.P.A.T.E. preschools pioneered the acceptance of all children, regardless of their disability condition or chronic illness. Boldt and Valente focus on how the school deliberately acknowledges and responds to students' and teachers' feelings of anger, aggression, and defensiveness when they arise in collective activity. At A.P.A.T.E, a "collectivist integration" approach obtains, one that stands in contrast to mainstream French approaches to special education. In this approach, difference is not positioned as an individual trait, but as an effect of a group coming together, as a group's collective responsibility to work in ways that are functional and adaptive in support of the well-being of every member. Boldt and Valente are decidedly unromantic in presenting the challenges of achieving a harmonious social group composed of people of divergent makeup and socialization. This effort, they argue, can nonetheless enable those involved to work toward their potential as a function of collective living amidst difference and the challenges it affords.

Conclusion

We hope that this volume can contribute to the work of practitioners, researchers, theorists, and educators dedicated to providing more affirming and fulfilling lives for people across the human spectrum. These lives include not only those with atypical bodily, neurological, cognitive, affective, and other aspects of human makeup, but those who surround them, through the construction of more sensitive and compassionate social settings that foreground assets and potential rather than difference and deficiency. We hope to situate human difference so that attention to context becomes foremost in how anomalous makeups are understood and respected by others, with contexts viewed as malleable and therefore amenable to adaptation so that greater, more valued participation becomes available to the greatest number of people possible. As educators, we are committed to educating the broadest spectrum of people imaginable, including those who surround people historically considered disabled. By expanding attention to human difference to the conduct of those whose presence shapes perception and possibility for others, we hope to provide more humane environments whose benefits afford new possibilities not only for individuals, but for the social relationships and trajectories available to all.

References

Blanton, L. P., Pugach, M. C., & Florian, L. (2011). *Preparing general education teachers to improve outcomes for students with disabilities.* Washington, DC: American Association of Colleges for Teacher Education & National Center for Learning Disabilities. Retrieved June 8, 2016, from http://www.ncld.org/wp-content/uploads/2014/11/aacte_ncld_recommendation.pdf

Burgess, R. (2016, May 24). Comic redesigns the autism spectrum to crush stereotypes. *The Mighty*. Retrieved May 30, 2016 from https://themighty.com/2016/05/rebecca-burgess-comic-redesigns-the-autism-spectrum/

Charlton, J. (1998). *Nothing about us without us: Disability oppression and empowerment.* Berkeley, CA: University of California Press.

Cole, M. (1996). *Cultural psychology: A once and future discipline.* Cambridge, MA: Harvard University Press.

Cook, L. S., & Smagorinsky, P. (2014). Constructing positive social updrafts for extranormative personalities. *Learning, Culture and Social Interaction, 3*(4), 296–308. Available at http://www.petersmagorinsky.net/About/PDF/LCSI/LCSI_2014.pdf

Danforth, S. (2005). Compliance as alienated labor: A critical analysis of public school programs for students considered to have emotional/behavioral disorders. In S. L. Gabel (Ed.),

Disability studies in education: Readings in theory and method (pp. 85–102). New York, NY: Peter Lang.
Dudley-Marling, C., & Burns, M. B. (2014). Two perspectives on inclusion in the United States. *Global Education Review, 1*(1), 14–31.
Eltman, F. (2016, April 6). Attorney: NY school ignored abuse by special ed teacher. The Associated Press. Retrieved May 31, 2016 from http://bigstory.ap.org/article/9830562560dc-45c296e8ac88f1791b88/attorney-ny-school-ignored-abuse-special-ed-teacher
Fenton, A., & Krahn, T. (2007). Autism, neurodiversity and equality beyond the "normal." *Journal of Ethics in Mental Health, 2*(2), 1–6. Retrieved April 5, 2016 from http://www.jemh.ca/issues/v2n2/documents/JEMH_V2N2_Theme_Article2_Neurodiversity_Autism.pdf
Gabel, S. L. (Ed.). (2005). *Disabilities studies in education: Readings in theory and method.* New York, NY: Peter Lang.
Gabel, S. L., & Connor, D. J. (Eds.). (2014). *Disability and teaching.* New York, NY: Routledge.
Garland-Thomson, R. (1997). *Extraordinary bodies: Figuring physical disability in American culture and literature.* New York, NY: Columbia University Press.
Goldsmith, S. (1963). *Designing for the disabled: A manual of technical information.* London, UK: RIBA Publications.
Goldsmith, S. (1997). *Designing for the disabled: The new paradigm.* New York, NY: Routledge.
Hayashi, A., & Tobin, J. (2014). The power of implicit teaching practices: Continuities and discontinuities in pedagogical approaches of deaf and hearing preschools in Japan. *Comparative Education Review, 58*(1), 24–46.
Learning Disabilities Roundtable. (2002). *Specific learning disabilities: Finding common ground.* Washington, DC: U.S. Department of Education Office of Special Education Programs, Office of Innovation and Development.
Lee, K. (2008). ADHD in American early schooling: From a cultural psychological perspective. *Early Child Development and Care, 178*, 415–439.
Lee, K. (2010). Who is normal? Who is abnormal? Rethinking child development from a cultural psychological perspective. In K. Lee & M. D. Vagle (Eds.), *Developmentalism in early childhood and middle grades education: Critical conversations on readiness and responsiveness* (pp. 35–58). New York, NY: Palgrave Macmillan.
Lee, K., & Neuharth-Pritchett, S. (2008). Attention deficit/hyperactivity disorder across cultures: Development and disability in contexts. Special Issue. *Early Child Development and Care, 178*(4), 339–346.
Lee, K., & Walsh, D. J. (2001). Extending developmentalism: A cultural psychology and early childhood education. *International Journal of Early Childhood Education, 7*, 71–91.
Nichols, T. (2017). *The death of expertise: The campaign against established knowledge and why it matters.* New York, NY: Oxford University Press.
Philips, S. U. (1983). *The invisible culture: Communication in classroom and community on the Warm Springs Indian Reservation.* New York, NY: Longman.
Smagorinsky, P. (2011). Confessions of a mad professor: An autoethnographic consideration of neuroatypicality, extranormativity, and education. *Teachers College Record, 113*(8), 1701–1732. Available at http://www.petersmagorinsky.net/About/PDF/TCR/TCR2011.pdf

Smagorinsky, P. (2012). Vygotsky, "defectology," and the inclusion of people of difference in the broader cultural stream. *Journal of Language and Literacy Education* [Online], *8*(1), 1–25. Available at http://jolle.coe.uga.edu/wp-content/uploads/2012/05/Vygotsky-and-Defectology.pdf

Smagorinsky, P. (2014, November 26). Taking the diss out of disability. *Teachers College Record.* Available at http://www.petersmagorinsky.net/About/PDF/TCR/TCR2014.html

Smagorinsky, P. (Ed.). (2016). *Creativity and community among autism-spectrum youth: Creating positive social updrafts through play and performance.* New York, NY: Palgrave Macmillan.

Smagorinsky, P. (2017). Misfits in school literacy: Whom are U. S. schools designed to serve? In K. Hinchman & D. Appleman (Eds.), *Adolescent literacy: A handbook of practice-based research* (pp. 199–214). New York, NY: Guilford Press.

Smagorinsky, P., Cole, M., & Braga, L. W. (2017). On the complementarity of cultural historical psychology and contemporary disability studies. In I. Esmonde & A. Booker (Eds.), *Power and privilege in the learning sciences: Critical and sociocultural theories* (pp. 70–92). New York, NY: Routledge.

Tobin, J., & Hayashi, A. (2015). Contesting visions in a Japanese school for the deaf. *Anthropology and Education Quarterly*, *46*(4), 380–396.

Tobin, J., Hsueh, Y., & Karasawa, M. (2009). *Preschool in three cultures revisited.* Chicago, IL: University of Chicago Press.

Tobin, J., Wu, D., & Davidson, D. (1989). *Preschool in three cultures: Japan, China, and the United States.* New Haven, CT: Yale University Press.

Underwood, J., & Mead, J. F. (2012, February 29). A Smart ALEC threatens public education: Coordinated efforts to introduce model legislation aimed at defunding and dismantling public schools is the signature work of this conservative organization. *Education Week.* Retrieved May 30, 2016 from http://www.edweek.org/ew/articles/2012/03/01/kappan_underwood.html

Vygotsky, L. S. (1987). Thinking and speech. In L. S. Vygotsky, *Collected works* (Vol. 1, pp. 37–285) (R. Rieber & A. Carton, Eds.; N. Minick, Trans.). New York, NY: Plenum.

Vygotsky, L. S. (1993). *The collected works of L. S. Vygotsky. Volume 2: The fundamentals of defectology (abnormal psychology and learning disabilities)* (R. W. Rieber & A. S. Carton, Eds.; J. E. Knox & C. B. Stevens, Trans.). New York, NY: Plenum.

Walker, N. (2012). Throw away the master's tools: Liberating ourselves from the pathology paradigm. In J. Bascomb (Ed.), *Loud hands: Autistic people, speaking* (pp. 225–237). Washington, DC: Autistic Self Advocacy Network. Retrieved April 5, 2016 from http://neurocosmopolitanism.com/throw-away-the-masters-tools-liberating-ourselves-from-the-pathology-paradigm/

Wells, H. G. (1904). *The country of the blind.* Retrieved June 8, 2016 from http://www.online-literature.com/wellshg/3/

PART ONE

Theoretical and Historical Perspectives

CHAPTER ONE

Learning Disabilities

Theory Matters

CURT DUDLEY-MARLING

The popular history of learning disabilities holds that the term "learning disability" was introduced by Samuel Kirk in 1963. *Learning disabilities*, as conceptualized by Kirk, captured significant numbers of otherwise bright children who, because of a neurologically-based *learning disability*, struggled academically but, to this point, were not seen as meriting any special consideration in school (Wiederholt, 1974). Kirk assumed—as others still do—that learning disabilities have always been present among school-age children, but the *discovery* of learning disabilities had awaited developments in the science of testing and evaluation (see Sleeter, 1986).

Animated in part by Kirk's call to action, parents and educators pressed Congress to officially recognize learning disabilities as a special education category. By 1969 Congress passed the *Specific Learning Disabilities Act*, part of the *Education of the Handicapped Act of 1970* (PL 91–230), which mandated support services for students with learning disabilities. By 1980 more than one million students were identified as having a specific learning disability. Currently, over 2.2 million students are *diagnosed* as learning disabled (National Center for Educational Statistics, 2016).

In the years following Kirk's talk, considerable attention has been given to identifying the cause(s) of learning disabilities. Despite continued uncertainties about the precise nature and causes of learning disabilities, the dominant narrative in special education situates learning disabilities in the minds and bodies of individuals. The Learning Disabilities Roundtable (2002), for example, defined specific learning disabilities (SLD) as involving "disorders of learning and cognition *that are intrinsic to the individual*" (emphasis added). Locating learning disabilities in the heads of individual, otherwise "normal" students focuses interventions on *fixing* students with learning disabilities, usually through the remediation of various cognitive and/or academic deficiencies, relying on educational strategies that target the (putatively) unique learning characteristics of students with SLD.

The narrative of learning disabilities as the benevolent outcome of scientific progress has been challenged by a number of researchers. Sleeter (1986, 2010), for example, offers a radically different history of the founding of the learning disability field. According to Sleeter, the ratcheting up of literacy standards following the Sputnik crisis in the late 1950s threatened to capture middle-class children who struggled to meet heightened standards with pejorative labels such as slow or mentally retarded. Learning disabilities, with its emphasis on organic causes and average or above average intelligence, provided a way to explain the academic failures of White, middle-class children without implicating the culture of middle-class families or the normality (i.e., intelligence) of their children.

Similarly, my colleague Don Dippo and I argued that the learning disability category benefits the institution of schooling by "preserv[ing] fundamental assumptions in the discourse of schooling about what schools are for and who should succeed in them" (Dudley-Marling & Dippo, 1995, p. 412). The dominant narrative of schooling in the U.S. presents the schools as caring institutions that generally act in the best interests of students. Implicit in the language of *No Child Left Behind* (NCLB), for example, is the assertion that rigorous standards, accountability, and high quality teachers will enable all children to achieve high levels of academic success.

Despite the rhetoric of NCLB, schools are about creating winners and losers. Indeed, school achievement is understood in terms of students' performance relative to their peers. Don Dippo and I asserted that constructs like learning disabilities function to obscure the ways schools operate as agents of failure and, in the process, perpetuate historical inequities based on race, class, language, and gender. As Booth (1998) observes, the creation of special education categories like learning disabilities "can be viewed as the means by which the failures of the system and the exclusionary pressures within it are transformed into the failings of students" (p. 83). In this way, learning disabilities act as "a safety valve for the failure of schools to include all comers" (Slee, 1998, p. 135).

Many scholars have been especially critical of the deficit thinking that underpins most definitions of learning disabilities. The "disorders of learning and cognition" referenced in the LD Roundtable's definition of learning disabilities, for instance, are typically conceptualized as discrete (measurable) deficits in various academic, linguistic, perceptual, or cognitive processes or skills presumed to be neurologically based. An alternative, social constructivist narrative contends that LD exists outside minds and bodies of students in the complex web of human relations (Gergen, 1990). As McDermott and Varenne (1999) put it, people can't be LD on their own. The performance of a learning disability requires the specific actions of a group of people (students, teachers, special educators, school psychologists) performing just the right moves at just the right time and place (McDermott & Varenne, 1999). The social construction of LD also requires an institutional framework that assigns particular meanings to students' behaviors that, in other cultural contexts, do not carry the same significance (Dudley-Marling, 2004).

This chapter builds on my earlier work on the social construction of learning disabilities (Dudley-Marling, 2004). I begin with a brief, critical overview of deficit-based perspectives on learning disabilities. In this context I also critique the assumption that students with LD are unique, that is, that there are instructional strategies particularly suited to children with LDs. Next I detail an alternative, social constructivist perspective of LDs that situates the problem, not in the minds and bodies of individual children, but in the complex web of relations among students, teachers, curricula, specialized staff, and other factors. Finally I consider what comes from a social constructivist perspective on LDs, including the implications of a social constructivist perspective on both the organization of schools and classrooms and the curricular opportunities for students who are deemed to be failing. I begin with a critique of deficit approaches to LDs.

Learning Disability as Deficiency

The dominant approach to theorizing about—and providing instruction for—students with LDs targets deficits presumed to be intrinsic to individual students. Early on LD remediation typically focused on deficiencies in visual and auditory processes and/or psycholinguistics abilities that were presumed to be neurologically based and fundamental to academic success (for a critique of these approaches see Hammill, Goodman, & Wiederholt, 1974; Hammill & Larsen, 1974). More recently, LD theory and practice has shifted toward a cognitive model that associates reading problems with such deficiencies as phonological processing (Thomas & Loxley, 2007) that are in turn related to neurological functioning (Shaywitz & Shaywitz, 2004).

The nature of deficiencies presumed to be associated with a learning disability has shifted over time, but *the problem of learning disabilities* continues to be seen in terms of deficits in underlying skills, traits, or abilities that reside in the minds individual children. These efforts to link learning disabilities with various neurologically-based deficiencies seek to explain learning difficulties in otherwise normal children "with the fabrication of an organizing capacity, some 'faculty'" lying beyond the learning problem itself (Thomas & Loxley, 2007, p. 71).

Following this logic, the locus of remedial instruction for students identified as LD has often targeted the underlying faculties "lying beyond the problem itself." However, this reasoning violates Vygotsky's "principle of unity," which "forbids the decomposition of a psychological phenomenon into elements which are below the level at which that phenomenon has meaning" (Harré, 1985, p. 14). From this perspective, the instructional emphasis for students labeled as having reading disabilities, for instance, ought to focus on meaningful texts, not decontextualized bits like phonemic awareness (see Dudley-Marling & Paugh, 2004; Smith, 1996). Neurologically-based, deficit perspectives on LD have also been criticized for their reliance on discredited cognitive-behavioral theories of human learning (see Dudley-Marling, 2015) as well as flawed brain research that is increasingly cited in support of these approaches (e.g., Strauss, 2004). Moreover, deficit-oriented, in-the-head conceptualizations of learning disabilities ignore the social, cultural, and institutional contexts within which LDs emerge.

Despite these critiques, deficit thinking remains the dominant way in which learning disabilities are conceptualized in schools. This is more than a theoretical debate, however. Deficit perspectives on learning disabilities affect both the quality of instruction for students labeled LD and how schools are organized to serve them. In the following section I consider what comes from a deficit orientation to LDs.

What Comes from a Deficit Perspective on LD

Paraphrasing Rist (1970), there is a greater tragedy than being labeled a poor learner, and that is being treated like one. There are consequences that come from various theoretical perspectives on learning disabilities. Certainly, parents and teachers hope that the LD label will give children access to appropriate special education services without the stigma attached to other special education labels (Sleeter, 2010). However, traditional, deficit-based models of learning disabilities often lead to instructional arrangements based on faulty assumptions about the nature of LDs and remedial instructional strategies that contribute to the ongoing failure of students who have acquired the LD label. In the following sections I consider effects of deficit-based models of LD, beginning with how deficit-oriented instruction exacerbates learning problems by limiting the learning opportunities of students labeled LD.

Organizing for Instruction of Students with LD Labels

Historically, the practical rationale for special education is that children with special needs—including students identified as LD—possess unique learning characteristics that require specialized teaching strategies provided by specially trained teachers. Specifically, it is assumed that students with learning disabilities share a set of common traits and abilities that distinguish them from non-LD-labeled students and more or less determine the kind of instruction provided to students labeled LD. In other words, there are presumed to exist research-based instructional strategies uniquely suited to the special needs of LD-labeled students. Increasingly, LD-labeled students are educated in inclusive settings. Yet the ways schools are organized to address the needs of LD-labeled students suggests that the "special" needs of these students are distinct from both normally-achieving students and students identified with other special education labels.

There are, however, no traits or abilities (i.e., deficits) or patterns of traits and abilities that are unique to students with learning disabilities. Nor are there any research-based teaching strategies that are effective for *all and only* LD-labeled students. For example, LD researchers have long been interested in identifying patterns of performance on intelligence tests that are characteristic of LD-labeled students. In an early analysis of research claiming "unique" patterns of performance on the Wechsler Intelligence Scale for Children (WISC), Dudley-Marling, Kaufman, and Tarver (1981) concluded that these patterns did not apply to all LD-labeled students, nor were these patterns uncommon in non-LD-labeled children. Similarly, an analysis of research seeking to identify instructional practices that "work" for LD-labeled students revealed considerable variability in the efficacy of various teaching strategies among individual students (Dudley-Marling & Gurn, 2012). The most effective strategies for LD-labeled students work, at best, for many or, perhaps, most LD-labeled students, but never with all and only with them.

Overall, research does not support organizing instruction for LD-labeled students based on assumptions of unique deficiencies or patterns of deficits shared by all—or even most—LD-labeled students. There is reason to believe, however, that dominant approaches to teaching students identified as learning disabled may exacerbate the learning difficulties of many of them by limiting their affordances for learning.

The Deleterious Effects of Deficit-Based Instruction

The idea that learning difficulties are linked to specific deficits in skills or abilities is closely associated with cognitive-behavioral models of instruction that equate learning with mastery of a finite scope and sequence of discrete skills and subskills. From this perspective, successfully learning to read depends on developing proficiency in various skills (e.g., phonemic and phonological awareness, sound blending, etc.) that are believed to undergird fluent reading. Weaknesses in any of these presumed foundational skills are assessed as deficiencies that, in turn, are targeted for remediation. This sort of intervention makes sense from the point of view of literacy as a decontextualized, technical activity (that is, decoding text), but is at odds with sociocultural models of literacy that position reading and writing as complex processes whose meaning is inextricably tied to social and cultural settings (e.g., Gee, 2012; Street, 1995). From a sociocultural perspective readers don't learn to read once and for all as much as they learn to read particular texts (e.g., religious texts, novels, operating instructions, webpages), in particular ways (e.g., skimming for main ideas, in-depth reading for understanding), for particular purposes (e.g., participation in religious rituals, gathering information, entertainment, studying for tests), in particular settings (e.g., church, school, coffee house, basement workshop, virtual space) (Gee, 2012).

Beyond these theoretical concerns, there is the more immediate problem of what comes from the perspective that equates learning disabilities with *deficiency*. The evidence indicates that when differences in learning are interpreted as deficiencies, students are more likely to be subjected to reductive, watered-down skill instruction (Trent, Artiles, & Englert, 1998; Wong, 2010). Curriculum focused on low-level skills limits students' affordances for learning by denying them access to the rich, challenging curricula experienced by high-achieving students (Elliot, 2015). Simply put, many LD-labeled students learn less because they are taught less. This claim is supported by the finding that LD-labeled students—as well as students considered disabled more generally—continue to lag far behind on a variety of measures of academic achievement (Newman, Wagner, Cameto, & Knokey, 2009; Samuels, 2015). The National Center for Learning Disabilities (2014) reports that 88% of LD-labeled students perform at "below average" and "very below average" on certain measures of reading comprehension, and that by the time they reach high school, LD-labeled students continue to significantly underperform on a range of academic measures including grades, various academic assessments, and graduation rates.

To be sure, some children are well served by the learning disability label and what it offers but, overall, traditional, deficit-oriented programs for LD-labeled students have had limited success. In the rest of this paper I consider a social constructivist perspective on learning disabilities.

A Social/Cultural Constructivist Perspective on Learning Disabilities

Historically, theory and practice in learning disabilities have focused on the identification and remediation of deficiencies presumed to reside in the minds and bodies of individual children. An alternative discourse focuses on the role that the structures of modern schooling play in producing high levels of failure among poor students, students of color, second language students, and students labeled as disabled. What is there about schooling that transforms so many children who have repeatedly demonstrated that they are good at learning outside school into children who are not good at learning (Gee, 2004)? As Cambourne (1995) put it, "how could a brain which could master such complex learning in the world outside school be considered deficient with respect to the kinds of learning that were supposed to occur inside school?" (p. 183). McDermott, Goldman, and Varenne (2006) answer that "the American classroom is well organized for the production and display of failure, one child at a time, if possible, but group by group if necessary" (p. 13). Varenne and McDermott (1999) discuss how this process works:

> A half-century of ethnographic studies has shown that American education is compulsively competitive. In American classrooms, every child not only has to learn, but to learn better or faster than his or her neighbors. As such, American education is well organized to make hierarchy out of any differences that can be claimed, however falsely, as natural, inherent, and potentially consequential in school. (p. 4)

The proof that some students have learned "better and faster" is the presence of students who fail. In other words, the success of some is determined in relation to the failure of others. Indeed, there is a sense in which school failure is inevitable, a *natural* outcome of the *normal* distribution of human behavior including academic achievement. The anomaly that some normally-intelligent children perform below average academically is the primary driver of the concept of LD.

A social constructivist perspective challenges the LD-as-deficiency position by asserting that the performance of an LD requires the coordination of just the right people doing just the right things in just the right time and place. I next offer a more detailed discussion of a social constructivist theory of LDs with a particular emphasis on what comes from this perspective.

Traditional psychology defines identity in terms of essential, often immutable traits that are presumed to be the possession of autonomous individuals (Schweder, 1990). It is generally assumed, for example, that people are happy or sad, outgoing or shy, smart or dull, engaged or distractible, calm or excitable, and so on. It is never quite so simple as this, however. The happiest person is sometimes sad, and a calm person can get excited. And, of course, a student labeled with a reading disability may have extraordinary mathematical abilities. Still, the popular assumption remains that, over time, there are more or less immutable, essential qualities that define who we are.

An alternative perspective rejects essentialist, in-the-head notions of identity in favor of the idea that identities are always constructed in relation to other people engaged in coordinated activity in particular social and cultural settings. Cole (1996) argues that "psychological processes do not stand apart from activity but, rather, are constituted by the activities of which they are a part" (pp. 33–34). Moreover, sociocultural contexts do not stand apart from human activity. Human beings both construct and are constructed by the sociocultural contexts in which they are situated. As Schweder (1990) cleverly puts it, "you can't take the stuff out of the psyche and you can't take the psyche out of the stuff" (p. 22). This reciprocal view goes beyond ecological perspectives in which individuals are simply inserted into various social contexts. From a sociocultural perspective, individual identities and contexts are mutually constituted (Gutiérrez, 1994). Moreover, individual identities are never autonomous or independent but "always acquire social meaning in relation to other available identity positions and other social actors" (Bucholtz & Hall, 2005, p. 598). Identities are produced in coordinated actions with others in cultural contexts that give meaning to these actions. But, because actors, actions, and contexts are always shifting, identities are never stable (Bucholtz & Hall, 2005).

At the most basic level, "identity emerges in discourse through the temporary roles and orientations assumed by participants, such as evaluator, joke teller, or engaged listener" (Bucholtz & Hall, 2005, p. 591). Consider, for example, the quality of "smart," which is generally considered to be an essential identity trait in Western cultures. The performance of *smartness* requires the production of certain behaviors valued by the culture (e.g., high academic achievement) performed at the right time and place (e.g., schools, certain workplaces), the presence of others authorized to adjudicate *smartness* (e.g., teachers, psychologists, supervisors) and, crucially, the presence of others *deemed not to be smart*. Ultimately, no one can perform the identities of smart, slow—or learning disabled—on their own. People do bring various traits to the different contexts in which they live, but it is the sociocultural context—full of actors, actions, institutional norms, and so on—that gives meaning to these traits (Gee, 2000).

Consider the following example, which illustrates how the identity "learning disabled" emerged in an instructional interaction between a special education teacher, Mrs. Stroh, and Regis, a student with learning disabilities. In this excerpt Mrs. Stroh and Regis were discussing a picture he brought to school.

S: What are you doing in the picture?
R: Skating.
S: Will you tell me a sentence about it?
R: I go skating.
S: Where?
R: In the Mill Pond.
S: In the Mill Pond? Are you right in the pond?
R: Yeah. No.
S: No [laughs]. Where are you?
R: Skating.
S: Yes, but you're not in the Mill Pond. You'd be all wet if you were in it. Where are you?
R: Skating, I think. I don't know. Icing, I think.
S: Sometimes we say, "Skating at the Mill Pond."
R: Yeah.

Through a "lens of disability" (Mehan, 1996) this confused and confusing interaction lends credence to the school's assessment that that there is something wrong with Regis, that he has a learning disability. Certainly, that's how Mrs. Stroh saw it. In a separate interview she indicated that this lesson demonstrated Regis's difficulties expressing ideas. Regis did seem to be having trouble expressing himself in relation to Mrs. Stroh's prompts, and even made up a word ("icing") to describe where he was and what he was doing in the picture. However, from Regis's point of view, such miscommunication takes place when one conversational partner (the teacher) treats another's utterances as nonsense (Gergen, 1990). Regis seemed more than a little mystified by Mrs. Stroh's interrogations. By treating Regis's language as problematic, Mrs. Stroh limited his possibilities, highlighting what it appeared he couldn't do and limiting opportunities to show what he could do. As Ladson-Billings argues, "when students are treated as competent they are likely to demonstrate competence" (p. 123). Similarly, when students are treated as incompetent they are likely to demonstrate incompetence.

It's not that there wasn't something *different* about Regis. But these differences were not the source of the problems he experienced at school. The problem did not consist in his *being* learning disabled as much as in his *living in* "a world well organized to label and disable him" (McDermott & Varenne, 1999, p. 42). As McDermott and Varenne argue,

> The problems many people have in the American School stem only incidentally from what they can or cannot do and much more radically from the way they are treated by others in relation to the designation, assignment, and distribution of more or less

> temporary or partial difficulties interpreted as success or failure and responded to in the terms of the testing world. (pp. 134–135)

To be clear, however, Mrs. Stroh isn't the villain here. Her interactions with Regis, situated in the context of a learning disability classroom, constructed her as a particular kind of person, too. As a special education teacher she's been deputized to police children's behavior, always on the lookout for deficiencies to be remedied. She invoked a familiar instructional script in response to Regis's perceived struggles with verbal expression made salient by his identity as an LD-labeled student. Together Regis and Mrs. Stroh engaged in a perverse, improvisational dance mediated by institutional scripts of schooling. In this way they performed particular identities that made them into particular kinds of people: Regis, a student with learning disabilities, and Mrs. Stroh, a teacher of students with LD.

But this performance goes beyond just Regis and Mrs. Stroh. Lots of people participated in the choreography of their interactions. McDermott, Goldman, and Varenne (2006) argue that

> The cultural work of LD is embedded in the concerted activities of millions of people engaging a surveillance system of professionals—doctors, psychologists, lawyers, educators, and parents are all involved and at the ready before the children show up—looking for and producing evidence of LD in educational settings designed for symptoms of LD to become visible. (p. 6)

If it takes a village to raise children like Regis, it takes a culture to disable them.

Social constructivism offers a theoretical rationale for rejecting deficit views of learning disabilities. But, as with deficit models of LD, what matters most is what comes from a social constructivist perspective. In the following sections I consider the effects of a social constructivist position on both instruction and how schools might be organized to accommodate the incredible diversity that exists among the student population.

What Comes from a Social Constructivist Perspective on Learning Disabilities

The hallmark of a social constructivist stance, which explicitly rejects "in-the-head" conceptions of disability, is a *presumption of competence* (Biklen & Burke, 2006), what Miller (1993) refers to as a philosophy of abundance that

> is based on capability and competence. It presumes an optimistic explanation for human thinking, learning, and ability … that each person, regardless of age, gender,

> economic circumstance, or geographic location, is constantly in the process of constructing meanings based on her or his own life experiences. (p. 56)

In other words, from a social constructivist perspective, it is taken-for-granted that all but the most seriously disabled students (a very small percentage of the overall special education population) are competent and capable learners. A philosophy of abundance has profound effects both on how students with learning disabilities are taught and how we organize schools in support of learning disabled and other students with "special needs."

Effect on Instruction: Engaging with High-Expectation Curricula

A personal anecdote helps frame this section. My first job was in a school for children with intellectual disabilities, teaching 6- and 7-year-old children with "IQ"s measured under 50. Our curriculum focused on oral language, socialization, and fine and gross motor skills. Notably absent from the curriculum was any explicit reading instruction beyond routinely reading stories to my class. The presumption was that our students were deficient in the cognitive skills necessary for learning to read. However, at the beginning of my fourth year of teaching, I was assigned a teaching aide who was a certified elementary teacher with experience teaching reading. Early in the school year she asked if she could try to teach reading to at least a few of our students and, within months, these children began reading children's books.

What we learned from this experience was that the students in my class weren't learning to read *because I wasn't teaching them to read*. But when we treated our students as competent learners, they acted competently. My students learned what they were taught, and they didn't learn what they weren't taught. Not all the students in my class learned to read, but before we started formally teaching them to read, none of them did. Subsequent research confirms the literacy learning abilities of children with low-measured IQs (e.g., Buckley, 2001; Kliewer, 2008). Similarly, researchers have routinely demonstrated the literacy learning abilities of children with learning disabilities in out-of-school settings where students were afforded opportunities to learn high-level reading practices (e.g., Collins, 2013; McDermott, 1993; Rogers, 2003).

Two instructional principles follow from a social constructivist stance on learning disabilities: All learners are smart (Miller, 1993), and students can learn what they are taught. If the instructional focus for students with LD is on low-level skills (e.g., sound blending, phonemic awareness, etc.), that is what they will learn. They will not, however, learn the rich, engaging practices afforded high-achieving students—unless they are taught them. Therefore, from a social constructivist perspective, what LD-labeled students need most is to be afforded the same opportunities and quality of instruction—what we have referred to as high-expectation curricula (Dudley-Marling & Michaels, 2012)—as that afforded the most academically successful students.

I next share and discuss a few examples of high-expectation curricula that have been successfully implemented with students with special needs, including children with LD. One of the most dramatic examples of a challenging, high-expectation curriculum with special needs students is the highly successful OLE (Optimal Learning Environment) project, which emphasizes progressive pedagogical principles such as student choice, active student engagement in learning, meaningful and authentic purposes for learning, and learning in social contexts. These principles are more often implemented in gifted classrooms and affluent suburban schools than in poor urban schools (Ruiz, García, & Figueroa, 1996) or special education classes. Similarly, Chapin and O'Connor (2012) document the remarkable success of Project Challenge, a demanding mathematics curriculum emphasizing mathematical reasoning skills implemented in high-poverty schools overpopulated by students who have been identified as having special needs.

The presumption of competence that underpins high-expectation curricula like OLE and Project Challenge transforms student identities by altering the shape of the *pedagogical dance* that makes teachers and students into particular kinds of people. In the earlier example, Mrs. Stroh and Regis engaged in a choreographed performance (Initiation-Response-Evaluation) that highlighted his identify as a disabled learner. The dance metaphor is useful here because it suggests that if teachers alter their interactions with students, they can affect both student identities and students' affordances for learning. As Gutiérrez (1994) has shown, even a small change in the pattern of interactions between students and teachers can have a significant impact. Consider the following example from 4th grade classrooms in a South Bronx elementary school that had adopted Shared Inquiry as part of their reading curriculum (see Dudley-Marling & Michaels, 2012).

Shared Inquiry is based on whole-class, evidence-based discussion of stories that students have read and re-read in preparation for the discussions. Shared inquiry begins with an open-ended question (based on the reading) for which there is no single correct answer. The example below is excerpted from a story called "Cedric" (Jansson, 1962), which is about a boy named Sniff who has a stuffed animal named Cedric who has Topaz eyes and a moonstone on his collar. The text says, "Possibly the moonstones were more important to Sniff than the dog's inimitable expressions." In the story Sniff gives the stuffed animal away after someone tells him that "if you give something away that you really love, you'll get it back ten times over."

Almost immediately Sniff regrets his decision "to [the point of] desperation." Sniff shares his distress with another character, Snuffkin, who tells him a parallel, story-within-a-story about a woman who collects beautiful things to the exclusion of friends or travel. She gets a bone stuck in her stomach and thinks she's going to die, so she decides to anonymously give away her things. Friends start to visit, and one day she laughs so hard that the bone comes out. She's changed, has friends, and goes off to travel the world. Eventually, Sniff finds Cedric, but the topaz eyes have been removed and made into eardrops, and the moonstone on the collar has been lost. But, as the story says, Sniff loves Cedric "all the same," but now "only for love's sake." The following excerpt from a 54 minute, whole-class discussion responds to the teacher's question, "Why at the end of the story does Sniff love Cedric 'only for love's sake'?" Cory is a student who his teacher, Ms. Cole, indicated had been identified as "dyslexic."

Ms. Cole:	Cory, what do you want to add?
Cory:	I … I think … um I think it's because, I think he loves for love's sake, it's because, um on page 85, [Teacher: uh huh] cause it's telling you, on page 80—on page um 84 and 85. On 84 it says, "AN IDEA … CAME. SHE W-- [THE AUNT]. AND SHE WAS GONNA GIVE AWAY EVERYTHING SHE OWNED. [Teacher: uh huh] Also, on page 85, it says SHE THOUGHT WISELY AND SHE GAVE UM, UM, WHAT EVERYBODY UM WOULD WANT. So …
Ms. Cole:	So what does that have to do with um Sniff loving Cedric only for love's sake?
Cory:	It means that, it's telling, cause that's how he um loves Cedric for, for who he, for who he is because when he [Snufkin] told him [Sniff] that part of the story, um he's telling him that, that that she didn't, that she loves him for— that she um, if you love
Student:	(… for who he is, not like what he got on)
Cory:	It tells me that, that um … she … that um if he loved him, then she wouldn't give away her jewels, cause she didn't really care about the jewels. So … so that means that if she—she didn't care about the jewels, she just cared, cared about the um, about her friends, the person, not the jewels.
Ms. Cole:	She cared about the persons there?
Cory:	Uh huh. It's sort of like that …
Students:	Her friends, the person, her friends
Cory:	It's sort of like she loved, she loved the um that, that he taught him to love somebody for who they are, instead of for the jewels.
Ms. Cole:	So how did he teach him that? I'm still not understanding that.
Cory:	He teached him—he teached him that because—
Ms. Cole:	With the story, you're saying that he taught him something. So how did he teach him—teach him that with the story?

Cory:	He taught him that in the story because in this part of the story it's telling her that, telling her that she didn't really like the jewels if she would've gave it away, if she would've gave it away for her friends.
Ms. Cole:	Does she not really like the jewels? I mean uh her material things?
Cory:	Yeah, she **likes** them, but then, … but then after, when you read on, she didn't really like them cause she liked her friends better.
Student:	She—she—she liked 'em before she had friends.
Student:	She liked 'em before she had friends.
Cory:	Yeah, because she didn't know all that was gonna happen and death was gonna happen and stuff.
Diarra:	I get—I understand what um, what Cory is saying. Cory is saying that um (what, um what) if it hadn't been for the bone, then she would've never changed … her um her um her manner. And she would've never met so many friends.
Ms. Cole:	Is that what you're trying to say, Cory?
Cory:	Yeah, yeah, that part if she—if sh—if that—if that part wouldn't have happened then she wouldn't change.
Ms. Cole:	So what does that have to do with Sniff?
Cory:	So that means, it's telling him, it's telling him that she didn't really, care about, care about (that like if). Like if you really love something, that um you wouldn't love something for the jewels, the jewels it has. Cause, on page 80 it says, POSSIBLY THE JEWELS WERE MORE IMPORTANT TO SNIFF THAN EXPRESSIONS BUT … BUT UM, BUT IN ANY CASE HE LOVED, HE LOVED CEDRIC. So, so that means that um … that he—he loved, that he's sp—you only s'posed, he um posed to —he's teaching him to love someone for um [Student: what they are] for who they are.

Cory's comments are, at times, confusing, and it would have been be easy for his teacher to have dismissed his initial comment as nonsense, further evidence of his learner problems. But Ms. Cole and the other students took Cory's comments seriously and, over a number of turns—and with the support of his teacher and several other students—Cory constructed a text-based argument for "Why at the end of the story does Sniff love Cedric 'only for love's sake?'" Specifically, Cory cited the lesson Sniff learned from Snuffkin's story about the woman with a bone stuck in her stomach; that is, "[Snuffkin's] teaching him to love someone for … for who they are." Notably, Cory was the only student who cited the parallel, story-within-a-story to support his claim for why Sniff loved Cedric "only for love's sake."

For her part, Ms. Cole employed various "talk moves" (Michaels & O'Connor, 2011) to orchestrate this discussion and scaffold her students' development of evidence-based reasoning. Over the course of the 54-minute discussion of Cedric, she asked students to expand or clarify what they've said (e.g., "What did you mean by that?"); pressed students for deeper reasoning (e.g., "Why do you think that?" "What's your evidence?"); solicited additional viewpoints ("Derrick, we haven't heard from you."); and encouraged students to connect their reasoning to the reasoning of other students (e.g., "Who agrees or disagrees with what Derrick has said?") (Michaels & O'Connor, 2011). Crucially, Ms. Cole avoided any form of evaluation of students' responses on the assumption that teacher evaluation constrains open discussion by leading students to believe there really is a right answer (i.e., the teacher's).

Shared Inquiry discussions created affordances that enabled students in a low-achieving, high-poverty school to display a high level of academic competence as students constructed sophisticated academic arguments while discussing challenging texts (Dudley-Marling & Michaels, 2012). In the case of Cory, Ms. Cole used a set of talk moves to draw out what he thought and, with the help of other students, to scaffold Cory's construction of a sophisticated, evidence-based argument. Presuming that Cory, like all of her students, was *smart*, Ms. Cole shifted the teacher's role from evaluator/teacher to facilitator and, in the process, significantly changed the shape of the instructional dance, transforming Cory's identity from a student who couldn't read (dyslexic) to a competent student able to participate in a highly valued academic practice. Collaboratively, Ms. Cole and Cory's classmates scaffolded his performance as a competent student. For Cory, "higher mental functions [were being] internalized through social and dialogic interactions with other members of a sociocultural group" (Trent et al., 1998, p. 286).

In contrast, in the earlier example of Regis and Mrs. Stroh, Mrs. Stroh took Regis's response to her question about his picture as evidence of a problem that needed fixing, leading to a series of instructional moves that scaffolded Regis's performance of a learning disability. At best, through his interactions with Mrs. Stroh, Regis learned how to participate in low-level interaction mainly associated with a particular way of doing school. However, unlike Cory, Regis was not afforded opportunities to engage in "higher mental functions."

I want to be clear that my argument that learning disabilities are socially constructed does not mean that I believe that there aren't differences among students or that all students can achieve the highest levels of success. Certainly Regis—like other students who have acquired the learning disability label—played a role in the instructional dance that constructed him as "disabled." It is also true that some children will require more frequent, intensive, and individualized support and direction than their peers (Dudley-Marling & Paugh, 2004). This need does not mean, however, that any student requires "special," qualitatively different instruction, since this designation tends to refer to learning low-level skills. As Wong (2010) observes, "Labels, which in essence name students' inabilities, offer little guidance for educators; in fact, they may influence teachers to intentionally or inadvertently set limits on the learning opportunities for these students" (p. 15). Ultimately, creating affordances for learning that allows all students to display competence demands that schools be organized to accommodate the range of human differences children bring with them to school.

Organizing Schools for a Diverse Population of Students

The concept of "normal"—the idea that human behaviors roughly distribute along the contours of a bell-shaped distribution with most people clustering around the mean or average—plays a significant role in how American schools or organized. Age-graded curriculum focusing on the putative "average" student shapes day-to-day instruction. Routine grading practices are based on the assumption of normality, justifying the practice of "grading on the curve." Students who deviate from "normal" are identified and classified through the use of norm-referenced testing. In this model of schooling, difference is a problem: a disability. Students who do not easily fit into the rigid structures of the modern school are pathologized as exceptional (in the negative sense) or disabled. These children are deemed to require special classes, specialized instruction, and specially-trained teachers, all targeted toward remediating student deficiencies so that they can assimilate into the normative structures of schooling. The problem of learning disabilities is the presence of students who are expected to do well in school—those presumed to be endowed with average or above average intelligence—but significantly underachieve.

There is, however, a fundamental problem with this model of schooling. It is based on a myth. The normal curve is a poor model of human behavior. Human behavior does not distribute normally—only truly random events distribute *normally*—and defining exceptionality in terms of deviations from the mean (normal) has no rational basis (Dudley-Marling & Gurn, 2010; Gallagher, 2010). As it turns out, human differences are not abnormal; instead, it is normal to be different.

Presuming difference to be a normal part of the human experience suggests a radically different approach to organizing schools. Instead of "fixing" children presumed to be "exceptional" so that they fit into the rigid structures of schooling, we have the capacity to create truly inclusive schools that accommodate the extraordinary diversity of U.S. school children. From this perspective, the goal is not getting children ready to fit into the *normal* curriculum but "getting the school 'ready' to serve increasingly diverse children" (Swadener, 1995, p. 18), including students labeled as learning disabled.

Creating inclusive environments for all students is, however, an aspiration, a problem to be solved. In the long term this effort will require the dismantling of the institutional structures of schooling that, in conception, never even imagined students with disabilities, students of color, or girls. Rigid, age-graded curriculum, normative testing practices, and tracking and ability grouping will never be congenial to the human diversity that exists in every school and classroom. In the place of these normalizing structures, we must create new institutional structures that offer welcoming spaces for all students, acknowledging and building on the competence of all children regardless of their differences and the communities from which they come.

Realistically, this long-term political project will encounter significant resistance from groups that benefit from current structures of schooling. Therefore, more immediate strategies are required for creating welcoming, inclusive classrooms within existing structures of schooling. Significantly smaller class sizes would help. Allington and McGill-Franzen (1989) argue that small class sizes would allow for more individualized instruction, mitigating the need for identifying students as disabled. Workshop structures for reading and writing that provide teachers with opportunities to provide individual support and direction for students as needed (e.g., Dudley-Marling & Paugh, 2004, 2009) are also helpful. Similarly, Universal Design for Learning (UDL) is a means to "leverage technology's power to make education more inclusive and effective … by offering [learners] 1) multiple means of representation … 2) multiple means of expression … and 3) multiple means of engagement" (Rose, Meyer, & Hitchcock, 2005, p. 3). Culturally-relevant pedagogies, which acknowledge and build on the linguistic and cultural knowledge all students bring with them to school (Gay, 2000, 2002), are also useful for creating inclusive schools and classrooms. Most important, however, is replacing deficit thinking that begins with the assumption of pathology with a philosophy of abundance that begins with the assumption that all students are competent learners entitled to the same rich, engaging curriculum provided to the highest achieving students.

Conclusion

Increasingly, U.S. politics are dominated by an extreme individualism that constructs people as lone actors, independent from social or cultural influences. From this perspective we're all "in it" on our own with no particular responsibility for our fellow citizens. Some reject any collective responsibility for the poor or disadvantaged as an impingement on their freedom (see Murray, quoted in Ketchum, 2012). Such views are repugnant to the benevolent spirit that has animated special education from its inception. Yet the ideology of individualism—in one form or another—has shaped common perceptions of people with disabilities even within the field of special education. The commonly held view is that school failure is intrinsic to solitary individuals who are deficient in the traits and abilities fundamental to high academic achievement. This stance directs academic intervention to fixing individual students, not the institution of schooling that created so much failure in the first place.

Recognizing that traditional approaches to special education derive from worldviews about individuals, communities, and institutions highlights the reality that social constructivism, as a counter-narrative that defines disability in terms of sociocultural factors, challenges the ideology of individualism that dominates U.S. culture. Seen in these terms, it's easy to see why social constructivist perspectives on disability have encountered such fierce resistance from traditional special educators (e.g., Kauffman & Sasso, 2006).

Perhaps the most effective argument for challenging traditional perspectives on disability critiques deficit thinking from a social justice perspective. Special educators—like educators more generally—are good and caring people who want to do the best for children in their care. My own experience as a teacher educator suggests that teachers and teacher candidates are open to rethinking their commitment to deficit thinking when they begin to understand how deficit thinking pathologizes—and stigmatizes—whole groups of people by conflating human differences with deficiency. However, our work with teachers also indicates that changing teachers' beliefs about the nature of disability doesn't easily translate into practice, given that teachers work in an institution saturated with deficit thinking (Dudley-Marling & Paugh, 2010). Challenging the status quo is hard, but doing so is an issue of social justice that affects how educators think about and behave toward students who embody certain human differences. This isn't a just a theoretical debate. It is part of a larger project of creating welcoming, supportive spaces for the range of human experiences in all our institutions, including public schools.

References

Allington, R. L., & McGill-Franzen, A. (1989). Different programs, indifferent instruction. In D. Lipsky & A. Gartner (Eds.), *Beyond separate education: Quality education for all* (pp. 75–98). Baltimore, MD: Brookes.

Biklen, D., & Burke, J. (2006). Presuming competence. *Equity & Excellence in Education, 39*(2), 166–175. Retrieved August 21, 2018 from http://dx.doi.org/10.1080/10665680500540376

Booth, T. (1998). The poverty of special education: Theories to the rescue? In C. Clark, A. Dyson, & A. Millward (Eds.), *Theorising special education* (pp. 126–136). New York, NY: Routledge.

Bucholtz, M., & Hall, K. (2005). Identity and interaction: A sociocultural linguistic approach. *Discourse Studies*, *7*(4–5), 585–614.

Buckley, S. (2001). *Reading and writing for individuals with Down Syndrome—An overview.* Kirkby Lonsdale, UK: Down Syndrome Education International.

Cambourne, B. (1995). Toward an educationally relevant theory of literacy learning: Twenty years of inquiry. *The Reading Teacher*, *49*(3), 181–190.

Chapin, S., & O'Connor, C. (2012). Project challenge: Using challenging curriculum and mathematical discourse to help all students learn. In C. Dudley-Marling & S. Michaels (Eds.), *High-expectation curricula: Helping all students succeed with powerful learning* (pp. 113–127). New York, NY: Teachers College Press.

Cole, M. (1996). *Cultural psychology: A once and future discipline.* Cambridge, MA: Harvard University Press.

Collins, K. M. (2013). *Ability profiling and school failure: One child's struggle to be seen as competent* (2nd ed.). New York, NY: Routledge.

Dudley-Marling, C. (2004). The social construction of learning disabilities. *Journal of Learning Disabilities*, *37*(6), 482–490.

Dudley-Marling, C. (2015). *Preparing the nation's teachers to teach reading: A manifesto in defense of "teacher educators like me."* New York, NY: Garn Press.

Dudley-Marling, C., & Burns, M. B. (2014). Two perspectives on inclusion in the United States. *Global Education Review*, *1*(1), 14–31. Retrieved July 27, 2018 from http://ger.mercy.edu/index.php/ger/article/view/10

Dudley-Marling, C., & Dippo, D. (1995). What learning disability does: Sustaining the ideology of schooling. *Journal of Learning Disabilities*, *28*(7), 408–414.

Dudley-Marling, C., & Gurn, A. (2010). Troubling the foundations of special education: Examining the myth of the normal curve. In C. Dudley-Marling & A. Gurn (Eds.), *The myth of the normal curve* (pp. 9–23). New York, NY: Peter Lang.

Dudley-Marling, C., & Gurn, A. (2012). Toward a more inclusive approach to intervention research: The case research in learning disabilities. *International Journal of Inclusive Education*, *16*(10), 1019–1032.

Dudley-Marling, C., Kaufman, N. J., & Tarver, S. G. (1981). WISC and WISCR profiles of learning disabled children. *Learning Disability Quarterly*, *4*(3), 307–319.

Dudley-Marling, C., & Michaels, S. (2012). Shared inquiry: Making students smart. In C. Dudley-Marling & S. Michaels (Eds.), *High-expectation curricula: Helping all students succeed with powerful learning* (pp. 99–110). New York, NY: Teachers College Press.

Dudley-Marling, C., & Paugh, P. (2004). *A classroom teacher's guide to struggling readers.* Portsmouth, NH: Heinemann.

Dudley-Marling, C., & Paugh, P. (2010). Confronting the discourse of deficiencies. *Disability Studies Quarterly*, *30*(2) (online). Retrieved July 27, 2018 from http://dsq-sds.org/article/view/1241/1285

Elliott, S. N. (2015). Measuring opportunity to learn and achievement growth: Key research issues with implications for the effective education of all students. *Remedial and Special Education, 36*(1), 58–64.

Gallagher, D. (2010). Educational researchers and the making of normal people. In C. Dudley-Marling & A. Gurn (Eds.), *The myth of the normal curve* (pp. 25–38). New York, NY: Peter Lang.

Gay, G. (2000). *Culturally responsive teaching: Theory, research and practice.* New York, NY: Teachers College Press.

Gay, G. (2002). Preparing for culturally responsive teaching. *Journal of Teacher Education, 53*(2), 106–116.

Gee, J. P. (2000). Identity as an analytic lens for research in education. In W. G. Secada (Ed.), *Review of Research in Education, 25* (pp. 99–125). Washington, DC: American Educational Research Association.

Gee, J. P. (2004). *Situated language and learning: A critique of traditional schooling.* New York, NY: Routledge.

Gee, J. P. (2012). *Social linguistics and literacies: Ideology in discourses* (4th ed.). New York, NY: Routledge.

Gergen, K. J. (1990). Social understanding and the inscription of self. In J. W. Stigler, R. A. Schweder, & G. Herdt (Eds.), *Cultural psychology: Essays on comparative human development* (pp. 569–606). New York, NY: Cambridge University Press.

Gutiérrez, K. D. (1994). How talk, context, and script shape contexts for learning: A cross-case comparison of journal sharing. *Linguistics and Education, 5*(3–4), 335–365.

Hammill, D., Goodman, L., & Wiederholt, J. L. (1974). Visual-motor processes: Can we train them? *The Reading Teacher, 27*(5), 469–478.

Hammill, D., & Larsen, S. C. (1974). The effectiveness of psycholinguistic training. *Exceptional Children, 41*, 5–14.

Harré, R. (1985). *Foreword.* In G. Claxton et al. (Eds.), *Psychology and schooling: What's the matter?* London, UK: Bedford Way Papers.

Jansson, T. (1962). "Cedric." In T. Warburton (Trans.), *Tales from Moominvalley* (pp. 150–161). New York, NY: Farrar, Straus and Giroux.

Kauffman, J. M., & Sasso, G. M. (2006). Toward ending cultural and cognitive relativism in special education. *Exceptionality, 14*(2), 65–90.

Ketchum, J. (2012, October 5). Is personal responsibility the key to ending poverty? *Marketplace.* Retrieved August 21, 2018 from https://www.marketplace.org/2012/10/05/wealth-poverty/commentary/personal-responsibility-key-ending-poverty

Kliewer, C. (2008). *See all kids as readers: A new vision for literacy in the inclusive early childhood classroom.* Baltimore, MD: Brookes.

Ladson-Billings, G. (1994). *The dreamkeepers: Successful teachers of African American children.* San Francisco, CA: Jossey-Bass.

Learning Disabilities Roundtable. (2002). *Specific learning disabilities: Finding common ground.* Washington, DC: U.S. Department of Education Office of Special Education Programs, Office of Innovation and Development.

McDermott, R. P. (1993). The acquisition of a child by a learning disability. In S. Chaiklin & J. Lave (Eds.), *Understanding practice: Perspectives on activity and context* (pp. 269–305). New York, NY: Cambridge University Press.

McDermott, R., Goldman, S., & Varenne, H. (2006). The cultural work of learning disabilities. *Education Researcher, 35*(6), 12–17.

McDermott, R., & Varenne, H. (1999). Adam, Adam, Adam, and Adam: The cultural construction of a learning disability. In H. Varenne & R. McDermott (Eds.), *Successful failure: The school American builds* (pp. 25–44). Boulder, CO: Westview.

Mehan, H. (1996). The construction of an LD student: A case study in the politics of representation. In M. Silverstein & G. Urban (Eds.), *Natural histories of discourse* (pp. 253–276). Chicago, IL: University of Chicago Press.

Michaels, S., & O'Connor, C. (2011). *Promoting academically productive talk across the curriculum: A high-leverage practice.* Unpublished paper.

Miller, L. (1993). *What we call smart: A new narrative for intelligence and learning.* San Diego, CA: Singular.

National Center for Educational Statistics. (2016). *Digest of educational statistics.* Washington, DC: U.S. Department of Education. Retrieved July 27, 2018 from https://nces.ed.gov/fastfacts/display.asp?id=64

National Center for Learning Disabilities. (2014). *The state of learning disabilities: Understanding the 1 in 5.* Retrieved July 27, 2018 from http://www.ncld.org/the-state-of-learning-disabilities-understanding-the-1-in-5

Newman, L., Wagner, M., Cameto, R., & Knokey, A. M. (2009). *The post-high school outcomes of youth with disabilities up to 4 years after high school: A report from the National Longitudinal Transition Study-2 (NLTS2).* NCSER 2009–3017. Washington, DC: National Center for Special Education Research.

Rist, R. C. (1970). Student social class and teacher expectations: The self-fulfilling prophecy in ghetto education. *Harvard Educational Review, 40*(3), 72–73.

Rogers, R. (2003). *A critical discourse analysis of family literacy practices: Power in and out of print.* New York, NY: Routledge.

Rose, D. H., Meyer, A., & Hitchcock, C. (Eds.). (2005). *The universally designed classroom: Accessible curriculum and digital technologies.* Cambridge, MA: Harvard Education Press.

Ruiz, N. T., García, E., & Figueroa, R. A. (1996). *The OLE curriculum guide: Creating optimal learning environments for students from diverse backgrounds in special and general education.* Sacramento, CA: California Department of Education.

Samuels, C. (2015, October 29). NAEP scores for students with disabilities show wide achievement gap. *Education Week.* Retrieved July 27, 2018 from http://blogs.edweek.org/edweek/speced/2015/10/naep_scores_for_students_with.html

Shaywitz, S. E., & Shaywitz, B. A. (2004). Reading disability and the brain. *Educational Leadership, 61*(6), 6–11.

Schweder, R. A. (1990). Cultural psychology—what is it? In J. W. Stigler, R. A. Schweder, & G. Herdt (Eds.), *Cultural psychology: Essays on comparative human development* (pp. 1–46). New York, NY: Cambridge University Press.

Slee, R. (1998). The politics of theorising special education. In C. Clark, A. Dyson, & A. Millward (Eds.), *Theorising special education* (pp. 126–136). New York, NY: Routledge.

Sleeter, C. (1986). Learning disabilities: The social construction of a special education category. *Exceptional Children, 53*, 46–54.

Sleeter, C. (2010). Why is there learning disabilities? A critical analysis of the birth of the field in its social context. *Disability Studies Quarterly, 30*(2), 210–237. Retrieved July 27, 2018 from http://dsq-sds.org/article/view/1261/1292

Smith, F. (1996). *Reading without nonsense* (3rd ed.). New York, NY: Teachers College Press.

Strauss, S. L. (2004). *The linguistics, neurology, and politics of phonics: Silent "E" speaks out.* New York, NY: Routledge.

Street, B. V. (1995). *Social literacies: Critical approaches to literacy in development, ethnography and education.* New York, NY: Longman.

Swadener, B. B. (1995). Children and families "at promise": Deconstructing the discourse of risk. In B. B. Swadener & S. Lubeck (Eds.), *Children and families "at promise": Deconstructing the discourse of risk* (pp. 17–49). Albany, NY: State University of New York Press.

Thomas, G., & Loxley, A. (2007). *Deconstructing special education and constructing inclusion* (2nd ed.). New York, NY: McGraw-Hill.

Trent, S. C., Artiles, A. J., & Englert, C. S. (1998). From deficit thinking to social constructivism: A review of theory, research and practice in special education. *Review of Research in Education, 23*, 277–307.

Varenne, H., & McDermott, R. (1999). Introduction. In H. Varenne & R. McDermott (Eds.), *Successful failure: The school America builds* (pp. 1–21). New York, NY: Westview.

Wiederholt, J. L. (1974). Historical perspectives on the education of the learning disabled. In L. Mann & D. Sabatino (Eds.), *The second review of special education* (pp. 103–152). Philadelphia, PA: JSE Press.

Wong, J. (2010). Exploring the construction/deconstruction of learning disabilities in an urban school: Revisiting Sleeter's essay. *Disability Studies Quarterly, 30*(2). (online). Retrieved July 27, 2018 from http://dsq-sds.org/article/view/1242/1286

CHAPTER TWO

Vygotsky, "Defectology," and the Russian/Soviet Approach to Human Difference

PETER SMAGORINSKY

In this chapter I review the Russian and Soviet tradition in what corresponds to U.S. "special education." To the Soviets, and to the Russia that both preceded and emerged from its dissolution, this field has been known by the unfortunate name of "defectology." I have hoped mightily that this term is a product of an awkward translation, yet my Russian colleagues assure me that it accurately captures the original. McCagg (1989) reports that Russian academic ideas about anomalous children were heavily influenced by the Germans when the first special research and training centers were opened in the early 20th century. This influence included the use of the term "defective" to characterize children with special needs. The Latin origins of *defectologia* suggest failure, shortcoming, and other terms associated with deficiency. McCagg confirms what most people with 21st Century ears would think: "this term would not survive 3 minutes in a discussion of the handicapped in the Western world today because it carries too much negative connotation toward the disabled" (p. 40). Three minutes? I can only hope that it wouldn't last nearly that long.

The term's deficit-drenched connotations, however, bely the fundamentally empathic and nurturing approach that Soviet and Russian defectologists have brought to their education of children either born with, or having developed through life traumas, bodies and minds—entities that I do not consider distinct from one another—that do not conform to the norm or that do not progress according to age-based schedules. The richest primary source of understanding of

Soviet and Russian defectology comes from the second volume of collected works of L. S. Vygotsky (1993), a Soviet psychologist whose major work was carried out between 1924 and 1934, when he died at 37 years of age after contending with tuberculosis his whole adult life. A principal secondary source is McCagg (1989), whose history of disability theory and practice in the Soviet Union includes specific attention to defectology while also historicizing this field within the broader stream of Soviet psychology and education and their European antecedents.

This attention to defectology is intended to broaden the range of theoretical streams informing the related fields of Disability Studies, Critical Disability Studies, Disability Studies in Education, and Critical Special Education. These perspectives collectively provide the foundation for critiques mounted against mainstream special education in the U.S. and in international circles, and the basis for pushback against any notion that "disability" diminishes human value. These perspectives tend to get traced historically to the Frankfurt School that emerged between the first and second World Wars, and its emphasis on deconstructing power hierarchies, including those associated with positioning people of cognitive, neurological, and physical difference as deficient.

Well before the Frankfort School began to assert the value of all humans using Marxist principles, a distinctively separate line of work emerged in the form of defectology. This school was also deeply indebted to Marxism once it was adapted by Soviet psychologist L. S. Vygotsky for the new Soviet Union's egalitarian founding principles (if not their actual practice under Stalin). This profoundly important body of work has been neglected not only in the context of Vygotsky's career, but in the formulation of current Western efforts at inclusive, respectful attention to all people available through the various Disability fields.

This chapter is designed to introduce this body of work's contributions to fields oriented to providing humane, sensitive educational and social opportunities to children and youth often viewed as hopeless and of little value to the broader culture. The goals and values of defectology and Disability fields are often remarkably similar, perhaps not a surprise given their shared Marxist heritage (Smagorinsky, Cole, & Braga, 2017). However, the Soviet attention to materiality and powerful theorization of long-term, socially-mediated human development appears to make a unique contribution to the education of those whose bodies and minds depart from evolutionary norms. Defectology is grounded in the field of cultural-historical psychology, a field that Cole (1996) presents as eclectic in its sources, as likely to draw on Russian poets as it is on rhetoric, psychology, or other fields. Nonetheless, its firm grounding in the emerging field of psychology of nearly a century ago provides it with a distinctive perspective that allows it both to complement the work of our contemporary Disability fields and offer insights that appear unique.

Defectology in Tsarist Russia and the Soviet Union

Retarded, defective, idiot … these are such harsh terms to the modern ear. But a century and more ago—and a lot more recently as well—they were accepted and widely used. Here I will rely on McCagg's (1989) account to historicize the emergence of the field of defectology in the European context, both in terms of the vocabulary of over a century ago and in the epistemologies that governed thinking about the norms of human development at the time.

Pre-Soviet European (and Current U.S.) Conceptions of Human Difference

McCagg (1989) is mindful of the time in which the field of defectology came into being, and the historical context in which it first appeared. Diagnostics in the 19th century were relatively primitive, especially with young children who often died before their conditions could be understood or treated, leaving the testimonials of those who survived to adulthood as the primary source of knowledge about people whose bodies and minds defied societal norms and expectations. Amidst this uncertainty, defectology provided a very broad way of studying people exhibiting a great range of evolutionary absences, particularly blindness, deafness, cognitive impairment, and other conditions considered physically debilitating to those adhering to ableist norms.

McCagg (1989) finds that the medical model for diagnosing difference was firmly established well before the emergence of defectology. In the late 1700s, for instance, Austrian emperor Joseph II set up special asylums for "weak-minded children, as well as separate school institutions for the blind and deaf" (p. 43). This sort of intervention was advanced during the French Revolution, when the Bicêtre Hospital in Paris was liberated to house and treat people considered insane separately from people jailed for poverty-driven crimes. This distinction decriminalized mental health and provided the basis for Superintendent Philippe Pinel's 1793 revolutionary introduction of humane methods to the treatment of those considered mentally ill (an approach retrospectively found by Foucault, 1961/1964, to be fraudulent in its purported humaneness). The primitive state of medicine, and great shortage of trained doctors of the era, contributed to the ignorance surrounding attention to anomalous bodies and minds and how best to either treat them or protect society from having to be concerned about them.

Meanwhile, the emergence of the European Enlightenment promoted the need for widespread education, for which "handicapped" children were ill-suited, leading to their segregation from mainstream education and society. Further, at that point, there was little to no differentiation among anomalous ways of being in Europe (and nascently in the U.S.): "the old etiological confusion of the handicapped groups, which had been based on sheer ignorance, gave way to a new lumping together of these people based on expediency, as well" (McCagg, p. 45). All handicapped conditions were considered more or less the same, because considering all departures from the norm to be all of a piece allowed authorities to manage the problem of variation through a single solution that both segregated students based on ableist assumptions and served the emerging economic interests of the ruling classes: exclusion. The slow progress in caring for people who fall outside norms and expectations remains shocking, shameful, and cruel at a historical period well beyond the ignorant beliefs extant during the 18th and 19th centuries.

The Enlightenment brought about both a reliance on scientific solutions and a need for more universal education. A medical approach to human difference proliferated, in part due to scientific and medical studies of "wild" people in Europe who lived in secluded areas, such as those exhibiting

> cretinism—an environmentally caused idiocy that was widespread in the valleys between the Alps. One could not help but guess, even in the days of primitive diagnostics, that the solution here would have to be medical, not just pedagogical. The cretins were clearly not just uneducated: they were physically defective. Their treatment could not be handed over just to educators, but clearly had to be retained in the hands of the medical profession. (McCagg, 1989, p. 45)

McCagg (1989), I infer, is not so much defending the development of medical views of human variation, as he is explaining how they came to take hold. In the 1800s, there was simply little understanding of human difference, and there were few avenues for addressing it. Enlightenment values suggested scientific solutions for social problems, and medicine was an emerging, if very imprecise, science. Further, education for the masses was a new phenomenon, itself barely ready to take on the challenge of educating the great range of humanity enrolled in its classrooms. The times, then, were ripe for making a "handicap" or "disability" into a medical condition amenable to a medical solution. Again, this conception remains alive and well in mainstream special education (Gabel, 2005), therapy (Smagorinsky, 2016a), and virtually any other field in which difference is constructed as deficit.

McCagg (1989) reports that in mid-nineteenth century Germany, a "medical curative pedagogy—*Heilpädogogik*"—was established specifically to address "the schooling of the handicapped" (p. 46). This approach became institutionalized late in the 19th century in Germany and elsewhere in Europe. The label of retardation was applied to anyone not progressing according to age-group norms, including immigrant children deemed "retarded" by natives.

These "curative" services expanded greatly during the 1800s, leading to both appropriate treatment and abuses. They were made available through crash courses offered to pedagogues over how to best educate the children enrolled, a problematic endeavor given that "abnormal" children were virtually all considered "retarded," whether they were deaf, blind, or cognitively behind their peers. This "scientific" conclusion has not stood up over time among specialists. In the U.S. and elsewhere, however, such assumptions remain in play in policy and practice.

Early in the 19th century, Dr. Jean Itard of the Paris Institute for the Deaf published his study of a "wild boy," leading him to seek, as a medical doctor during the Enlightenment, a form of special education that attempted to get down to the "natural mind" of people considered handicapped. In Germany, according to McCagg (1989), disability "seemed in general more a social question than in France, and the result was a holistic tradition of disability rehabilitation, which increasingly contrasted with the individualistic pedagogical tradition of the Atlantic countries. Some well-known historical factors reinforced this tradition, which—to repeat—was in no small degree appropriate, given the extreme difficulty of disability diagnosis" of the day (p. 45). McCagg notes that politics contributed to the different national conceptions of how to address human difference, with Germans rejecting French ideas (e.g., Rousseau's naturalistic views) in favor of Germanic philosophy according to Kant and Herbart, producing a conception of comprehensive rehabilitation. The Germans took the approach "that all varieties of human deficiency be studied together, rather than separately; that medical doctors as well as pedagogues be deeply involved in the care of the handicapped; and that science, not accident, dominate such serious matters" (McCagg, p. 46).

Approaches based on primitive efforts to medicalize disability produced a number of misguided, ultimately abusive treatments. McCagg (1989) notes in particular the German insistence that lip reading, rather than sign languages, be used exclusively for deaf education, under the assumption that "a mode of thinking dominated by images, and allegedly encouraged by sign language, was inhibitory to the abstract mode of thinking that was considered necessary to produce a cultured person. This was science and holism carried to unintelligent excess" (p. 46). Normalizing deaf communication thus involved cutting deaf people off from approaches that have now proven highly effective, under the guise of a "scientific" assumption with no basis, one extensively refuted since.

The curative approach developed in Germany, a nation whose cultural imprint on Europe was powerful, found receptive audiences across the continent, at least where political affiliations and nationalistic loyalties allowed. To McCagg (1989), in addition to these tribally-motivated concerns,

> *Heilpädogogik* and the *Hilfsschulen* may have seemed extremely interesting to an Eastern European government [Hungary] faced with the problem of spreading education among a large population that the ruling classes had traditionally regarded as stupid peasants. In the socio-economic backwardness of Hungary, defectiveness may have seemed a far broader phenomenon than the officially recorded statistics regarding the deaf, blind, and weak-minded might imply. (p. 48)

These pathologizing assumptions based on the SES group into which one is born remain in play today, with both class-based intelligence and class-based morality presumed to be the province of the affluent and with immigrants, the impoverished, and the socially othered assumed to be deficient and in need of educational reformation (Smagorinsky & Taxel, 2005). This perspective helped to provide the context in which other approaches such as defectology came into being around the turn of the 20th century.

The Emergence of Defectology Prior to World War I

In 1908, Tsarist Russian psychiatrist and special education school organizer V. P. Kashchenko founded what he called a "sanatorium school, implying a joint medical and pedagogical approach to retardation" (McCagg, 1989, p. 48). Kashchenko in turn introduced the term defectology in Moscow in 1912. According to McCagg (1989), "the word defective did not conjure up, even in the West, the connotations of prejudice it does today. One may find it as a classifier term in the New York Public Library catalogue, for example, which was composed in that day. It was perfectly respectable" as a term applied to those exhibiting makeups that departed from the evolutionary norm (p. 40). In 1919, Kashchenko used the term "medical pedagogical station," a literal translation of *Heilpädogogik*, for his Moscow clinic.

Kashchenko himself, as this timetable suggests, was an old-school Tsarist who adapted to the Bolshevik turnover and became established as among the leading Soviet architects of what became known as schools of defectology, at least until Stalin deposed him in the 1930s. This term referred to a range of "defects" including deafness, blindness, and various forms of cognitive impairment viewed as "retardation" in his day. Even in the midst of the turmoil that eventually produced the Soviet Union in December, 1922, Kashchenko and colleagues had begun setting up institutes and congresses, such as the First All-Russian Congress for Struggle against Child Defectiveness, Delinquency and Homelessness in 1920 as part of a broader effort to found "a new centralized Soviet system for educating physically abnormal and mentally retarded children" (McCagg, 1989, p. 41). Again, these terms were standard at the time, only later to be replaced by means of reference more in tune with the ears and sensibilities of later generations. According to McCagg, by the 1930s, when the term "defectology" might have begun to sound outdated, "there was no going back for Soviet defectology. Perhaps its label was by then too well established, too revolutionary-national, to be cast aside" (p. 42). The political, nationalist shading of human understanding remains a theme in the development of philosophies and practices attendant to the manner in which the lives of those considered "disabled" are conceived and cultivated.

Along with Kashchenko, Drs. Rossolimo and Griboedov are credited by one authoritative source with establishing *Heilpädogogik* and defectology in Russia and the ensuing Soviet Union. McCagg (1989) finds no definitive pathway from Germany to Russia for this adoption, noting that

> the transfusion of ideas is not surprising, given the universal prestige of German science at the time, its dominance in Russian universities, and the frequency with which Russian intellectuals visited the German lands. It thus seems most probably that what these Russians came to call defectology derived from this transfusion. … The diagnostic and rehabilitative tasks they faced in Russia were enormous. … Especially when the Revolution of 1917 provided both an opportunity and a demand for quick solutions to enormous social problems, the hardly tried German model for remedial education must have seemed the answer to a prayer. (p. 49)

As McCagg (1989) notes, the nationalism that helped to shape educational politics later created divisions between Germany and Russia that prevented such cross-national sharing of intellectual contributions and practices. Initially, however, the German model easily made its way into Soviet thinking, along with the foundational ideas of Karl Marx in forming a political economy.

McCagg (1989) finds that the original conception of defectology has undergone significant changes over time, "perhaps most of all because of the work of L. S. Vygotsky, the revolutionary of early Soviet psychology" from Belarus's Jewish population, a heritage despised by the Romanov dynasty of Russia to the point of banishment and reprisal by pogrom (p. 51). I next turn to Vygotsky's much-overlooked contributions to this field and how his attention to the anomalous child, to use his translated parlance, fits within his broader conception of a comprehensive, socially-mediated developmental psychology.

Setting the Historical Stage for Vygotsky's Dramatic Appearance

McCagg (1989) relates how the Bolshevik Revolution produced a purge of established, bourgeois, and anti-revolutionary psychologists from positions of authority in Moscow. Some of the old-school psychologists pragmatically shifted to Bolshevism to save their careers, without substantially incorporating Marxist principles into their conception. Toward the goal of making psychology more of a Marxist discipline, K. N. Kornilov was appointed head of the Moscow Psychology Institute due to his greater value on materialism than many of his colleagues held.

At roughly the same time, Vygotsky, still in his 20s and working on his doctoral dissertation (a work of literary criticism produced from his sickbed, focused on "the psychology of art" through textual analysis; see Smagorinsky, 2011a), gave a talk at a 1924 congress in Moscow that shook the field and launched his stardom. As described by McCagg, "Vygotsky was an ardent, believing Marxist, and was possessed by a nigh messianic energy. He had a dynamic effect on the younger members of the institute. He soon seemed to incarnate the revolution there" (p. 52). This stunning entrée gave him revolutionary authority to establish a Laboratory for Study of the Psychology of Abnormal Childhood modeled on a school he had set up in Gomel before his ascendance to greater fame and influence in Moscow. This lab in turn put him in contact with the defectologists working in the *Heilpädogogik*. However, the defectologists working from older traditions worked from a doctrine that "insisted on medical involvement in the education of abnormal children, on a vague linkage between various social and physical abnormalities, and on an activist approach to all of them. Now, Vygotsky made it over into a specifically Marxist, high philosophical science" far more robust than what had previously been conceived of (McCagg, 1989, p. 53), abetted by the extraordinary intellectual firepower of the psychologists whom Vygotsky recruited to work with him on this great national challenge.

Once again, however, the reigning political forces compromised advances in the field. Stalin was paranoid about academia and generally suppressed their influence, often through violent means (Zinchenko, 2007). Vygotsky himself found his work under attack because he did not fully embrace a Stalinist orthodoxy and, by the end of his brief and infirm life, feared death through other means. Although his work experienced a later revival, what he produced during his own lifetime was airbrushed out of the picture of Soviet psychology and education, replaced by more congenial perspectives that Stalin found less threatening. The death blow, or at least a knockout punch followed by decades on the canvas, came in the 1936 proclamation by the Central Committee of the Soviet Communist Party, "On

Pedagogical Perversions in the Commissariat of Education," which produced a Pedology Decree that, among other things, essentially banned the practice of defectology and villainized the likes of Vygotsky for practicing such bourgeois forms of education. Just a year later, Stalin launched the Great Terror in which all dissent was treated with deadly response.

Only after Stalin's death in 1953 was the door opened to a rediscovery of Vygotsky's contributions, often in other languages than Russian before becoming available in his own adopted country. I next review Vygotsky's contributions to defectology, working from the primary sources now available in translation from his prolific career as distilled in his writing and in lectures and transcriptions of his sickbed articulation of his ideas.

Vygotsky's Cultural Historical Theory

Vygotsky's work has variously been characterized as sociocultural, sociocognitive, cultural-historical, social constructionist (or constructivist), and other terms that locate the process of cognition first in the environment, and only later, through a process of appropriation, as an individual mental function. Contexts in this sense are never static, but founded on cultural history such that they have specific properties and values that are continually refined as people occupy and transform the settings of human development. This attention to contexts does not mean that biology is irrelevant, however; Vygotsky (1929) distinguished between the biological and cultural lines of development through which "psychological functions [involve] the working out of new methods of reasoning, the mastering of the cultural methods of behavior" (p. 415). These lines converge early in life, perhaps with the first human contact (Cole, 1996).

Yet any disruption in either line may amplify its presence, as when a person becomes blinded. Schools have long been dominated by an extrapolation of Piaget's stage theory that has been used to justify institutionalized age-level schooling schedules as the norm and considered those who lag in conventional developmental ways to be deficient and behind, a problem evident in much mainstream special education (see the contributors to Gabel, 2005). A cultural-historical approach would view development according to more local norms, and even so, not treat deviations as deficiencies. Further, sudden changes, such as those affecting Eastern Europe during a decade of continual warfare between the beginning of the first World War and the end of the Russian Civil War, had the tragic consequence of hundreds of thousands of damaged and traumatized children and youth, who in turn became the responsibility of the public education system. This change in physical capabilities, to the Soviet defectologists inspired by Vygotsky, did not indicate a suddenly degraded life. Rather, it suggested the need for the people in the context to help construct new and different developmental pathways to allow for participation in society's practices and processes.

Vygotsky's Approach to the Anomalous Human

The field of defectology provided an education for the many children and youth who were maimed, dismembered, blinded, deafened, or cognitively impaired by the violence of the first World War, the Bolshevik Revolution, and Civil War that produced the Soviet Union in 1922, coinciding with the beginning of Vygotsky's career in Moscow. This important research program has largely been overlooked by scholars over time, perhaps overshadowed by his broader developmental research program and the small number of key ideas—the zone of proximal development, the role of play in development—that have reductively and inadequately been distilled from his career project (see Smagorinsky, 2018a, 2018b).

This period coincided with Hitler's embrace of eugenics, an ableist perspective enforced with deadly vengeance on those whose bodies did not meet the Aryan ideal. Yet Vygotsky challenged debilitating views of the physically different by arguing that they comprise a *social problem* rather than one of the individual presumably disabled by difference. Defectology was designed to construct more humane settings to help cultivate the potential of those generally felt to have little potential for living a satisfying life or contributing to a broader society's possibilities. Their lives, according to common perception, became stunted at the point of departure from the norm. Their presumed deficiencies framed their humanity; and their prospects for development into prosperous people were shut down by assumptions of limitation among those who surrounded them.

Vygotsky (1993) found that the "old defectology" viewed "a handicapped condition as a purely quantitative developmental limitation. … Reaction against this quantitative approach to all theoretical and practical problems is the most important characteristic of modern defectology" (p. 30). Rather, he believed,

> a child whose development is impeded by a defect is not simply a child less developed than his peers but is a child who has developed differently. … A child in each stage of his development, in each of his phases, represents a qualitative uniqueness, i.e., a specific organic and psychological structure; in precisely the same way, a handicapped child represents a qualitatively different, unique type of development. … Only with this idea of qualitative uniqueness (rather than the overworked quantitative variations of separate elements) in the phenomena and processes under examination, does defectology acquire for the first time, a methodological basis. (p. 154)

Vygotsky's (1993) rejection of quantitative assessments concerned their reductive, normative way of establishing a proper developmental growth trajectory from which deficits can be measured. His criticism is congruent with critiques from the various Disability fields with respect to modern-day special education based on biological stages and diagnosis of developmental lags requiring remediation. To Vygotsky, this "mechanistic notion is unfounded methodologically speaking." Rather, he argued, the appropriate approach is to consider "the alliance of social and biological regularities in child development" in a dialectical fashion (p. 124).

Vygotsky (1993) regarded the biological difference—in defectology, blindness, deafness, and cognitive impairment—as a person's *primary disability*. This point of difference served as the sole focus of attention for the diagnosticians prior to the development of defectology, and remains a continuing problem in 21st century diagnostics. However, the primary disability is mainly a problem *when people in the environment treat the person as inferior* for exhibiting these non-normative bodily functions. Unfortunately, this social belief in a person's inferiority may be appropriated by the affected individual, producing the far more damaging *secondary disability* of feelings of low self-esteem in response to the way societal treatment of a primary disability makes the disability disabling. The "problem" of disability is in this conception *a social problem* that requires a re-education of the general population, who then work to provide avenues for participation in cultural practices through which people of anomalous makeup develop feelings of affirmation and inclusion.

Attempting to repair the defective person, Vygotsky (1993) believed, was misguided; and this medical model of viewing difference as a curable problem remains in effect today in many special education programs (Danforth, 2009). Rather, he sought to include those lacking normative functions by making available "roundabout" or alternative means of mediation, such as the use of a braille to assist the unsighted. Vygotsky's approach to the anomalous human makeup was thus positive, optimistic, and future-oriented; "no theory," he maintained, "is possible if it proceeds from exclusively negative premises" (p. 31). This future-oriented perspective was designed to help all people lead fully productive lives, particularly those whose bodies do not conform with the evolutionary norm.

Social Esteem

Vygotsky argued that feelings of inadequacy may be resolved in two very different ways for those who live with physical or cognitive "disability." First, he asserted that the feelings of inadequacy could serve to motivate positive new ways of engaging with society. Through Vienna-based Alfred Adler's (1933) influence,

Vygotsky (1993) argued that "*Via subjective feelings of inadequacy, a physical handicap dialectically transforms itself into psychological drives toward compensation and overcompensation*" (p. 33; emphasis in original). Adler is often viewed as a disciple of Sigmund Freud, yet like Vygotsky, he broke with Freud's individualistic emphasis in psychotherapy and his focus on past life events. Both Adler and Vygotsky took a social perspective on the human psyche, one that was concerned with one's forward trajectory more than its early, traumatic experiences. Adler's notion of *social interest*—an individual's personal interest in furthering the welfare of others—is central to Vygotsky's view that "disability" is a social problem rather than a problem held by individuals.

Vygotsky's view of compensation was thus oriented to the future. Compensation allows a bypass of obstacles via adjustments that represent "a continually evolving adaptive process. If a blind or deaf child achieves the same level of development as a normal child, then the child with a defect achieves this *in another way, by another course, by other means*" (p. 34; emphasis in original). A person considered "disabled" makes adaptations through mediational means that allow for participation in society's cultural practices.

Human difference thus needs to be valued for its potential to motivate a personally-initiated productive adaptive response that allows for cultural participation and thus feelings of affirmation: "Cultural development is the main area for compensation of deficiency when further organic development is impossible; in this respect, the path of cultural development is unlimited" (Vygotsky, 1993, p. 169). He thus sees the need for mutual adaptations. Society must provide environments that promote development toward cultural ends via roundabout means. At the same time, individuals should appropriate alternative means of mediation to compensate for their ill-fit with conventional societal structures so as to navigate their surroundings with greater facility.

A feeling of inadequacy can thus have a beneficial effect *when learners are treated as productive people adapting to, and contributing to, their environments.* These alternative developmental pathways, made available in a supportive setting, make it so that "the most important and decisive condition of cultural development—precisely the ability to use psychological tools—is preserved in such children" (Vygotsky, 1993, p. 47). Vygotsky offered this view to counter the prevailing perspective, one that he located in European Christian traditions, that people of anomalous makeup should be pitied or treated with charity, both of which to Vygotsky contributed to the feelings of deficiency that comprise the secondary disability.

A reciprocal process of adaptation, he emphasized, must be undertaken *by the people surrounding the anomalous child*, who accept these alternative means of navigating the physical and social worlds nonjudgmentally and respectfully. People surrounding those considered "disabled" have an adaptive responsibility to construct alternative pathways that allow for satisfying navigation of the world such that one's positive sense of self is affirmed. Vygotsky's approach was thus oriented to *assets* rather than *deficits*, a view well-aligned with the various Disability fields and their attention to both the discursive environment of social interaction and the material means through which its navigations become possible.

Vygotsky (1993) thus addressed the notion of "disability" through attention to the environment, where the creation of future-oriented, affirmational mediational settings, and alternative pathways of development are provided for people of anomalous makeup such that their points of difference are not foregrounded in people's construction of their potential. Vygotsky shifted the terms of the debate *from re-mediation of the deficit to education of the surrounding community*. This attention to *settings* was a critical dimension of Vygotsky's (1993) broader psychological project that emphasized the necessary integration of all aspects of human development with one's affective engagement with the world (Vygotsky, 1971, 1994, 1999a, 1999b). "Full social esteem," he insisted, "is the ultimate aim of education inasmuch as all the processes of overcompensation are directed at achieving social status" (1993, p. 57). What matters is that children are provided the means through which they have the potential to develop higher mental functions—those that are developed within cultural contours and that distill value systems, appropriate practices, and teleological goals—even in the absence of a phylogenetically typical capacity, e.g., seeing or hearing.

Those who can compensate for a "disability" by learning roundabout means develop unconventional ways of integrating themselves into society. In doing so, they may develop capacities for insights not available to those whose makeup does not require adaptation, because they learn to see the world through other means and from other perspective. In Vygotsky's (1993) ideal society, those who develop such capabilities are encouraged and embraced as valued productive members, appreciated and understood by fellow citizens whose own willingness to shift their understanding of difference helps to construct and support those alternative means of participation.

"Mental Health" from a Defectological Perspective

I close with a brief account of how I have adapted Vygotsky's defectological approach to the issue of what is widely, and I believe deceptively, called "mental health." Vygotsky himself was never concerned with neurological variation that produces a host of what are called mental disabilities and disorders; and most of what I read in the Disability fields concerns physical differences more than those associated with what is understood as the mind. I undertook this adaptation for very practical purposes when I began to accept the presence of neurodiversity in my own family and in myself (see Smagorinsky, 2011b), particularly with respect to what are known as autism spectrum *disorder*, obsessive-compulsive *disorder*, and chronic anxiety *disorder*, all of which run through my own system and that of family members.

My pathway to Disability fields thus began through a personal recognition that I was different in ways I had trouble understanding, rather than through empathy for others or formal learning via the reading of Disability field scholarship. This pathway led me to Vygotsky's work in defectology, although quite indirectly; and ultimately led me to see the relation between what I was learning and what has been articulated by Disability scholars and practitioners. In other words, I have ended up in Disability fields through an alternative route, one that I hope has some value for those whose pathways have been much more conventional: as special education practitioners disillusioned by common practice, as humanities scholars concerned with discursive constructions of difference, and other routes. Rather, I arrived at this point as a person who might be considered mentally ill according to the *Diagnostic and Statistical Manual of Mental Disorders* (American Psychiatric Association, 2013), yet who resists being considered disabled, disordered, handicapped, or other pejorative and debilitating term in common diagnostic and social parlance.

In a series of publications (Cook & Smagorinsky, 2014; Smagorinsky, 2011b, 2012a, 2012b, 2014a, 2014b, 2016a, 2016b, 2016c, 2016d), I have seized especially on Vygotsky's (1993) notion of the secondary disability and his view that human difference is primarily a social problem to help me frame my understanding of what it means to live a neuro-atypical life. I have argued that neurodivergence is a social problem more than a problem of the individual, with the education of those surrounding the neuro-atypical person more important than trying to normalize people manifesting unusual neurological makeups.

I have also argued that any notion of "disability" is situational, using the example of the blind person in a room with sighted people in which the lights go out and the room is pitched into darkness, leaving the blind person the only one able to navigate easily to find a way out. "Disability" is also relational, a function of how other people relate to difference, providing avenues for acceptance and appreciation rather than pity and rejection. In this sense, I have argued (2014b) that as an academic, I have an *Asperger's Advantage* because my career rewards those who can pursue narrow interests in excruciating detail, an Asperger's trait that I believe has helped distinguish my research and publications. When bundled with chronic anxiety and obsessiveness-compulsiveness, this disposition both works efficiently at a rare level of detail, and drives a need to complete tasks ahead of schedule. As an academic, I have benefitted enormously from what is generally considered disabling.

I have also developed the notion of *positive social updraft*, a set of conditions that allows for constructive, affirmational participation in valued social activities. This notion is directly adapted from Vygotsky's (1993) romantic belief that the Soviet Union could provide young people with opportunities to become involved in Soviet social movements oriented to promoting their egalitarian national culture, a belief shattered by Stalin's shifting of these group's responsibilities to becoming tattletales on behalf of the state, including reporting actions of their own parents considered dangerous to the Soviet mission (Snyder, 2010).

Less idealistically, I have formulated the notion of positive social updraft to describe the manner in which neuro-atypical youth may become involved in cultural practices that foreground their assets and minimize their shortcomings. For instance, Cook and Smagorinsky (2014) describe a young woman on the Asperger's spectrum whose awkward social skills were minimized and her artistic abilities amplified through the online anime culture to which she contributed. Shunned by others in her material world and considered a problem in her family, she found affirmation through this medium and, as Vygotsky would assume, developed a positive self-image through the online response to her chosen personas. Her "disabilities" thus receded and her potential became ripe for development as the social context of the online community allowed her to prosper as a valued participant by means of the positive social updraft afforded by the online community.

Discussion

In this chapter I have introduced the Soviet defectological tradition to the Disability fields, contextualizing its development and providing extensions to areas not part of defectology's original purview and generally not written extensively about in Disability publications. In doing so I hope to have provided the field with an intellectual stream rooted in 1700s Europe, adapted and developed in the first decades of the 20th century in Russia and the Soviet Union, still practiced in modern-day Russia, and amenable to adaptation to new areas of human difference moving forward. I have found Vygotsky's principles to be quite durable and informative to my interests in neurodiversity, and I hope to Disability scholars interested in the broadest possible application of their work.

I do not contend that defectology has solved all problems uniquely. Indeed, it shares many assumptions with the various Disability fields. It does emerge, however, from a different cultural context and provides a language for identifying problems such as the secondary disability, which has been hiding in plain sight for some time now. I hope that my own realizations have some value to those who share my concerns for the diverse human species and aspire to cultivate the potential of all people, regardless of how they are made up, through more sensitive and appreciative beliefs and contexts and through the provision of positive social updrafts through which they may most fruitfully realize their human potential.

References

American Psychiatric Association. (2013). *Diagnostic and statistical manual of mental disorders*, 5th ed. Washington, DC: Author.

Cole, M. (1996). *Cultural psychology: A once and future discipline*. Cambridge, MA: Harvard University Press.

Cook, L. S., & Smagorinsky, P. (2014). Constructing positive social updrafts for extranormative personalities. *Learning, Culture and Social Interaction, 3*(4), 296–308. Retrieved December 17, 2015 from http://www.petersmagorinsky.net/About/PDF/LCSI/LCSI_2014.pdf

Danforth, S. (2009). *The incomplete child: An intellectual history of learning disabilities*. New York, NY: Peter Lang.

Foucault, M. (1961/1964). *Folie et déraison: Histoire de la folie à l'âge classique* (*Madness and civilization: A history of insanity in the age of reason*). (R. Howard (abridged edition); J. Murphy & J. Khalfa (unabridged edition), Trans.). New York, NY: Taylor & Francis.

Gabel, S. L. (Ed.) (2005). *Disability studies in education: Readings in theory and method*. New York, NY: Peter Lang.

Judd, A. (2017, May 11). Deaths, delays paint grim picture of Georgia mental health reform. *Atlanta Journal-Constitution*. Retrieved October 17, 2017 from http://www.myajc.com/news/state--regional-govt--politics/deaths-delays-paint-grim-picture-georgia-mental-health-reform/myjKGIHosiV0KLWxv2h0oM/

McCagg, W. O. (1989). The origins of defectology. In W. O. McCagg & L. Siegelbaum (Eds.), *The disabled in the Soviet Union: Past and present, theory and practice* (pp. 39–62). Pittsburgh, PA: University of Pittsburgh Press. Retrieved December 16, 2015 from http://digital.library.pitt.edu/cgi-bin/t/text/pageviewer-idx?c=pittpress;cc=pittpress;idno=31735057895033;node=31735057895033%3A1.6.2.2;frm=frameset;rgn=full%20text;didno=31735057895033;view=image;seq=0049

Smagorinsky, P. (2011a). Vygotsky's stage theory: The psychology of art and the actor under the direction of *perezhivanie*. *Mind, Culture, and Activity, 18*, 319–341. Available at http://www.petersmagorinsky.net/About/PDF/MCA/MCA2011-Psychology of Art.pdf

Smagorinsky, P. (2011b). Confessions of a mad professor: An autoethnographic consideration of neuroatypicality, extranormativity, and education. *Teachers College Record, 113*(8), 1701–1732. Available at http://www.petersmagorinsky.net/About/PDF/TCR/TCR2011.pdf

Smagorinsky, P. (2012a). Vygotsky, "defectology," and the inclusion of people of difference in the broader cultural stream. *Journal of Language and Literacy Education* [Online], *8*(1), 1–25. Available at http://jolle.coe.uga.edu/wp-content/uploads/2012/05/Vygotsky-and-Defectology.pdf

Smagorinsky, P. (2012b). "Every individual has his own insanity": Applying Vygotsky's work on defectology to the question of mental health as an issue of inclusion. *Learning, Culture and Social Interaction, 1*(1), 67–77. Available at http://www.petersmagorinsky.net/About/PDF/LCSI/LCSI_2012.pdf

Smagorinsky, P. (2014a). Who's normal here? An atypical's perspective on mental health and educational inclusion. *English Journal, 103*(5), 15–23. Available at http://www.petersmagorinsky.net/About/PDF/EJ/EJ2014.pdf

Smagorinsky, P. (2014b, November 26). Taking the diss out of disability. *Teachers College Record.* Available at http://www.petersmagorinsky.net/About/PDF/TCR/TCR2014.html

Smagorinsky, P. (Ed.). (2016a). *Creativity and community among autism-spectrum youth: Creating positive social updrafts through play and performance.* New York, NY: Palgrave Macmillan.

Smagorinsky, P. (2016b, May 22). University of Georgia professor explains his "Asperger's Advantage" and disabling assumption of disorder. *Atlanta Journal-Constitution.* Available at http://getschooled.blog.myajc.com/2016/05/27/university-of-georgia-professor-explains-his-aspergers-advantage-and-disabling-assumption-of-disorder/

Smagorinsky, P. (2016c, July 8). Is mental health strictly mental? *Psychology Today.* Available at https://www.psychologytoday.com/blog/conceptual-revolution/201607/is-mental-health-strictly-mental

Smagorinsky, P. (2016d, August 2016). Foregrounding potential, not disorder, in neurodiverse students. *Literacy & NCTE.* Available at http://blogs.ncte.org/index.php/2016/08/foregrounding-potential-not-disorder-neurodiverse-students/

Smagorinsky, P. (2018a). Deconflating the ZPD and instructional scaffolding: Retranslating and reconceiving the zone of proximal development as the zone of next development. *Learning, Culture and Social Interaction, 16,* 70–75.

Smagorinsky, P. (2018b). Is instructional scaffolding actually Vygotskian? And why should it matter to teachers? *Journal of Adolescent & Adult Literacy, 62*(3), 253–257.

Smagorinsky, P., Cole, M., & Braga, L. W. (2017). On the complementarity of cultural historical psychology and contemporary disability studies. In I. Esmonde & A. Booker (Eds.), *Power and privilege in the learning sciences: Critical and sociocultural theories* (pp. 70–92). New York, NY: Routledge.

Smagorinsky, P., & Taxel, J. (2005). *The discourse of character education: Culture wars in the classroom.* Mahwah, NJ: Lawrence Erlbaum.

Snyder, T. (2010). *Bloodlands: Europe between Hitler and Stalin.* New York, NY: Basic Books.

Vygotsky, L. S. (1929). The problem of the cultural development of the child. *Journal of Genetic Psychology,* 36, 415–432. Retrieved December 16, 2015 from https://www.marxists.org/archive/vygotsky/works/1929/cultural_development.htm

Vygotsky, L. S. (1934/1987). Thinking and speech. In L. S. Vygotsky, *Collected works* (Vol. 1, pp. 39–285) (R. Rieber & A. Carton, Eds.; N. Minick, Trans.). New York, NY: Plenum.

Vygotsky, L. S. (1993). *The collected works of L. S. Vygotsky. Volume 2: The fundamentals of defectology (abnormal psychology and learning disabilities)* (R. W. Rieber & A. S. Carton, Eds.; J. E. Knox & C. B. Stevens, Trans.). New York, NY: Plenum.

Zinchenko, V. P. (2007). Thought and word: The approaches of L. S. Vygotsky and G. G. Shpet. In H. Daniels, M. Cole, & J. V. Wertsch (Eds.), *The Cambridge companion to Vygotsky* (pp. 212–245). New York, NY: Cambridge University Press.

PART TWO

Emic and Autoethnographic Perspectives

CHAPTER THREE

Blind and in Technicolor

A Personal Account of Adaptation

GINA MARIE APPLEBEE

Blindness and neurologic divergence have been unique, integral parts of a journey full of adversity, adventure, and adaptation. Personally, I would not trade this rich, unusual life experience for 20/20 vision and all the money in the world, and have come to hold an affirmative social view of diverse abilities as essential aspects of human diversity, and significant factors in my own being and growth. In this chapter, I offer a brief autoethnographic account of lessons learned through losing my sight, being neurologically divergent, and developing a type of pan-sensory synesthesia. Additionally, I aim to share insights into inclusion and adaptive accommodation in our educational systems gained through these life experiences, for the purpose of promoting alternative understandings of diverse abilities and transforming such systems.

At first glance, it seems easy for casual observers to assume that my life, and perhaps my identity, have been primarily shaped, or even defined by, my blindness and adversities associated with it. Though losing my sight and developing subsequent adaptation has played a pivotal role, such a view is reductionistic and simply incorrect. Progressively going blind over the first 23 years of my life was indeed a difficult, important part of my development, but has by no means been the only or the most challenging and influential factor.

Intersectionality among being neurologically divergent, losing my sight, being blind and post-trauma, becoming a synesthete, and living my entire adult life below the poverty line as a woman with these diverse abilities paints a more complex and adequate picture of my path and ongoing situation. Indigence and post-trauma have been without question the most challenging parts of my path, but cannot be understood separately from these other experiences, as part of a whole complex human life. Although my focus in this chapter is on my experience as someone with diverse abilities, the reader is encouraged to remember that these are embedded in the broader, distinct dynamics of my development.

Beginnings: Going Blindly Into the World

My twin sister and I were born with a type of genetic difference, which eventually came to be described as Atypical Clumped Pigmentary Retinal Degeneration, or Advanced S-cone syndrome. This difference, combined with conditions in my incubator following an embattled and almost deadly entrance to life, caused me to become legally blind by age 12, and I entered college with an extremely limited central visual field and vision worse than 20/800. Having lost most of my sight as a young girl, and showing an unusual degree of resilience from an early age, I accepted and adapted quickly as my vision faded, first to blurry, then to shimmering, through double vision to massive central field loss. This is not to say I did not have moments of teenage angst about my vision, and more especially the social responses to it. These were passing moments, however, and the radical acceptance and resilience that is the gift of childhood overruled them. These are gifts I have never had the luxury or desire to grow out of. The parade of retinal specialists and grueling tests came to the conclusion that I was going blind, with no clue as to the rate or shape of the trajectory.

Despite having accepted my vision loss when I began my undergraduate career, I remained very uncomfortable explaining it to others or admitting my situation to my teachers. I had tried a variety of approaches to this challenge, and was not fond of the pity, patronization, and overall awkwardness that so often seemed to result from talking about my vision. Having lost the vision somewhat gradually, I had succeeded in adapting as I grew, and was still able to "pass" as a "normal" person with ridiculously thick reading glasses most of the time. In this way, I spent my first year of college struggling, being unable to read slides and chalkboards, straining to pretend I could see what was in the microscope or textbook figures. I did not want to be treated differently from other students, or have some special, attention-drawing assistance. It was the kindness of an introductory geology professor who broke this stubborn silence, and he opened a door to a much more honest, cooperative world of learning with a simple, inclusive gesture.

I highlight this experience because it illustrates how even the smallest inclusive acts of an instructor can trigger a major, positive shift for students with disabilities. The professor noticed I was struggling with figures on a test, despite being a very hard-working student. When he asked about it, I admitted I had very bad vision, and was not registered with disability services. To be clear, many instructors to this day would insist on a formal letter requesting accommodations. Instead, he offered his slides on CDs so I could view them with my glasses, and told me the story of a totally blind paleontologist he had gone to graduate school with. Before long, I declared my major, registered for accommodations, and got my Leaderdog, Mitchell. The slum was my home, my teachers were my heroes, and geology provided my path to building a real, decent life. It was around this time that I began diligently exercising my non-visual senses, and mapping my perceptual world outside of what I knew was fading, ephemeral remaining vision.

With the help of Mitchell the dog, teachers, and friends, I gradually became more open about my blindness, beginning to develop much more socially distributed ways of adapting and learning with very low vision. Although we used some traditional accommodations (e.g., extended test time), my geology teachers and I worked together to find many other creative, effective learning strategies. The enlarged protractors, blown up notes, microscopes plugged into projectors, and stash of snacks to keep me from having to steal all my food were just manifestations of what really made the difference in my inclusion: their belief in me and willingness to work together to make things work. Many years later, when inclusive pedagogical training was my main occupation, I emphasized these generous provisions to current and future teachers. Planning is important; access tools and strategies are important. But what matters most is the welcoming, inclusive attitude teachers have toward their students with diverse abilities.

Not all my college professors were so enlightened and accommodating. I had some patiently spend office hours writing equations with giant markers, while others refused to comply with disability service's requests for copies of notes. I had some say "I think you can do this," and others tell me that even attempting to learn about the basics of their field without vision was a pointless waste of time. I was determined, though, and the more I experienced this range of responses, the better I became at navigating them with minimal damage to my own efficacy. I used zoom options on computers, closed caption TVs, binocular glasses, and all my powers of imagination to access learning, and the teachers who genuinely cared did their part to adapt alongside me.

When Mitchell the dog and I walked the graduation stage, I was 20. Having grown from the directionless, street-scampering punk to someone with recognized potential, who travelled and did research, I figured I had "made it" past the hard part. I had a degree, and was on my way to a summer fellowship I was certain would be a gateway to that real, decent life. For a few months, it was. Then, following a violent attack on me, trauma became the new and most difficult part of my experiential landscape. In the years that followed, post-trauma and post-traumatic growth, invisible to others, marked my path more than blindness or any other facet of my life. Invisible challenges were not altogether new to me, however, as I had lived with a growing awareness of being a neuro-cognitive outlier for many years.

It became apparent, even as a young, home schooled girl, that I learned a little differently than did my twin sister and other children. My mother was convinced I had severe ADHD, although I was never tested. In high school, and even through college, my cognitive and learning differences were largely masked by the pedagogical challenges presented by failing vision. But, I knew they were there and gradually became better acquainted with how my mind worked, and did not work, as I tried out various ways to befriend and make healthy use of my undomesticated intelligence. Understanding and tapping into the currents of motivation, flexible structure, and a long-cultivated patience have been the keys to remaining functional and sustainably productive. Over the years, I have come to identify strongly with the autism spectrum, although I have never sought formal testing or diagnosis. Throughout college, and later graduate school, I grappled with a layer of perceptual difficulty associated with blindness, along with this other layer of processing and expression difficulties associated with being neuro-cognitively divergent.

I can grasp highly complex concepts with ease and enthusiasm, but to this day struggle to fill out basic bureaucratic paperwork or simple forms. I am capable of mentally exploring three and four dimensional structures, but unable to perform the most menial of assigned tasks that do not interest me. I have lived fearlessly, at times a little recklessly, in the face of difficult circumstances, but may be engulfed in physical anxiety while engaging in ordinary activities, such as walking into a bank, or introducing myself at a meeting. Similar to my orientation toward losing my vision, I came to view my unusual, pattern-hungry, systems-loving mind as a kind of difficult blessing, and one I would not trade for any other.

There are certainly former teachers who would have contrary opinions, but for those who cared about my learning, tapped into my motivation, and saw past my difficulties to my potential, my different ways of thinking were refreshing, creative, and otherwise worth the trouble. One of the idiosyncrasies that comes with the way my mind works is the occasional learning binge, during which I would throw myself into a thorough exploration of or devour huge amounts of reading about whatever it was that had captured my interest. Often I turned this learning on my own perceptual processes, exploring and integrating my non-visual perception in an iterative effort to discover how best to appreciate and navigate the world with blindness. This learning paid off, years after, with the sudden loss of my remaining vision, and the later neurological revision that came in the form of synesthesia. What may have seemed to be deficits in attention or inhibitors to expression early in my schooling turned out to be an unconventional style of building and integrating knowledge in a way that was extraordinarily adaptive in my particular case.

During my master's program in marine geophysics, I lost the rest of my remaining vision suddenly at age 23. Following a few days of dazed disbelief, and onset of a bright blue, flashing light that was to illuminate my darkness for the next 5 years, I was relieved and very happy with the unexpected, early arrival of what I had known would be an inevitable development. Instead of struggling to make the last shreds of visual perception function, constant eye strain, migraines, and what seemed to be wasted cognitive processing, I was free to explore non-visual perception without distraction or any attempt at living between blind and sighted worlds.

Adapting quickly, I turned my tendency to binge-learn on the new challenge. I made a host of healthy life changes, learned braille and text-to-speech technology, and began building an extensive toolbox for non-visual living and learning. I began seeking out and learning from first other people who were blind, then people with a wide array of diverse abilities. My new experience with total blindness was hard, and did not always meet with a positive response, particularly from my master's advisor, but I held a strong affirmative view, and I had fun with it. I discovered a variety of data sonification software applications, experimented with tactile graphics, and exercised my capacity for auditory learning as much as possible. I came to know many people with a diversity of degrees and types of blindness, and became well aware that my affirmative view was not always shared, nor did I insist that it should be. For myself, however, given my way of seeing the opportunities of adversity, I embraced blindness as an interesting way of being. I have often been asked if I would accept a cure, if such were possible, and the answer was, and is, absolutely not. At no point have I sought a cure, treatment, or medication for my differences. Rather, my treatment of choice has been adapting, learning, and sometimes teaching.

My master's in the geology department allowed me many opportunities to travel the world, explore wild landscapes, and do research at sea. I loved learning and teaching about the Earth, and I still do. After losing the rest of my vision, however, I became highly motivated to contribute to the much-needed work of making our higher educational systems more accessible and inclusive for students with diverse abilities, and found a practical path in pursuing this through a PhD in science education. I began by building communities for students with diverse abilities, giving talks, running panels, starting a Celebrate Ability Week at the university, and otherwise advocating as much as possible. Universal design quickly became my framework of choice, leading to extensive work in implementing Inclusive Design for Learning (IDL). The inclusive design and work with the students, staff, administrators, and current and future faculty would become my whole-hearted vocation for the next 4 years. It is the most rewarding, worthwhile work I have done thus far, and I am honored to share some of the insights from it here.

Lessons from Inclusive Design for Learning

Working with students with a wide array of diverse abilities, I began to develop a much more nuanced and complex understanding of the range and degrees of challenges we face, as well as attitudes toward these trials and means of adapting. At the same time, there were experiences we shared across our differences. These stories included experiences with adversity, social obstacles, and barriers to work and employment, but also a sense of just being people who are different in some significant way, whether these departures were immediately noticeable or not to others. One of the many lessons I learned through this diversity and solidarity was that all individuals are impaired, and all have strengths and weaknesses in their distinct, dynamic ability spectra. Some of these differences are extreme enough, or have consequences such that we become labelled with or identify as people with disabilities.

So, in addition to numerous accommodation strategies and diverse-ability specific learning tools, I came to see the challenge of improving inclusion in this light. The challenge became one of opening up and adapting our systems in ways that are potentially beneficial to all people, none of whom is perfect or particularly normal in any meaningful sense. I adopted the phrase "diverse abilities" at that time, not in some effort at political correctness, or to put a warm, fuzzy spin on life experiences that are hard, and made harder still by social constructions. Instead, this phrase reflects what I mean when speaking of variations in human ability that represent often-overlooked aspects of diversity. Among the student groups, the phrase soon replaced "disability" in our references to ourselves and each other, and I found some faculty refreshingly changing their language as well.

The essential concept of universal design, and my IDL expansion of it, is a fundamental shift in thinking, from seeing students as individual problems, to viewing challenges in the context of the learning environment. What began as an architectural philosophy became a set of guidelines and principles called *universal design for learning*, and a promising, proactive complement to rigid accommodation plans assigned to a subset of students with disabilities. At its core, universal design is an approach that seeks to construct products or environments that are accessible to all people, while minimizing the need for modification. My own expansion into IDL simply sought to move further away from any conception of a one-size-fits-all approach, toward a flexible framework that acknowledges and incorporates the need for adaptive accommodation and informed, iterative re-design.

For years, I worked locally at my university, and nationally at conferences and other institutions, to train instructors in IDL implementation. I taught an IDL course, started a learning community, and began offering workshops with the International Association for Geoscience Diversity (IAGD) and many other organizations. As a framework, IDL is quite simple. Its guidelines include multiple means of representation, engagement, expression, and accommodation strategies. Principles (e.g., flexibility, perceptibility, tolerance for error) seek to further inform design. Much of IDL aligns with established good teaching practices, and students and faculty alike found the results positive and effective. While universal design was gaining in popularity and enjoying more awareness, there was still little work being done on the practicalities of implementation in a variety of specific contexts, and attention to these factors became the focus of my pilot study and dissertation work.

During my comprehensive exam, my neurological diversity began to show more strongly in the form of a deep fascination with Chaos theory and complex adaptive systems. These frameworks soon became a solid epistemological ground that I applied to theory, educational systems, and my IDL work in particular. Although my committee seemed baffled by my obsession with theory, I kept it coherent and, for the most part, relevant through the dissertation proposal stage. I was implementing IDL in introductory geology labs with a team of teaching assistants for my pilot study, enjoying teaching, and feeling comfortable with blindness. To my absolute shock, however, blindness was not the end of my perceptual adventure, and before long, everything changed, again.

Developing Pan-Sensory Synesthesia

Suddenly, in the fall of 2013, the flashing blue light that had illuminated my blindness for years became more colorful and dynamic, often overwhelming and distracting. I was working too hard, deep in theory, cognitively and energetically running at maximum capacity. The migraines became more intense and frequent, I had an odd burning sensation in my brain, and I often took short naps to recover and keep working. Upon waking from one of these naps, I began to "see" with my eyes closed. In the following months, I came to "see" myself, objects, and surfaces (i.e., the whole phenomenological world) with eyes open and closed, in a dazzling and astonishingly beautiful technicolor light. This phenomenon later became known as "non-optic vision," or a type of pan-sensory synesthesia (PSS), but at the time it was a reality-shattering experience reaching the level of spiritual emergency.

I have written at some length about the PSS in the *Psychology Today* blog *Superhuman Minds* (Applebee, 2015), and preliminary neurological studies have been published in the journal *Brain & Cognition* (Roberts & Shenker, 2016) and continue at the Medical University of South Carolina. For the purposes of this chapter, however, I will focus on two aspects of the experience: the social response, and the impact it had on my understanding of human ability.

With a great deal of work at learning about and improving my new visualization, at attempting to understand, at letting go of the need to understand, I slowly came to some degree of dynamic coherence with the novel new situation. There was far more to the experience than the new technicolor vision, much of which I later identified as a kind of kundalini awakening, and I cannot overstate the difficulty of this adjustment period. Of course, I kept working and teaching, and successfully defended my comps, but meanwhile I was revising my relationship with reality. Suddenly, my neurological diversity was much more apparent, and I became extremely sensitive and often phenomenologically overloaded. Making peace with the PSS was not made easier by initial social responses.

People are somewhat alarmed when a blind person claims they can suddenly "see" in technicolor, including with their eyes closed. I had a whole complex adaptive systems explanation, and early neurological reports, but these interpretations did little to mediate a perception by some that I was merely "crazy." Precious few people were supportive of my odd situation, and fewer made an effort to genuinely understand it. At one point, a woman tricked me into going to a psychiatric ward under the guise of exploring another counseling option, and rumors circulated around the university concerning my sanity. My response was, and often still is, I would like to see you go blind, then turn into a glowing technicolor being immersed in a world of liquid, psychedelic light, and see how you handle it.

I rapidly suspended and revised much of my understanding, but at no point did I manifest behavior worthy of such harmful labelling. In the end, my funding was cut, despite my having completed all of my program except my dissertation, and I was handed an Education Specialist degree and encouraged to seek employment elsewhere. I found myself working on grant money back at my undergraduate institution, as I was still adjusting to the PSS and my new phenomenological landscape. I continued IDL workshops wherever I could, but these jobs did not take institutionalized root or provide a stable income. When the grant ran its course,

I took up one of my many old undergraduate jobs as a figure model, and began auditing philosophy courses and doing the hard psychological work of rebuilding my reality. On the one hand, I am certain an individual with my level of education and skills, who was not blind, would have found more gainful employment. On the other, the absence of better employment has motivated me to continue and expand the scope of my education beyond what would otherwise be considered necessary. So, I am poor financially, but have a wealth of knowledge that few have the privilege of acquiring in the course of their relatively ordinary lives.

Navigating the New World

Fortunately after returning to Charleston, SC, I found acceptance and support for my unconventional neuro-phenomenological synesthesia in my communities. Over the next few years I became better at navigating my new visual and intense sensory experience, making lifestyle changes and habits of somatic and meditation practices that supported me. Occasional and very intense conversion anxiety — anxiety associated with somatization, i.e., the expression of mental phenomena as physical—was part of this process, and I found diet changes (e.g., removing caffeine, reducing alcohol consumption), trauma releasing exercises, breath work, and other non-medicinal approaches to work through these experiences. In writing, this sounds like a simple process. But in life, it took time, trial and error, and a lot of help from my friends and teachers.

As it turns out, the kundalini[1] experience, often labelled as merely "crazy" in U.S. culture, is celebrated and cultivated in the East and many other societies, and there is a growing body of literature and tools for supporting people who have such experiences (Grof & Grof, 2017). This availability illustrates the pathologizing tendency of traditional Western psychology and culture, which is quick to demonize differences that do not conform to its outdated paradigms. Given support, and some degree of social understanding, the very same non-normative experience can be viewed as non-pathological, positively transformational, and successfully integrated through a contextualized, whole-person approach (Greyson, 1993). Now, the slum is again my home, but my tiny house is under construction. My yoga, meditation, and martial arts teachers are my heroes, and I am starting my second year of a PhD in transpersonal psychology.

Lessons from a Life that Transcends Disability

Looking across this trajectory of development, I have arrived at a number of insights about human ability. First, drawing from the work of Lev Vygotsky

(1993) as well as social constructivism, I understand that disability itself is largely an artifact of social construction. What Vygotsky called the "secondary disability," or the barriers imposed by socio-cultural contexts, has indeed been amongst my greatest obstacles as a blind person whose mind functions in a noticeably different way. Secondly, the dynamic nature of ability and potential for adaptivity are apparent.

Clearly, ability spectra are not fixed throughout the human lifespan. Despite this variation, there is a common misconception that ability, and disability, are fixed attributes that, if they do change, are assumed to change for the worse. Those who lose their sight over time still fit within this way of thinking, but someone with fully progressed blindness would subsequently develop an adaptive, synesthetic sight challenges the observer into an alternative, more dynamic understanding. Changes in ability, even if they are initially culturally perceived as deficits or impairments of some kind, could later be viewed as adaptive and otherwise beneficial to individuals experiencing them, suggesting that such initial assumptions are limiting and not quite right.

When speaking of the benefits of diverse abilities, I am often met with surprise if not skepticism. To be clear, it is not my intention to downplay the difficulty of living with impairments, or claim that all differences in human ability are inherently adaptive. Rather, I choose to focus on the benefits of living with diverse abilities, and I see these as falling into two broad levels. The first is that, in having these differences, I am directly forced into unique ways of perceiving, appreciating, and expressing myself that are inherently valuable in their distinctness. Second, the opportunities emerging through adversity associated with living differently challenge me into exercising extraordinary levels of adaptability and growth that I otherwise would never find in myself.

At the end of the day, just because it is difficult does not mean I would have my life be any other way. What I feel as someone who is continually conditioning myself through the limits of my so-called flaws, impairments, or weaknesses is that some of my greatest strengths and adaptive skills are rooted in these conditions, and they are part of this complete, fully human experience. In this sense, instead of wishing for or compensating toward some superficial concept of wholeness, I have found my path to be one that is deeply generative, meaningful, and profoundly human.

Note

1. Kundalini is a Sanscrit term that refers to the arising of an energy and consciousness from the base of the spine and its source as the life force.

References

Applebee, G. M. (2015, September 11). Out of darkness and into a glowing world of technicolor. *Psychology Today*. Retrieved August 1, 2018 from https://www.psychologytoday.com/us/blog/the-superhuman-mind/201509/out-darkness-and-glowing-world-technicolor

Greyson, B. (1993). The physio-kundalini syndrome and mental illness. *The Journal of Transpersonal Psychology, 25*(1), 43–58.

Grof, C., & Grof, S. (2017). Spiritual emergency: The understanding and treatment of transpersonal crises. *International Journal of Transpersonal Studies, 36*(2), 30–43.

Roberts, M. H., & Shenker, J. I. (2016). Non-optic vision: Beyond synesthesia? *Brain and Cognition, 107*, 24–29.

Vygotsky, L. S. (1993). *The collected works of L. S. Vygotsky. Volume 2: The fundamentals of defectology (abnormal psychology and learning disabilities)* (R. W. Rieber & A. S. Carton, Eds.; J. E. Knox & C. B. Stevens, Trans.). New York, NY: Plenum.

CHAPTER FOUR

On Becoming a Number

Lessons Learned While Adjusting to Life with Multiple Sclerosis

DOROTHY BOSSMAN

> There is a burden that we the chronically ill in general and we the physically handicapped in particular carry. In every interaction, our baggage includes not only our own physical infirmity but the sense of infirmity we evoke in others and their consequent incapacity to deal with us.
>
> —Zola (1982, p. 202)

I have never had much interest in medicine. I remember taking a career aptitude test in high school and being surprised to see "general practitioner" at the top of the list of suggestions. I imagine my love of school and my concern for the welfare of others led to that result, but a medical doctor was never a viable career choice for me. First, I was shy, and the thought of touching the bodies of strangers made me squeamish. Second, I was terrified by hospitals and most medical procedures (during my only attempt to donate blood, just the sight of the needle had made me faint). I wonder how different it would have been to develop Multiple Sclerosis (MS) if I had been starting a career as a physician when it happened, rather than one as a teacher. Would I have denied and hidden my symptoms for as long as I did? Would I have been better prepared to face the ever-evolving forms of pain and disability that accompany my condition? Would I have expected my diagnosis to be so impersonal? I am not certain it would have been *better* to know what was waiting for me once I became a resident of "the kingdom of the sick" (Sontag, 1978); however, the move might have been less of a shock if I had at least been a student of that realm.

Hearing Something like a Diagnosis

A week before I received a name for my physical trials, I took myself out for a long lunch before driving to an appointment with a general practitioner I had seen once before. Like many individuals who develop serious illnesses, I knew something was wrong but was reluctant to see a doctor to find out what was happening. It had been years since all of it began, but I had sought to hide my symptoms (like shameful secrets) from everyone. After a brief discussion of my health concerns, the general practitioner with whom I met suggested I check in to the hospital. She ordered a series of tests that might be able to explain why my legs were getting weaker, why my balance was getting worse, and why pain made it increasingly difficult for me to concentrate. Looking back now, it was obviously MS, something I would have recognized if I had been to medical school. In the hospital lobby, I gave my name to several people, and after a tedious admission process, I received an official hospital bracelet and a room assignment. My first test was going to be the spinal tap, which I had *heard of*, but I only knew it as something bad that my father-in-law had endured during a hospital visit.

The procedure began in a cold, white room filled with stainless steel medical accessories and a plethora of cupboards. Wondering if this was actually a supply room, I put on a horrifyingly giant hospital gown and sat anxiously on the edge of a paper-covered examination table. A nurse came in and asked me the exact questions I had just answered in the lobby. "No, nothing has changed in the last hour, except that I am shivering now," I thought, as I offered my responses again. Impassively, she noted my answers and told me that she would inject my spine with a numbing medicine to make this procedure go smoothly. I sat up taller and looked away as she gave me a shot in my back, which surprised me with its burning pain. I hoped that it would be the worst part, but I braced myself for more unpleasantness.

A graying, serious-looking doctor came in the room, but he did not introduce himself. As he perused the papers the nurse had attached to a clipboard, I read his name from a lanyard with the hope that we might have a conversation after this event was over. The nurse came over and placed a pillow on my lap. I was puzzled, but it was nice to hold something soft, even if it was encased in stiff, abrasive material. She told me to lean over and hold the pillow tightly while they did the test. "Keep your eyes on me," she said firmly. I felt the cold, dry hands of the doctor on my back and then a series of unbelievably strong undulations of heat, pressure, and nauseating pain followed. I closed my eyes and pulled the pillow into my stomach. The nurse placed her hands on my shoulders, and I managed to open my eyes. She was smiling slightly, offering some comfort inside this frozen well of disorientating pain. While the excruciating procedure continued, I managed to look at my surroundings again. There were windows, covered with white blinds, but I focused on the sunshine that managed to seep through. I looked for a clock, but I imagined that time was not moving anyway.

When it was finally over and I was alone again, I reached around to feel a series of small bandages on my spine. They did not feel big enough to be the only physical reminders of *that* event. I began to feel dizzy as I struggled to dress myself. Just then, my husband, David, arrived from work, and I was thrilled to see him. He helped me get back into my real clothes, so I could head to a hospital room to wait for more tests. I allowed myself to believe that none of them could be as awful as the first. As we walked, and I leaned heavily on him for balance, I squeezed his arm and said, "I am glad you weren't here for *that,*" although we both knew it was a lie.

There were other tests (and many more needles) before I would hear anything that sounded like a diagnosis. Even when I did, it was an event without fanfare or a personal touch. The doctor who had sent me to the hospital came into to my room where I was trying to sleep in the hideous hospital gown I had worn for days. I was on strong medication for pain—narcotics that made me feel sicker—and I longed to recover from what had been a disorientating, difficult week. I sat up and ran my fingers through my hair, wishing I had on clothes. She sat down next to the bed and told me, matter-of-factly, that a neurologist had read the results of my spinal tap and other tests and had concluded that I had a condition "consistent with the symptoms of Multiple Sclerosis." I avoided looking at her while I tried to process this information.

That befuddling description of my condition was the closest thing I got to a diagnosis during my first hospital stay. It was as carefully worded as they have all been. I do not remember my response, but I recall the urge to get myself out of there before the words could be affixed to me permanently. As long as I was in this bland room, stuck in this bed, attached to IVs and monitors, doctors and other nameless hospital employees could read my posted medical information and know I was someone with this awful thing "consistent with" MS. At that moment, I fantasized that I could sneak out between visitors, keep the outcome of this hospital visit a secret, and return to my normal existence.

Adjusting to a New Reality

My reaction that day was an attempt to deny the truth, but I was not really *surprised* by the test results. It was the irony of the situation that got to me. I had just started a teaching career that gave me satisfaction, but then I discovered that my body might not let me pursue it. With the comfort of two incomes, we had just rented a larger place and had started making plans to have children. Our charming new house had more space, but it also had several flights of stairs that had become difficult for me to climb. In addition, I had no idea if I could or should have a baby, just when I realized I wanted one.

At that point in my life, I was proud of certain labels for myself: teacher, wife, reader, scholar, traveler, graduate student, sister, scrabble player, writer, grammarian, comedian, foodie, and poetry lover. Yet none of these distinctions mattered in the hospital, except perhaps "wife," which explained why David was a regular visitor. On a whiteboard in my room under the label "patient," various medical personnel wrote my name, then mostly numbers: my temperature, my heart rate, my medications and dosages, my husband's phone number, the date I arrived, my weight, the number for food service, and so on. Under a second heading of "goals," the board remained blank. More irony, I thought.

Being reduced to numbers and categories did not end when I was discharged, although I hoped that things would be different when I sought treatment on my own. After I received a diagnosis (or what had to pass for one) and left the hospital, I was grounded by pain—made worse by the figurative weight of the situation—and I spent a week in bed. Once I was able to walk, aided by the first of many courses of steroids, I scheduled a visit with the neurologist who had performed the spinal tap. As I drove to the appointment, I felt optimistic that the doctor and I would find a way to manage this disease with medication. This ugly episode would end, and then I would be able to get back to my job, my marriage, and my plans for the future.

This time, the doctor introduced himself, but he stayed far across the examination room and glanced at papers as he talked. He recited what sounded like a memorized description of relapsing-remitting MS, the condition "most consistent with" my test results. I noticed that he never said that I *had* a disease, a fact I had been struggling to digest since I heard the news. He explained that most people have a gradual increase in symptoms in the first ten years, a process that can be slowed with the use of the right medication. After that, unless the condition goes into remission, many people develop a more progressive form, which leads to increased disability and generally shortens the life span.

Spontaneously, I interrupted his lecture with an attempt to make a joke, "Well, that's a relief," I spouted with ironic enthusiasm, "My grandma died at 104!" The doctor, suddenly looking more human, raised his eyebrows and looked directly at me. After several awkward moments, he looked back down and began discussing the drug therapy he recommended for me: It was an interferon delivered weekly through intramuscular shots. It would begin with a training program at home, with a nurse who would help me learn to administer the medicine myself.

Wait! I wanted to stop him. I felt an urge to scream that all of this was too much. The information was too overwhelming to be coming from someone who did not know me. This stranger did not grasp how afraid I was to even *see* a needle, much less give myself or anyone else a shot. He was not aware of the interesting trio of health conditions that ran through my family—infertility, dementia, and longevity—and he had never heard the macabre joke we tell regarding these proclivities. "We live forever, albeit alone, but we enjoy not knowing it is happening." I do not know what the doctor would have done if I said all of this, but I did not risk it. He only knew my test results, which put me into a category I did not want to join. This man had no understanding of how strange it all was for me. I began weeping.

I am not someone who cries, not even when I might like to, not even when I am alone. Coming from a long tradition of stoicism, a family within which stories of keeping cool in a crisis are celebrated (like my mom, at 15, who did not cry at her mother's funeral), I have always taken pride in my self-control. Yet here I was, looking at this stone-faced doctor, crying. Trying to regain composure, I wiped my eyes and said I needed to go to the restroom. "We are done here," he said with finality. I was surprised, but nodded silently as I gathered my belongings. Before I left the room, I turned back to see him poring over paperwork again. With a shaky voice, I asked him if we could "talk about all of this," motioning toward my face and then in the direction of his clipboard. He looked squarely at me without offering a new expression. We regarded each other for a moment and then he said plainly, "You come back after you've sorted this out. Then we can talk." I stifled my crying and marched out without another word. As I drove home, without tears, I added finding a new neurologist to my list of problems to solve.

I wish that was the only time I was treated impersonally as I learned to live with MS. Coming to terms with this disease was the most personal ordeal I have ever experienced, but my changed body forced me to depend on a depersonalized system. Although the general perception that those in the medical field do good work is not wrong, the avenues available to patients are limited. The apparatus of medicine of which doctors are part feels like a gargantuan, inescapable labyrinth with entrenched traditions, detailed laws, and little room for negotiation. I was surprised how often individuals who work in medicine seemed unable to understand the profound effect that pain, decreased mobility, and the loss of independence had on me. Once I had a diagnosis, I found that there was not space in the treatment of this disease or in the realm of mainstream medicine for me to be anything but a patient. My story became a case of MS, my living became a series of statistics and probabilities, and my future aspirations dwindled down to one goal: get well again.

Getting worse or better, according to the medical world I had begun to inhabit, was depicted through numbers. When practitioners read the results of my tests, uninspiring statistics spoke on my behalf. Weakness, dizziness, lost appetite, myelin reduction, numbness, pain, low vitamin levels, thyroid dysfunction, weight loss, blurred vision, depressive ideations, and infections were all quantified. They replaced whatever else I was without MS. When I saw doctors (and there were suddenly many), I was shocked at the incredible amount of detail contained in my burgeoning medical files, which told them almost nothing about *me*. I thought of inserting pages detailing my favorite novels, ideal vacation spots, or memories in which I made a fool of myself. I longed for something personal, or even something "consistent with" personal.

Seeing Connections to Students I Have Taught

As I became a more seasoned sick person, I began to connect my experiences with some of my middle school and high school students who had felt alienated by a depersonalized system. I had always been on the lookout for "caring occasions" (Noddings, 1988) when I was teaching English, but this experience sharpened my senses. The systematic reactions to my own illness brought me closer to understanding the negative influences of many of the institutional practices, such as resource periods for special education students or the creation of individual education plans (IEPs), that are designed to help students. I remembered, with shame, reading the files of students I had not met so I could invent strategies to prevent catastrophes in my classes.

Thinking of the profound effects of the words and actions of medical practitioners I had encountered, I found truth in Nodding's (1988) assertion that goodness and wickedness "are both, at least in part, induced, supported, enhanced, or diminished by the interventions and influence of those with whom we are related" (p. 176). My disease made me exposed and vulnerable; those involved in my care had tremendous power to affect my experience and to direct the course of my treatment. Was this how it felt to be designated as ADHD or learning disabled, for all teachers and school personnel to know? I wondered if placement into a category was too much of a price to pay for access to services and accommodations.

I did not previously appreciate how terrible it could feel to be reduced to numbers and set categories until something as personal as my physical well-being was represented that way. In seeking medical treatment, I was defined by my diagnosis (as affirmed by a thick folder of records), more than any personal trait, skill, or attitude. Someone with "a condition consistent with relapsing-remitting MS" was just the same as any other person with that designation, as far as the recommended course of action was concerned. The standardized approach I experienced from medical professionals was not a comfort during the chaotic period of adjusting to reality with this disease. I felt reduced from full person to a case, filed neatly away in a neurology office alongside similar patients. But this crisis was uniquely mine. My experience with this disease was always going to be personal, and I longed for medical personnel who would treat it that way.

Reflecting on the Necessity of Numbers

I have been assigned numbers for many reasons, all of which make sense from a functional point of view. Entities like banks, school districts, government offices, and airline companies cannot deliver their products or serve their clients well according to names or personal attributes. The same applies to the industry of medicine, which serves a large clientele and cannot afford to be bogged down with facts that cannot be represented numerically. But when you are one of the clients who has an extenuating circumstance, like someone who must change a flight for significant personal reasons, someone who has a panic attack during a timed test, or someone who is sick in more dimensions than just those that fit into extant categories of modern medicine, these situations reveal the rigidity of a quantified approach to serving humans.

Laura Nader (1996) was right when she argued: "Questions of civil rights, of freedom, of social structure, of democracy, of quality of life, or of equality are not easily discussed numerically or through modeling. Numbers also dilute the dangerous and the unthinkable: the distancing function" (pp. 263–264). The remoteness I felt from the very places and people I went to for help with something as personal as my health was palpable. I also felt, more viscerally than I had before, the danger of bureaucratic systems (like schools, prisons, and hospitals) that observe to collect information and classify individuals as normal or abnormal or healthy or unhealthy. As someone who suddenly found herself on the wrong side of this "binary branding," I gained a new empathy for the individual who becomes "the object of information, never a subject in communication" (Foucault, 1977, p. 200). Having a disease has made me visible to my health providers, but only in terms of my symptoms and the information they gather about this particular case of MS. My humanity is diminished by contrast.

This lesson reminds me of certain students I have known: those who did poorly on standardized tests, those who did not speak English, those who were terrified of peers, those who struggled to stop taking drugs, those with adult-like burdens at home, those who missed school for illness, and all those who did not succeed in regular classes for whatever reason. Although there are networks of assistance for young people who do not fit into the mainstream program (e.g.,

IEPs, resource periods, social workers, personal aides, counseling sessions, foster homes, mentoring programs, home-bound education, tutoring, behavior plans, modified schedules), the safety nets are often delayed, inadequate, not well-designed, stigmatized, and accessible only after crisis conditions emerge.

If "don't fit" students (Deschenes, Cuban, & Tyack, 2001) realize that they are always left out by the program of school that fits everyone else, what effect could that awareness have? I think about my bitterness toward a certain airline or a particular doctor and wonder what it would be like if I had to keep depending on the measly accommodations they were willing to make. If I could not just take my business elsewhere, there would be no relief and no looking back on a situation I would rather forget. For students who feel as though they do not belong in class with their peers (or who have been told they do not belong there), life in school could be comprised of simultaneously being dehumanized and subordinated by a label or a number that is integral to their identity. Like me, they are branded as abnormal, and they become *known* principally by the information gathered about their condition rather than their individuality.

Before I was diagnosed with a chronic illness, I felt compassion for students who were left out or marked in some way. I do not think one must experience something as acutely as I have to feel sympathy. That said, my experience with this disease has shown me the frustration and pain of confronting an inescapable system that cannot or will not bend its rules, despite extenuating circumstances. These situations feel like a betrayal, particularly when the rule-keepers claim that their actions are in the best interest of the individual, and even more so when that individual has always believed that claim. My point is not to lament my medical care, but to critique its incessant subjugation. In the treatment of my disease, I do not get to be agentive. I am never a peer, never a collaborator, but instead I am just a recipient of care: a patient.

It has hurt emotionally and physically when I have hit dead ends I did not anticipate. However, I am glad for the deeper understanding of hardships some individuals experience while the majority lives happily protected by a system, unaware of the harsh realities outside it. Perhaps less acutely than long-term medical patients, students and teachers are also reduced to numbers in a depersonalized machine, based on administrative logistics, legal mandates, financial constraints, and convenience. I wonder if everyone needs a chance to step outside of the shallow protection of this system to see its flaws, and to imagine a different way of dealing with idiosyncratic, live human beings.

I wish I could have learned these lessons without getting sick, but I can testify, in the words of Audre Lorde (1980), "I would never have chosen this path, but I am very glad to be who I am, here" (p. 77). I am grateful to know how it feels to become a number. For other teachers, doctors, and anyone who wonders how they should treat individuals who have physical differences, I can offer the lessons I have gained from what I have experienced in schools and hospitals. For others who will become sick or disabled, I can only hope that my work can prepare them to teach the world to see their humanity as more essential than their numbers.

References

Deschenes, S., Cuban, L., & Tyack, D. (2001). Mismatch: Historical perspectives on schools and students who don't fit them. *Teachers College Record, 103*(4), 525–547.

Foucault, M. (1977). *Discipline and punish* (A. Sheridan, Trans.). New York, NY: Vintage Books.

Lorde, A. (1980). *The cancer journals.* Argyle, NY: Spinsters, Ink.

Nader, L. (1996). *Naked science: Anthropological inquiry into boundaries, power, and knowledge.* New York, NY: Routledge.

Noddings, N. (1988). An ethic of care and its implications for instrumental arrangements. *American Journal of Education, 96*(2), 215–230.

Sontag, S. (1978). *Illness as metaphor and AIDS and its metaphors.* New York, NY: Picador.

Zola, I. K. (1982). *Missing pieces: A chronicle of living with a disability.* Philadelphia, PA: Temple University Press.

PART THREE

Challenges of Inclusion and Practice

CHAPTER FIVE

"There is nothing to do with these girls"

The Education of Girls with Rett Syndrome

USREE BHATTACHARYA

"Tape des mains, ne t'arrete pas"
[Clap your hands, don't stop yourself]

My daughter had been moving in beat to this Congolese Francophone number since she was six months old, a song darkly prescient in ways we could never have anticipated. The image of silhouetted, burnt-orange hands swaying in rhythm to earthy African drums flashes across the upbeat YouTube video that she has watched nearly a thousand times in her life. Three months before she was finally diagnosed, she began to clap every waking minute. My husband said: "You know, she heard that line so many times that she ***really*** *took it to heart." I cried.*

"Clapping" hands are perhaps the most recognizable symptom of Rett Syndrome (RS), a rare neurological disorder. Occurring in about 1 in 10,000 births, the disease is said to be characterized by "profound intellectual and physical disability" (Sigafoos, Woodyatt, Tucker, Roberts-Pennell, & Pittendreigh, 2000, p. 203). In terms of its etiology, it arises as a result of "mutations in the methyl-cytosine-phosphate-guanine binding protein 2 (MECP2) gene located on Xq28" (Djukic, McDermott, Mavrommatis, & Martins, 2012, p. 25). After a short period of "normal" development, girls[1] with RS will experience "gradual reduction of speech and purposeful hand use, seizures, autistic like behaviour, ataxia, intermittent hyperventilation and stereotypic hand movements" (Lotan, Isakov, & Merrick, 2004,

p. 731), among other symptoms. The RS population is heterogeneous, with severity of symptoms being related to genotype, thus manifesting across a spectrum (Bartolotta, 2014; Rose et al., 2013; Sigafoos et al., 2011; Urbanowicz, Downs, Girdler, Ciccone, & Leonard, 2015).

The first scholarship in English on RS appeared in the early 1980s, and has slowly grown over the years (Bartolotta 2014). After my daughter's devastating diagnosis, I searched for educational literature on the topic, trying to find comfort and hope in the familiar. However, multiple searches yielded little insight; the interest in girls with RS appeared to arise primarily from a pathological perspective, with literacy a neglected, marginal aspect of their lives in scholarship. This chapter offers a review of the limited educational literature on girls with RS, a category of girls that has been starkly underrepresented in our broader field.

I begin with an overview of a core issue that affects the educational prospects of the girls: the lack of knowledge about their cognitive abilities. Their communicative difficulties are at the heart of the difficulty in assessing their cognitive capacity, which, fortunately, new advances in eye gaze technology may help overcome. Next, I review the sparse literature in the educational context, before finally delving into proven practices culled from different studies. We are at the cusp of exciting gene therapy human trials, commencing in early 2019, with the aim of curing RS. While we await results from the most promising medicinal intervention to attack this disease in the near future, we have to create a rich, nurturing learning environment for them so that they can live their best possible lives.

Unlocking their Cognitive Worlds

In terms of cognition, the scholarship suggests that girls with RS "function at a severe/profound level of mental retardation" (Brown, 2008, p. 1746), with individuals experiencing "severe cognitive deficits" (Bartolottoa, 2014). Perceived to be at the developmental level of infants (Demeter, 2000; Fabio, Castelli, Marchetti, & Antonietti, 2013; Kerr, 2002), they are considered to stagnate at the "presymbolic level" (Bartolotto, 2014, p. 2689). Over the decades since the earliest reports of this disease, the categorization has shifted to it being seen as a *neurodevelopmental* rather than *neurodegenerative* disorder (Lotan, 2006), meaning "that subjects may have the capacity to learn new skills" (Leonard, Fyfe, Leonard, & Msall, 2001, p. 104). But the cognitive worlds of the girls remain shrouded in profound mystery (Rose, Djukic, Jankowski, Feldman, & Rimler, 2016). Fabio et al. (2013) point out the "general 'resignation'" that pervades RS research around the girls' cognitive abilities: "it is widely assumed that there is nothing to do with these girls" (p. 2).

The reason that uncertainties abound regarding the cognitive phenotype of the girls is that "profound impairments in expressive language and hand use that characterize RTT preclude most standard neuropsychological testing" (Rose et al., 2016, p. 23). The issue thus is that regardless of their actual cognitive abilities, girls with RS cannot measurably display their understanding (Nash, 2007). A comment by a substitute teacher working with a girl with RS poignantly captured this conundrum: the girl's "body betrays her intelligence" (Nash, p. 155). Although the larger scholarship has consistently articulated a call for more appropriate assessment measures (Demeter, 2000; Nash, 2007), reports by parents and some scholars suggest that girls with RTT are cognitively more capable in ways that the relevant literature does not legitimize, capture, or acknowledge (Bartolotta, 2014; Rose et al., 2016).

Furthermore, as von Tetzchner et al. (1996) have argued, some conventional methods of assessment of girls with RTT "may be appropriate indicators of a child's ability to act on the environment but not for making assumptions about the child's cognitive skills in general" (p. 221). Demeter (2000), for example, claimed similarly that traditional models of cognitive assessment arose from Piagetian theory, "focused on the knowledge which a child acquires about their 'material' world" (p. 230), which is a serious constraint for girls with RS (cf. Lewis & Wilson, 1998). Lindberg (2006) likewise noted that "part of their handicap is caused by those of us who form their outer world. We are not used to conscious and varied analysis and interpretation of nonverbal signals. Although we do know that these children are met with certain difficulties it is often very hard for us to put this knowledge into practice" (p. 64). As a result, girls with RS experience underestimation of their cognitive capabilities (Baptista, Mercadante, Macedo, & Schwartzman, 2006; Bartolotta, Zipp, Simpkins, & Glazewski, 2011; Elefant & Wigram, 2005). Ultimately, the attention has most often focused on "their disturbing deficiencies" (Demeter, 2000, p. 227), rather than what it is they *can* do.

One of the core concerns is that most of the RS population is and will remain nonverbal, with a highly constrained communicative repertoire overall (Bartl-Pokorny et al., 2013; Bartolotta, 2014). Only a small minority of RS patients "may retain a few single words, simple phrases or, even more rarely, sentences" (Skotko, Koppenhaver, & Erickson, 2004, p. 145). As Kraayenoord (2001) noted in her editorial for a special issue in the *International Journal of Disability, Development and Education*, "communication is fundamental to life and … colours what it means to be human" (p. 327). People with limited speech due to multiple disabilities, including RS, are thus debilitated in a speech-oriented society.

The literature on the communicative abilities of RS patients is mixed, with their capability described variously as pre-intentional, pre-linguistic, pre-symbolic, or nonsymbolic (e.g., Woodyatt & Ozanne, 1992), though some scholarship in the area has challenged these traditional categorizations (e.g., Bartolotta, 2014; Fabio et al., 2013). There has also been interest in the informal and formal reports of RS girls using "alternative modalities" and "nonstandard" behaviors that may be imbued with intentional, communicative function (Bartolotta, 2014). These findings are consistent with scholarship that has previously demonstrated "that children with multiple disabilities, including RS, use various and, often, unconventional modalities to communicate" (Hetzroni & Rubin, 2006, p. 49). Within this context, augmentative and alternative communication (AAC) is a highly promising frontier in communicative intervention (Bartolotta, 2014).

Specifically, eye-tracking technology is a "hot topic" (Townsend et al., 2016, p. 102) in the field of RS research, since the gaze is considered "the most significant modality used during interventions" (Hetzroni & Rubin, 2006, p. 58). In fact, "[v]ision and gaze are considered the most important ways in which girls with Rett syndrome relate to the world" (Djukic et al., 2012, p. 25). In addition to enhancing patients' engagement within their communicative universe, eye-tracking offers new insights into the cognitive potential of those "who were previously thought to be at the very lowest end of the cognitive spectrum" (Loffler & Gordon, 2018, p. 2). This line of research was inspired by multiple observations that girls with RS "are able to establish eye contact, visually track, and communicate through eye gaze, suggesting that they may have more cognitive capabilities than are apparent" (Rose et al., 2013, p. 23). Some of the exciting research to emerge in the field includes the finding of intentionality in gaze (Baptista et al., 2006) as well as individuals' "preference for novel and salient stimuli in a way that normally developing children do" (Djukic et al., 2012, p. 27). However, this is a nascent field of research, with concerns that assessments using eye-tracking devices suffer from issues such as the "restlessness and overactivity, poor engagement, limited joint attention, and decreased alertness" of patients (Djukic et al., 2012, p. 28). Regardless, eye-tracking appears to be a powerful way "to gain more realistic insights into their minds, revealing perceptual and cognitive abilities including memory, attention, and receptive language" (Djukic et al., 2012, p. 28).

Literacy: A Tale of Low Expectations

As noted earlier, there is a dearth of research specifically related to the education of individuals with RS (e.g., Bartolotta, 2014; Katsiyannis, Ellenburg, Acton, & Torrey, 2001; Nash, 2007; Skotko et al., 2004). Furthermore, published scholarship on the topic has largely appeared in medical or specialized, disability-focused journals, out of the immediate reach of general educational researchers. In fact, during my initial searches on the topic of education of children with RS, I found so little that I questioned if educating them were even *possible*. Bartolotta (2014) cited several reasons for this paucity, specifically the perplexing nature of disabilities that characterize the RS population, as well as its complex articulation along a spectrum.

Within this limited literature, scholars cite several obstacles that individuals with RS experience within the educational context. A fundamental one is medical. Zurynski, Frith, Leonard, and Elliott (2008) highlighted how children with rare diseases such as RS experience multiple constraints that either seriously interrupt schooling or render it entirely impractical for children to continue with. Annually, a child with RS "attends an average of nine medical appointments, [and] one third require hospital admission" (Zurynski et al., 2008, p. 93). In addition, a large majority of individuals require intensive speech, occupational, and physical therapy sessions (among others) on a routine basis. The substantial time spent away from the classroom for a typical child with RS thus adds to their already significant schooling struggles. Related to the medical issues are the impediments posed by three specific aspects of RS: hand dysfunction, unconventional response to stimuli (and added response times), and global apraxia. There are intensive therapeutic interventions that may help support girls with these issues, if only to a limited extent (Lewis & Wilson, 1998).

Another formidable challenge is that there is little clarity or consensus about the cognitive capacities of individuals with RS (discussed previously), as well as limited information available on effective practices from a pedagogical standpoint (Elefant & Wigram, 2005). Children with RS constantly struggle with the underestimation of their capabilities in their schooling as a result of the multiple debilitations arising from their disease. This is not an unusual experience for those who grapple with disabilities in general. In their study on phonics instruction at the middle school level to children with special needs (including a teenager with RS), Ainsworth, Evmenova, Behrmann, and Jerome (2016) noted that, unfortunately, "literacy expectations for students with severe disabilities and communication disorders have historically been low. Thus low expectations begin the cycle of a self-fulfilling prophecy in which opportunities are not presented and then a student's disabilities are blamed for a lack of literacy acquisition" (p. 175). As Nash (2007) also showed in her study of a girl with RS in a general education classroom, assumptions can play a pivotal role in the classroom context. She made the case that "Those who assume the child is only physically unable to participate in the classroom may assume the child is capable and find an alternate method of presenting the information to the student. Those who assume the child is incapable of participating in the activities may not make accommodations at all" (p. 36).

Fortunately, over the last two decades the scholarly literature has pushed back against a deficit-oriented approach to individuals with RS, toward an *assume competence* model when it comes to children with RS (Baptista et al., 2006; Bartolotta, 2014; Demeter, 2000; Djukic et al., 2012; Elefant & Wigram, 2005; Loffler & Gordon, 2018; Nash, 2007; Rose et al., 2016). Critical to the educational success of a child with RS, they argue, is presuming that the child has intellectual capabilities and working within that framework to teach them (Lotan, 2006).

What can teachers do? Katsiyannis et al. (2001) emphasized that they "need to be aware of a variety of behavioral interventions found in the literature, focus on individualized approaches, consider contextual factors, work closely with physical and occupational therapists, and employ the least intrusive interventions" (p. 78). Scruggs (2009) similarly argued that educators need to be aware of "research-validated interventions and approaches to treat and improve the symptoms associated with Rett syndrome" (p. 14). Likewise, Sigafoos et al. (2009) pushed for teachers to adopt "well-designed educational interventions … [with] a careful prioritization of treatment goals followed by skilled use of the best available interventions" (pp. 305–506). Children with RS are educated in a wide variety of educational contexts (e.g., homeschooling, mainstream, special education), but research remains sparse, often being too narrow in focus for generalizations (e.g., a single case study in a classroom) or too broad for an understanding of specific cases (e.g., general studies of children with significant disabilities). Scholars such as Lotan (2006) and Nash (2007), however, have made a strong case for inclusion of the girls with RS as part of a mainstream educational context. Lotan, for example, argues that

> The importance of the educational environment lies in the fact that school represents many academic and social learning opportunities, beyond traditional classroom instruction. Students who are integrated in to the mainstream educational environment are exposed to those opportunities. All students require support from teachers, classmates, family, and friends in order to thrive and to gain full benefit from their school experience. Students with RS have special needs that require additional supports beyond those ordinarily received in the school setting. Students with RS must have access to an education that will enable them to develop the knowledge and skills they need in order to participate in their surrounding society to their fullest ability. (p. 1506)

Nash (2007) found that "students with disabilities tend to do better academically and socially in the general education classroom as opposed to a special education classroom" (p. 166). Being part of the general education classroom, in as many ways as possible, was critical for the educational growth of the child with RS that Nash followed through her study.

Although there is limited information about the actual impact of this line of work on pedagogy, there are practices that have been articulated within the research that are helpful:

- Lewis and Wilson (1998) offered multiple approaches for maximizing learning, discussing the importance of assessing schooling ideologies, examining the curriculum, and implementing innovative teaching strategies.
- Skotko et al. (2004) examined storybook reading events with mothers and their daughters with RS, discovering that simple but scaffolded reading practices and the purposeful use of assistive technologies led to increased and powerful communicative interactions. They argue that similar interventions could have a robust impact in the classroom as well.
- Hirano and Taniguchi (2018) focused on what interested RS patients, including "people, music, things to see, animations, or books" (p. 258). These interests, they argued, could be tapped for therapeutic and pedagogical purposes (cf. Demeter, 2000).
- Coyne, Pisha, Dalton, Zeph, and Cook Smith (2012) found that contextualized reading practices incorporating multimedia e-books can lead to remarkable gains for children with severe disabilities.
- Lotan (2006) recommended that the instructional plan be organized in a manageable sequence, and emphasized the importance of continual repetitions to assist in learning.
- Fabio et al. (2013) highlighted the need for "well-structured procedures repeated constantly every day for a long time, connected to each other hierarchically so that each level constitutes the ground for the next one" (p. 2).
- Ryan et al. (2004) stressed the importance of giving additional time for girls with RS to accomplish learning goals, as well as building cues into the instructional plan.
- Koppenhaver et al. (2001) recommended attributing meaning to vocalizations and gestures even when they did not "appear" communicative, as well as giving additional time for responses and scaffolded support to be offered after posing questions.
- Fabio, Antonietti, Castelli, and Marchetti (2009) highlighted the importance of "posture and physical containment" (p. 334) as critical to allowing the girls to focus on the task at hand.
- Nash (2007) suggested a range of practices derived from her study, including building regular and predictable routines, developing a relationship with the child, assuming competence, offering extra time to achieve lesson objectives, giving positive reinforcement, providing inclusion, and allowing girls to be in charge of their own learning.

This list is not comprehensive, providing instead a road map to consider in the difficult but important journey in educating girls with RS. There is considerable variability in terms of individual abilities among girls with RS (as a result of variation in genotype); it is thus pivotal to keep in mind that practices will have to vary and be tailored specifically for an individual with RS, rather than applied similarly for all girls with the condition (Bartolotta, 2014).

Finally, Ahonniska-Assa et al. (2018) contested the prevailing belief that there is "uniform and severe intellectual impairment among all females with RS" (p. 43). This assertion poses an intriguing and exciting moment for intervention and rehabilitation. If there is the possibility that these girls are "functioning at a level of mild cognitive impairment, or even within the normal range of intelligence" (Loffler & Gordon, 2018, p. 2), it calls for a complete reconceptualization of what we can do with these girls in the educational context. And it's not nothing.

Note

1. Girls comprise the large majority of patients with RS, a disease that only rarely affects boys.

References

Ahonniska-Assa, J., Polack, O., Saraf, E., Wine, J., Silberg, T., Nissenkorn, A., & Ben-Zeev, B. (2018). Assessing cognitive functioning in females with Rett syndrome by eye-tracking methodology. *European Journal of Paediatric Neurology*, *22*, 39–45.

Ainsworth, M. K., Evmenova, A. S., Behrmann, M., & Jerome, M. (2016). Teaching phonics to groups of middle school students with autism, intellectual disabilities and complex communication needs. *Research in Developmental Disabilities*, *56*, 165–176.

Baptista, P. M., Mercadante, M. T., Macedo, E. C., & Schwartzman, J. S. (2006). Cognitive performance in Rett syndrome girls: A pilot study using eyetracking technology. *Journal of Intellectual Disability Research*, *50*(9), 662–666.

Bartl-Pokorny, K. D., Marschik, P. B., Sigafoos, J., Tager-Flusberg, H., Kaufmann, W. E., Grossmann, T., & Einspieler, C. (2013). Early socio-communicative forms and functions in typical Rett syndrome. *Research in Developmental Disabilities*, *34*(10), 3133–3138.

Bartolotta, T. E. (2014). Communication skills in girls with Rett syndrome. In V. B. Patel, V. R. Preedy, & C. R. Martin (Eds.), *Comprehensive guide to autism* (pp. 2689–2709). New York, NY: Springer.

Bartolotta, T. E., Zipp, G. P., Simpkins, S. D., & Glazewski, B. (2011). Communication skills in girls with Rett syndrome. *Focus on Autism and Other Developmental Disabilities*, *26*, 15–24.

Brown, R. T. (2008). Rett syndrome. In E. Fletcher-Janzen & C. Reynolds (Eds.), *Encyclopedia of special education* (pp. 1745–1748). London, UK: Wiley.

Coyne, P., Pisha, B., Dalton, B., Zeph, L. A., & Cook Smith, N. (2012). Literacy by design: A universal design for learning approach for students with significant intellectual disabilities. *Remedial and Special Education, 33*(3), 162–172.

Demeter, K. (2000). Assessing the developmental level in Rett syndrome: An alternative approach? *European Child & Adolescent Psychiatry, 9*(3), 227–233.

Djukic, A., McDermott, M. V., Mavrommatis, K., & Martins, C. L. (2012). Rett syndrome: Basic features of visual processing—A pilot study of eye-tracking. *Pediatric Neurology, 47*, 25–29.

Elefant, C., & Wigram, T. (2005). Learning ability in children with Rett syndrome. *Brain Development, 27*, S97–S101.

Fabio, R. A., Antonietti, A., Castelli, I., & Marchetti, A. (2009). Attention and communication in Rett syndrome. *Research in Autism Spectrum Disorders, 3*(2), 329–335.

Fabio, R. A., Castelli, I., Marchetti, A., & Antonietti, A. (2013). Training communication abilities in Rett Syndrome through reading and writing. *Frontiers in Psychology, 4*(911), 1–9.

Hetzroni, O. E., & Rubin, C. (2006). Identifying patterns of communicative behaviors in girls with Rett syndrome. *Augmentative and Alternative Communication, 22*(1), 48–61.

Hirano, D., & Taniguchi, T. (2018). What are patients with Rett syndrome interested in? *The Journal of Physical Therapy Science, 30*(2), 258–261.

Katsiyannis, A., Ellenburg, J. S., Acton, O. M., & Torrey, G. (2001). Addressing the needs of students with Rett syndrome. *Teaching Exceptional Children, 33*(5), 74–78.

Kerr, A. (2002). Annotation: Rett syndrome: Recent progress and implications for research and clinical practice. *Journal of Child Psychology and Psychiatry, 43*(3), 277–287.

Koppenhaver, D. A., Erickson, K. A., Harris, B., McLellan, J., Skotko, B. G., & Newton, R. A. (2001). Storybook-based communication intervention for girls with Rett syndrome and their mothers. *Disability and Rehabilitation, 23*(3–4), 149–159.

Kraayenoord, C. V. (2001). Literacy for all: Reading, writing, speaking, listening, and viewing. *International Journal of Disability, Development and Education, 48*(4), 327–329.

Leonard, H., Fyfe, S., Leonard, S., & Msall, M. (2001). Functional status, medical impairments, and rehabilitation resources in 84 females with Rett syndrome: A snapshot across the world from the parental perspective. *Disability and Rehabilitation, 23*(3–4), 107–117.

Lewis, J., & Wilson, D. (1998). *Pathways to learning in Rett syndrome.* New York, NY: David Fulton Publishers.

Lindberg, B. (2006). *Understanding Rett syndrome: A practical guide for parents, teachers, and therapists* (2nd ed.). Cambridge, MA: Hogrefe & Huber Publishing.

Loffler, G., & Gordon, G. E. (2018). Cognitive function in Rett syndrome: Profoundly impaired or near normal? *European Journal of Paediatric Neurology, 22*, 2–3.

Lotan, M. (2006). Rett syndrome. Guidelines for individual intervention. *The Scientific World Journal, 6*, 1504–1516.

Lotan, M., Isakov, E., & Merrick, J. (2004). Improving functional skills and physical fitness in children with Rett syndrome. *Journal of Intellectual Disability Research, 48*(8), 730–735.

Nash, K. M. (2007). *Rett syndrome in the general education classroom*. Unpublished doctoral dissertation, Arcadia University, Glenside, PA.

Rose, S. A., Djukic, A., Jankowski, J. J., Feldman, J. F., Fishman, I., & Valicenti-McDermott, M. (2013). Rett syndrome: An eye-tracking study of attention and recognition memory. *Developmental Medicine & Child Neurology*, *55*(4), 364–371.

Rose, S. A., Djukic, A., Jankowski, J., Feldman, J. F., & Rimler, M. (2016). Aspects of attention in Rett syndrome. *Pediatric Neurology*, *57*, 22–28.

Ryan, D., McGregor, F., Akermanis, M., Southwell, K., Ramke, M., & Woodyatt, G. (2004). Facilitating communication in children with multiple disabilities: Three case studies of girls with Rett syndrome. *Disability and Rehabilitation*, *26*(21–22), 1268–1277.

Scruggs, A. (2009). *Rett syndrome: Characteristics, causes, and treatment*. Unpublished paper, Lynchburg University. Retrieved September 18, 2018 from https://www.lynchburg.edu/wp-content/uploads/volume-4-2009/ScruggsA-Rett-Syndrome-Characteristics-Causes-Treatment.pdf

Sigafoos, J., Green, V. A., Schlosser, R., O'Reilly, M. F., Lancioni, G. E., Rispoli, M., & Lang, R. (2009). Communication intervention in Rett syndrome: A systematic review. *Research in Autism Spectrum Disorders*, *3*, 304–318.

Sigafoos, J., Kagohara, D., van der Meer, L., Green, V. A., O'Reilly, M. F., Lancioni, G. E., Lang, R., Rispoli, M., & Zisimopoulos, D. (2011). Communication assessment for individuals with Rett syndrome: A systematic review. *Research in Autism Spectrum Disorders*, *5*(2), 692–700.

Sigafoos, J., Woodyatt, G., Tucker, M., Roberts-Pennell, D., & Pittendreigh, N. (2000). Assessment of potential communicative acts in three individuals with Rett syndrome. *Journal of Developmental and Physical Disabilities*, *12*(3), 203–216.

Skotko, B. G., Koppenhaver, D. A., & Erickson, K. A. (2004). Parent reading behaviors and communication outcomes in girls with Rett syndrome. *Exceptional Children*, *70*(2), 145–166.

Townsend, G. S., Marschik, P. B., Smeets, E., van de Berg, R., van den Berg, M., & Curfs, L. M. (2016). Eye gaze technology as a form of augmentative and alternative communication for individuals with Rett syndrome: Experiences of families in the Netherlands. *Journal of Developmental and Physical Disabilities*, *28*(1), 101–112.

Urbanowicz, A., Downs, J., Girdler, S., Ciccone, N., & Leonard, H. (2015). Aspects of speech-language abilities are influenced by MECP2 mutation type in girls with Rett syndrome. *American Journal of Medical Genetics Part A*, *167*(2), 354–362.

von Tetzchner, S., Jacobsen, K. H., Smith, L., Skjeldal, O. H., Heiberg, A., & Fagan, J. F. (1996). Vision, cognition and developmental characteristics of girls and women with Rett syndrome. *Developmental Medicine & Child Neurology*, *38*(3), 212–225.

Woodyatt, G., & Ozanne, A. (1992). Communication abilities and Rett syndrome. *Journal of Autism and Developmental Disorders*, *22*(2), 155–173.

Zurynski, Y. A., Frith, K., Leonard, H., & Elliott, E. J. (2008). Rare childhood diseases: How should we respond? *Archives of Disease in Childhood*, *93*, 1071–1074.

CHAPTER SIX

Confronting My Disabling Pedagogy

Reconstructing an English/ Language Arts Classroom as an Enabling Context

CHRISTOPHER BASS

I first realized that my ableist bias informed my teaching when I was a first-year English Ph.D. student. I clearly remember this moment of realization. I was doing research for my humanities seminar in the cavernous university library at the University of Illinois-Chicago and stumbled upon Owen and Gabel (2010), who argue that my home state of Illinois has always ranked near the bottom of the 50 states for inclusion practices. When I first read their statistics, I was shocked. I had been a high school English teacher in Illinois for eight years and almost all of my classes had at least one student with an Individualized Education Plan (IEP), 504 plan, or accommodation. Up until this point, I considered myself a successful inclusion teacher of English—the subject encompassing literature, composition, and language use. I quietly closed the book and placed it back on its shelf. I was sure they were describing other teachers in other schools. However, despite my confidence, the chapter's findings pushed me to reflect on my own inclusion training.

I still have memories of the Special Education course that I took as a requirement for my state licensure. The professor focused on the legal requirements of inclusion and methods to accommodate students. The overall tone of the course stoked fear and resentment amongst my peers. We got the message: You must meet the legal requirements or be sued, period. I don't remember learning any positive strategies for inclusion in that class. My own education had led me to expect all of my students to acquire the skills and knowledge that I valued.

Moreover, the culture of the first school at which I taught reinforced these beliefs. The administration believed that the purpose of education was to assure that all students, whatever their "problems," achieved the same standards. IEP and 504 plans, formative assessments, and teacher evaluations revolved around the belief that success occurs when *all* students achieve the same goal within a set timeframe. The school administrators evaluated inclusion teachers with a deficit mentality. They assumed that a successful teacher was one who could find a solution to the "problems" associated with a child's diagnosis. These solutions had to occur without affecting the expectations of their presumably "normative" peers in the class.

Through these reflections, it became clear that, though I always maintained the required IEP accommodations for students and was rated a successful teacher per administrative evaluations, I supported the systemic assumption of deficiency around differing abilities, if implicitly and complicitly. My experience is not unique. Unconscious enforcement of the ableist logic to which I adhered at the time often interferes with the success of inclusion practices (Allan, 2008; Smith, 2010). Otoole (2015), a disability activist and scholar, points out, "nearly every article about disability in mainstream media is by nondisabled people for nondisabled people. These articles focus on the imagined distress at the losses that will occur if nondisabled people become disabled and almost never on the systems that create the perceived losses" (p. 14). As a teacher of English, who worked with all forms of media, I rarely challenged the portrayal of disability, because the same deficit narrative surrounded me in all textual forms. In turn, my inclusion classroom unconsciously perpetuated the deficit narrative around disability. This realization shifted both my graduate research and teaching. I became more interested in how I could disrupt the conventional culture of my school that had forged a deficit mentality around disability.

Ultimately, through a better understanding of neurodiversity, I became determined to conceive and construct a classroom environment that sought to enable broader participation in cultural practice amongst all of my students. This classroom became a space for constructing an inclusive classroom, one in which the potential of those classified as "disabled" and "disordered" may be more fully realized than schools are typically designed to cultivate. As a teacher, I want to disrupt the conventional approaches to inclusion instruction and encourage an appreciation for the diverse abilities of all students. Such an approach reverses the customary focus of instruction, which remains focused on accommodating "disabled" or "disordered" students so that they may appear more like their typical peers. Rather, my approach to teaching aligns with others in this volume who argue that teachers should shift their attention from individual students and their differences to the disabling environment of the classroom and school.

First Attempt—Taking Disabilities Studies Solo

I quickly encountered my first dilemma in creating a more inclusive classroom while researching inclusive teaching methods. It was difficult to find published teacher-research on expanding inclusion practices such that no single type of student occupies the role of what Garland-Thomson (1997) calls the *normate*, an idealized conceptualization of able-bodiedness that governs schools' and society's notion of the optimal way of being. Although there were many articles emerging from the field of Disability Studies in Education (DSE), these pieces typically focused on the failures of district policies around inclusion. I found few pieces *written by teachers* who did the work of implementing Disability Studies into the classroom. There was a lack of looking *from the inside out* as Cochran-Smith and Lytle (1993) would say, of taking an emic perspective on disability from the K-12 classroom. Despite reading much DSE work, I was left wondering how English teachers could do inclusive education better. Ultimately, I turned toward research from the field of Disability Studies and Composition. This research is rooted in the experiences of teaching disability in college composition programs and the humanities, and I attempted to bring those theories into my high school classroom in more concrete ways.

In particular, I focused on Brueggemann's (2002) notion of *enabling pedagogy*. As an undergraduate composition professor, Brueggemann acknowledged the variation of ability amongst the members of the classroom and noted the different portrayals of abilities in the various texts that they encountered throughout the semester. She defines this approach to teaching as an enabling pedagogy, which she claims is "a theory and practice of teaching that posits disability as insight" (p. 321). This theory views ability differences as strengths that encourage students to critically analyze the power structures that create normative assumptions and regulations that disable. She claims that engaging with disability reveals the manner in which dominant social power structures set expectations and norms around differing abilities. In turn, enabling pedagogy is a process of questioning regulations that help construct identities. An enabled classroom becomes a space that nurtures the potential for students to challenge these dominant expectations while re-imagining alternative possibilities of identity and power structures. It is thus both an enabling pedagogy, and a critical pedagogy.

I decided to restructure my high school 11th-grade English composition course in a manner that would foster an enabling pedagogy amongst the students. This curricular restructuring led to a central research question: What will be the impact of integrating neurodiverse literature into the inclusion classroom? Broadening the range of authors included for study has been recommended to break up the monopoly of White male authors in the established literary canon, as urged by Lee (1993) for African American students. I thought that broadening the literacy perspective with which the students engage might create opportunities to enable conversations around neuro-atypical people, another demographic group typically short-changed in the curriculum such that its members rarely see their experiences reflected in school studies and such that neurotypical students have few opportunities to learn about their perspective. Throughout the semester, I kept a research journal, collected student work, and asked targeted reflective questions that encouraged students to express how they felt about concepts of neurodiversity.

Of the three English courses available to 11th-grade students at the high school at which I taught, the composition course enrolled the largest number of students with required accommodations. As I reworked the curriculum, it became clear that this grouping together of students in need of accommodations was not an accident. I noted that my composition course had five students with IEPs for neurodiversity while my Junior Advanced Placement course only had two. It seemed that this divide was likely the result of assumptions made by the registrar's office that the honors track was too rigorous for the school's neuro-atypical students. In assigning the majority of students with IEPs to the composition course, the School District could ensure that very few "disabled" students mixed with the honors students in the Advanced Placement track.

In recognizing the presumed bias of the School District, I became more determined to rework my inclusion practices and implement an enabling pedagogy. The School District's stated objective for the composition course was that students develop as writers in preparation for the rigor of their Senior English College Prep course. Often, these students considered themselves weak writers and admitted to having had negative writing experiences in previous courses. The Composition curriculum was genre-based; the students explored five different written genres throughout the semester. Each genre was introduced to the students through model texts of varying styles and authors. After reading the texts, the students wrote their own pieces that fit within the expectations of the modeled genre. The final project of the semester was a larger research-based argument paper, which led to an informal presentation in the school library, and the school community was always invited to attend.

I reconceived the goal of the composition course to be a space that allowed students to interrogate their assumptions and prejudices through daily exploratory writing. Daily writing provided the space in which students would develop as writers while they questioned and challenged assumptions and norms that create disability both in our class and in the community. I first attempted to implement enabling pedagogy through replacing several traditional model texts with contemporary texts written by neuro-atypical authors. I hoped that students would feel comfortable engaging with the neurodivergent voices and topics that these authors explored. I knew, for many students, it would be the first time that they ever challenged notions of disability. It was certainly my first time acknowledging the normative nature of deficit thinking around diverse abilities.

I hoped that an enabling pedagogy would lead us (both the students and me) to recognize the deceit of the normate. As Otoole explains, "acknowledging that there is no 'normal' creates a society where difference can be recognized without being diffused or ignored" (p. 21). I wanted the classroom to recognize the potential in difference. I believed that an enabling pedagogy had the potential to create a classroom space for difference and in turn decenter the ableist gaze that too often determined normative approaches to learning and pushed alternative possibilities and identities to the fringes of the classroom.

However, while working with the first set of neurodiverse pieces, I quickly discovered how difficult it would be to establish the kind of space that Otoole and Brueggemann describe. The first genre of the curriculum was the short story. For this unit, I paired the short pieces, "Pretend you Good at It" by Jenny Lawson and Sloane Crosely's "Lost in Space." I structured the introduction of these pieces in the same manner that I did with each paired reading in the curriculum: I shared a shortened author's biography, provided a description of the setting and characters, and a read a brief introduction to the main conflict. Though I mentioned that the author of each piece explores experiences with atypicality, I did not draw attention to their specific conditions (for Lawson it is anxiety and depression while Crosley writes about experiences with severe temporal spatial deficit, a pathologizing term that left her feeling, in an oft-listed quote, replete with "a learning disability that means I have zero spatial relations skills. It was official: I was a genius trapped in an idiot's body.").

I purposefully chose not to define the diagnoses because I didn't want to limit the students' focus to the authors' atypical makeups. Rather, it was my hope that the students would independently note the manner in which authors wrote about their differing abilities. I then let the students choose one of the pieces to read. This was one of the few story pairings that was split almost evenly between students (11 students chose Crosley while 10 chose Lawson). The students selected the pieces with enthusiasm. Though they were excited to choose from two contemporary authors (especially after our previous pairing of Nathaniel Hawthorne stories), several students were also interested in reading pieces that felt "more relatable" as one student claimed in his reflection. A few students picked up both of the stapled story packets claiming that they were "curious about each of the characters." The students began reading silently for the remaining 12 minutes in class and were asked to finish the piece for homework. After all of the students selected a story, the class quickly quieted down to read, and there were dampened laughs throughout the room as the students began their encounter with each author's humor.

At the end of that day, I was sure that I was on track to implement Brueggemann's theory of enabling pedagogy. My research notes were filled with possible questions that I would ask the students the following day. I was outlining the many ways that neurodiversity and other atypical ways of being could provide insight into differing life experiences that had gone overlooked in our previous class conversations. However, at start of class the next day, I quickly realized that an enabling pedagogy in the high school classroom would be much more challenging than expected.

Class began with a journal response about the readings. In the journals, I asked students to respond to the texts using a variety of reader response questions: What did you like/not like about the story, what surprised you, did the story impact you, could you relate to this story? I had hoped that these journal questions would become the springboard for a class conversation that I would facilitate; however, once the conversation began, I sensed that the students were unsure how to talk about the readings. The students offered "safe" comments about generally appreciating the narrative voice, the humorous tone, and the general descriptions of the settings.

I was quickly disappointed that no students mentioned the portrayal of neurodivergence. In fact, when I asked the students if anyone noticed the portrayal of a neurodiverse perspective, students' eyes darted toward the windows as their feet shuffled. I thought that this discomfort likely stemmed from confusion about the concept of neurological diversity, so I attempted to ease their discomfort by explaining that there are many different labels that fit within the definition of neurodiversity; however, despite my attempt to clarify, the term remained too vague for the students. I was experiencing one of the moments most teachers seek to avoid: standing in front of the 21 students who stare back with complete confusion on their faces. No matter how clear I thought I had made neurodiversity, the students did not seem to understand.

This struggle led me to rely on simplistic, ableist jargon in an effort to better explain who may be considered neurodiverse. I found myself defining conditions like autism, and ADHD. Though I tried to assure that neurodiversity is an inclusive category that breaks down divisions between diagnoses, I reverted to the very labels that I wanted to avoid. All the while, the students stared skeptically as I spoke. One student eventually pointed out additional attributes of autism that I did not mention. She claimed to have done well on a research paper for biology and confidently asserted stereotypical terms to describe the condition. Suddenly another student chimed in with the claim that her health teacher said depression was a "controllable" condition that should be medicated. In response, I suggested that we turn to the text to consider how the authors had positive experiences with their neurodiversity. I was surprised that no students vocalized support for the positive portrayal of neurodiversity in the texts. At the bell, the neuro-atypical students silently walked out of the classroom with looks of embarrassment after being diagnosed and defined by their peers. I had failed.

Driving home from school that day, I got stuck at train tracks as a freight train slowly trundled forward. While I was waiting in the motionless car, my mind raced as it recreated the image of the neuro-atypical students with IEPs slumped in their chairs and zoned out while the two students spoke as if "experts" on depression and autism. I tried to count the train cars to distract from my guilt. I had to admit that I didn't realize what I had asked my students to do. Neurodiversity demands that students take a risk and leap into a large pool of undefined, unordered notions of identity. As a concept, neurodiversity disrupts the norm and suggests that all individuals process and communicate ideas differently. Eliminating the boundaries that define normal and abnormal can be quite unsettling for teen-aged students—particularly for those two students who had been positively rewarded for memorizing the definitions, symptoms, and labels of differing abilities in previous courses.

I want to say that I managed to improve my instruction the following day; however, as I planned for the course, I found myself fearful that I might offend students, reinforce stereotypes, or instill a deficit mentality around abilities. I also felt pressured by my curricular calendar. I worried about falling behind the schedule so early in the semester. Rather than verbally address the previous conversation, I stuck to the planned calendar and began class with a free writing prompt that referenced the neurodiversity readings: Have you ever been falsely defined by society? In what ways might you be judged for a thing that most people assume is negative? After giving time to respond, I reviewed the elements of short stories that we had studied earlier that week. The students then were encouraged to expand upon either today's prompt or one from an earlier reading. I did hope that independent writing might provide the space the students needed to process their thoughts around the paired neurodiverse readings; however, many students flipped back through their journals and chose earlier pieces that were written in response to more traditional short stories.

After a week of writing and revising these short narratives, the students shared a rough draft. Only one of the narratives engaged with atypical mental makeups. This student, Tommy, who had an IEP, created a protagonist who hid his depression and anxiety for fear of being mocked by his peers. The story ended with him being "cured of the disease" and "making a lot of friends." As feedback, I noted in the margins, "for many people, anxiety and depression don't need be 'cured' in order to be happy. In both of the pieces that we read, the neurodiverse authors have happy lives with many friends! Tommy—Happy to answer any questions you may have about either writing or neurodiversity." Ultimately, he asked me about neither writing nor neurodiversity, and Tommy didn't turn in a final draft by the deadline. When I asked him about missing the deadline, he claimed that he did not want to share it with his peers at our class-reading day. It was clear that he did not feel enabled by his differences. Rather, Tommy felt isolated. My first attempt to apply Disability Studies and engage with neurodiversity ended with me feeling like a failure.

The struggle to enable our classroom continued well into the semester. By the fourth month of class, we had engaged with five pieces that explored neurodiversity. After reading each piece, I asked the students to consider how the writer engaged with differing abilities. The students then would discuss the structure of the genre. Often the majority of students criticized the stories written from outside mental health norms, which were more experimental in organization and voice than the other traditional pieces that we read. For example, we read a short chapter written by D. J. Savarese, which is a part of his father R. J. Savarese's larger novel (2007), *Reasonable People.* I introduced the chapter as a model of argumentative essay; however, the students were confused by the hybridity of Savarese's writing structure, which combines verse, formal prose, and letter writing to make an argument about testing. Several of the students criticized the hybridity. One student claimed, "no one would take my argument seriously" if he wrote in such a way. The overall lack of interest in neurodiversity was most apparent in student writing. The students neither wrote about nor challenged concepts of disability in their own pieces. If anything, notions of difference felt more silenced. Disability became the proverbial elephant in the room. Though the students had read neuro-atypical writers in several different genres, no students were actually engaging with those voices. The students' writing was modeled more on the traditional typical pieces. Not only was the curriculum resistant to inclusion. The students themselves seemed to struggle to engage with neurodiversity, even as its membership shared the classroom with them.

A little more than half way through the semester, I had collected enough evidence to suggest that integrating atypical perspectives into the inclusion classroom had made a negligible impact at best. Perhaps most disappointingly, I noticed that the neuro-atypical students did not engage with the curriculum any more than in previous courses without the inclusive perspective. After reflecting on why this might be, I had to admit that I was unprepared for the challenge of disrupting the normative approach to teaching. I didn't know how to answer student questions around neuro-atypicality without using ableist terms. Moreover, I had been at the center of these classroom conversations. I wanted to *lead* the discussion and didn't allow students to *engage* in one. My desire to lead was rooted in my fear. I was very aware of the harms of ableist jargon and wanted to keep the definitions around differing abilities open, unstable, and fluid. I had hoped that the students and I could engage with differences without doing any of the hard work that should be expected when teachers disrupt norms and bias. I realized that I could not implement the theories of Disability Studies alone. On a late Friday drive home that felt, once again, longer than usual, I decided to stop the project altogether.

Admitting defeat led me to a surprising place. The following week, I began an email exchange with a colleague in the Special Education Department of my school. I reached out to her with concerns about Tommy, who had continued to miss deadlines since writing his short story. At this point in the semester, he was struggling. At first, I was hesitant to reach out to my colleagues because much of the scholarship in Disability Studies bemoans Special Education Departments; however, I realized that Tommy had worked with her since freshman year whereas I'd only had him for four months. It was also clear that he respected her as both a teacher and mentor. Though Disability Studies often positions itself against Special Education's methods, it soon became clear that my Special Education colleagues might have something to offer. An important collaboration began.

Second Attempt: A Collaborative Approach to Changing the Context

I continued to communicate with two Special Education teachers who had already developed relationships with several students in the composition class. The more I met with my colleagues in the Special Education Department, the more I realized that I had never reached out to collaborate and share instructional methods with these teachers. This lack of intellectual exchange, in many ways, reinforced the barrier between the stigmatized Special Education Department and the teachers in the general curriculum departments. Previously, I only met with Special Education teachers at the annual student case meetings. I dreaded these meetings, which were very structured and focused exclusively on specific accommodations and learning goals per student IEP.

In contrast to the formal IEP meetings, our conversations were collaborative. I was surprised to learn that the Special Education teachers did not know any of the authors that I implemented in the classroom. While they learned of new authors, I gained invaluable insights into the particular needs and strengths of the students that we shared, information that was not available on the IEP contracts. Based on our conversations, I developed methods that would help me broaden my focus from textual changes to a complete redesign of my classroom's physical layout, a reworking of my pedagogical pacing, and a modification to the structural aspects of my course.

Our collaboration helped me realize that the environment of my classroom remained challenging. As a result, I created a more fluid instructional space and expanded my expectations for student learning. My colleagues recommended some of these changes: Move the desks out of rows, allow students to choose where to sit (one student with anxiety and obsessive-compulsiveness focused best when he sat nearest the classroom door), and consistently begin class with a clear outline of the lesson plan. However, I also made revisions to the structural elements of the course that I thought would make the classroom a more positive environment for differences: Students were allowed to leave the room when needed; I dimmed the classroom florescent lighting to help a student with anxiety; I also allowed this student to communicate via email or online discussion boards rather than in classroom conversations, which were too pressured for her; certain students with A.D.H.D. were allowed to move freely around the classroom when needed; I was also prepared to loosen the deadlines for my student with anxiety. These particular changes were made in response to individual student needs and strengths, which I had learned from both my collaboration with colleagues as well as my observations throughout the semester. I hoped that these changes would promote new opportunities for individual student success.

Fortunately, I managed to implement these changes by the start of the final assignment. Traditionally, I would have introduced the entire final assignment, a problem-solution research project, all in one day; however, rather than overwhelm the students with many details so quickly, I began the assignment with a day of creative brainstorming. At this point of the semester, the students had encountered 20 differing model texts, of which ten were written by neuro-atypical authors.

I started the brainstorm session by referencing these pieces. I noted that the authors argued that their differences were not the problem. Rather, the problem was *the manner in which society disables people based on individual differences.* Each writer had described how their differences enabled them to be strong members of society. For these authors, their positive portrayal of neuro-atypicality was a solution to the problem created by society's ignorance around difference. I then asked the students to reflect on whether they had ever been marginalized by a societal norm. I pushed them to consider how this marginalization may have been disabling. In asking this question, I encouraged them to return to their previous writings and revisit their responses to the readings. Finally, I asked them to imagine a solution to this stigmatization that could be implemented locally.

The following day, I introduced the full assignment. I mentioned that each of the ten divergent authors made a persuasive argument about the harms of societal norms, and each of the authors had chosen to write in a genre that best matched the persuasive purpose. Therefore, rather than just assign an argumentative essay for all students, I encouraged the students to consider which genre best matched their persuasive purpose. We returned to the brainstorming journals from the previous day, and the students partnered-up to talk about what genres might work best. We ended class with an informal sharing of genres. I was surprised by the variety of texts that students suggested: short story, essay, newspaper editorial, poem, and research poster.

After introducing the flexible-genre project, I dedicated the following two weeks to in-class writing and researching. Though I wanted to make the classroom structure as flexible as possible, I distributed an outline of blank writing benchmarks to assure student accountability. I first asked the students to create an individualized writing schedule. This plan allowed the students to map out and visualize a writing process that worked best for them. The students then transferred their writing process to the outlined benchmarks. I assured the students that I would hold them answerable to their schedule; before moving onto the next benchmark, each student had to do a brief review with me. In developing their benchmarks, I reminded the students that everyone's writing process is different, that there is no "normal" mode of writing. Therefore, all writers need an opportunity to work in an environment in which they can succeed. In response, the students had many requests: students wanted to listen to music, work in the library, type on laptops, write in journals. Some students worked better at home and preferred to research during class, some students wanted to reference printed texts while others wanted to cite from online research. By the end of the period, each student had produced a custom outline for an individual writing process and described a writing environment that worked best for them.

The development of custom writing benchmarks highlighted the differences among all of the students. Some students preferred more time for research while others wrote in small drafts and wrote while researching. As the week developed, there was an understanding that there is no "normal" way to read or write. This flexibility created a more comfortable working environment. The neuro-atypical students focused on their writing in a way that I had not noticed all semester. Each of the students had established a distinct environment in which to work. In his reflection, one student with severe anxiety noted, "writing with my music on and sitting in the corner of the room helped me to see my argument. I usually get distracted when I face the classroom." Another student, with an IEP for ADHD, explained, "I liked that we could do whatever. For my research, I interviewed my uncle who has ADHD like me. It was good to talk about this with him, and he helped me start the paper." Both of these students had struggled to submit earlier assignments on time; however, each of them worked diligently on this final piece.

Tommy, who had struggled with deadlines all semester, created a reasonable set of writing benchmarks and developed a creative piece that explored the problem of early school start times. He managed to reference many studies that found teenagers' circadian rhythms often work against the traditional school schedule. Early school start times hinder the opportunity to succeed for many students. The protagonist of this short story was about a kid who struggled to get up every day. When I asked him about the piece, Tommy explained, "Sometimes people assume that I am lazy or party a lot because I sleep through my alarm and come late to school. That's not true. I just think I would do better in school if we started later into the day—wouldn't be late as much." After I eliminated many of the classroom structures and expectations that are the norm in schools, neuro-atypical students like Tommy, who had felt disengaged from previous writing activities, were involved from the brainstorming through the writing.

Eliminating the normate also emboldened students without IEPs. I noted a change in the manner in which all students collaborated and sought help from each other; there was a sense of shared purpose amongst the students that I had not felt previously. Overall, the students were more empathetic and refrained from judging a student whose writing process may have seemed atypical previously. No one could stand out because the relaxing of rules had enabled each student to do what personally worked best. Moreover, my assurance that there was no "correct" way to write created a space in which students could experiment with what might work best for them.

As the project progressed, I also settled into a routine. Each class would begin with mini-lessons on either research or writing. However, rather than occasionally posting notes on the course website after instruction, I flipped the routine: The class mini-lessons always developed from the notes that I had posted online the day before. I found that some students preferred to interact with the slides at their own pace while others liked to listen to the lesson, then refer to the PowerPoint as they worked. Additionally, the students with IEPs could access the notes in their resource course with the Special Education teacher.

Similarly, I would post links to databases, articles, and videos; or model persuasive pieces prior to talking about them in class. Again, early posting allowed students to interact with the materials in a manner that best fit them. There were even a few mini-lessons that developed unexpectedly from in-class conversations that students started about a post I had made earlier. One student, who had severe social anxiety, would review the notes in her resource course, and then email questions that I could address in the mini-lesson. Additionally, updating the website facilitated collaboration among both my colleagues in the Special Education department and parents who wanted to work with their students.

On an old table in the corner of the classroom, I stacked nine writing manuals that had been discarded by the library. I marked specific sections of each text with post-it-notes. This feature was helpful when students had questions about in-text citations, creating a bibliography, or even a grammar question. Although these books were not new, I noticed that students with ADHD used the books most often. When I asked about this choice, they quickly agreed it was easier to use the books than search for information online.

When I collected the final projects, I was happy to find that about half of the students had challenged assumptions around differing abilities. Of those, three neuro-atypical students wrote about disabling experiences in the school. Each of them claimed to have been stigmatized by the ableist school culture. The three students proposed solutions that involved structural changes to the normative school curriculum. One student asserted that he valued having ADHD and felt that teachers did not like teaching students like him. Based on his research on ADHD, he claimed that many major world leaders had ADHD, but teachers never mentioned that in history class. He argued that history teachers should be required to acknowledge that many historical leaders had differing abilities and often succeeded because of their differences. In his reflection, he mentioned that Lawson's short story style encouraged him to experiment with his own style of writing. The six-page persuasive piece was written in stream-of-consciousness style because he felt that the reader would understand how he processed thoughts. Another neuro-atypical student argued that the school should add a course that focused on injustice in all its forms, including stigmas against depression. She felt that the students needed more space to hear stories, like those we read throughout the semester, about differing abilities. She chose to create a cover letter and lengthy lesson plan that outlined her objectives. I learned of several more neuro-atypical authors because of her work.

When I first read these projects, I felt that I had heard these passionate concerns for the first time. I had neither considered a course dedicated to differing abilities nor questioned the history curriculum. All of the neuro-atypical students stated in their reflections that it was the first time identifying with their learning difference on an assignment. Moreover, these students claimed to feel empowered because the assignment enabled them to find a solution that focused on societal change and not individual change.

In addition to pieces by the three neuro-atypical students, writing by roughly half of their classmates described problems within the school structures and dreamed of solutions that created a more inclusive environment. These problems included early school start times, heavy homework loads, the rigor of daily school routines, and the continual pressure to take AP courses. Although these problems were not explicitly about disability, each of the projects noted how school structures disable student success. Though the solutions to these problems varied, each student described a more humane learning environment that was responsive to differing student abilities. It was clear that these projects did not envision implementing mere accommodations; rather, students described a new school environment that encouraged the development and appreciation of differing abilities.

Implications

What has surprised me most is the manner in which working with inclusive narratives encouraged students to think critically about injustice. However, narratives only had an impact after I restructured both the material environment and the structural elements of the class. I needed to create a space that enabled differences to succeed. I could only make the class work by creating an environment that encouraged the students to articulate and take ownership of their differences. Such an environment developed after professional collaboration with colleagues. As the final project advanced, I reworked my original research question. Rather than examine the effects of literature, I continually asked, how might individual differences empower or enable my students to become more active participants in the community? In teaching to answer this question, I structured the classroom to enable difference, listened to my colleagues in all departments, and continually added new texts into the curriculum.

I began this project without having stopped to acknowledge the manner in which my school and my classroom often perpetuated deficit thinking around disability. Because of this oversight, my work was doomed to fail as it first did. Engaging with texts centered on neuro-atypicality did help the students and me understand the variations among us. However, it is not enough to just read the stories. These perspectives must be applied to the classroom through pedagogical methods that are inclusive and open to diverse perspectives and actions, and that involve the material reconstruction of the teaching and learning context. Once I altered the classroom structure to provide the space for student differences, individuals were enabled to write better. But more importantly, they were able to envision a world in which structural powers no longer disable.

References

Allan, J. (2008). *Rethinking inclusive education: The philosophers of difference in practice.* Amsterdam, NL: Springer.

Brueggemann, B. J. (2002). An enabling pedagogy. In S. L. Snyder, B. J. Brueggemann, & R. G. Thomson (Eds.), *Disability studies enabling the humanities* (pp. 317–336). New York, NY: Modern Language Association.

Cochran-Smith, M., & Lytle, S. L. (1993). *Inside/outside: Teacher research and knowledge.* New York, NY: Teachers College Press.

Crosley, S. (2010). *How did you get this number?* New York, NY: Riverhead.

Davis, L. (2009). *Obsession: A history.* Chicago, IL: University of Chicago Press.

Garland-Thomson, R. (1997). *Extraordinary bodies: Figuring physical disability in American culture and literature.* New York, NY: Columbia University Press.

Lawson, J. (2015). Pretend you're good at it. In J. Lawson, *Furiously happy: A funny book about horrible things* (pp. 45–50). New York, NY: Flatiron.

Lee, C. D. (1993). *Signifying as a scaffold for literary interpretation: The pedagogical implications of an African American discourse genre* (NCTE Research Report No. 26). Urbana, IL: National Council of Teachers of English.

Otoole, C. J. (2015). *Fading scars.* New York, NY: Autonomous.

Owen, V., & Gabel, S. (2010). Lack of vision? Lack of respect? Exclusion in Illinois. In P. Smith (Ed.), *Whatever happened to inclusion? The place of students with intellectual disabilities in education* (pp. 86–100). New York, NY: Peter Lang.

Savarese, R. J. (2007). *Reasonable people: A memoir of autism and adoption.* New York, NY: Other Press.

Shor, I. (2009). What is critical literacy? In A. Darder, M. Baltodano, & R. Torres (Eds.), *The critical pedagogy reader* (2nd ed., pp. 282–304). New York, NY: Routledge.

Smith, P. (2010). *Whatever happened to inclusion? The place of students with intellectual disabilities in education.* New York, NY: Peter Lang.

CHAPTER SEVEN

Refusing to Become a Drifter

A Preschooler's Resistance to the Transition to a Special Education Classroom

KYUNGHWA LEE, JAEHEE KWON, AND JOOEUN OH

Vignette 1

It's around at 8:40 AM. Children at Young Kids' Academy,[1] a public pre-Kindergarten (pre-K) program in the Southern United States, are having breakfast in their school cafeteria. A special education (SPED) class taught by Claire is the first group to line up at a corner of the cafeteria to go back to their classroom. While the rest of her students are still having breakfast, Heather, the lead teacher of a pre-K class, helps Shantie, a boy from her class, line up with the SPED class. Waiting for the line to move, Shantie leans on Heather and holds her hand tight. The line begins to leave the cafeteria, and Heather walks down the hallway with Shantie.

As they approach the entrance of the SPED class next door to their pre-K class, Shantie says in a complaining tone, "I don't wanna go in there." He now tries to shake off Heather's hand. Still holding Shantie's hand, Heather tells him, "Hold my hand." She tries to look into Shantie's eyes, asking, "Do you want to hold my hand? Or do you want to walk by yourself?" She holds Shantie's hand tight, and Shantie whines, "I don't wanna go in there." Heather responds, "Well, tomorrow we're gonna go on a field trip. So you don't have to." As they enter the SPED classroom, Shantie stops moving forward and squats down by the entrance. Heather reminds him, "Watch out! There are people behind you." Then, she asks Misha, an assistant teacher of the SPED class who comes in with another child, "Y'all are cool if I just walk out?" Misha says fine, and Heather leaves. Shantie lies curled up in a corner by the entrance. Misha tries to take his hands, saying, "Come on Shantie, come to the rug. Come on Shantie, stand up." She takes Shantie's hands and struggles to make him stand up and walk a few steps toward the rug where the class is gathering. She then sees another boy who has been just dropped at the entrance and takes him to the rug.

Meanwhile, Shantie quietly goes out of the classroom and peeks at the room through a small window next to the entrance door. Claire, the lead SPED teacher, spots him and walks toward him. Shantie begins running away from the classroom and back toward the cafeteria. Running behind him, Claire tells him in a calm and yet firm voice, "Stop. No, sir!" Heather comes out of the cafeteria and then stops, seeing Claire behind Shantie. Shantie now moves toward an exit of the building, and Claire grabs him. Shantie lies down on the floor. Showing him a large laminated card which says "*Sit*" and shows a drawing of a child sitting on the floor, Claire tells Shantie, "Your body needs to be ready in our classroom now. Stand up and walk. Stand up and walk."

Through a case study of young children considered at risk of being diagnosed with Attention Deficit/Hyperactivity Disorder (ADHD), we met Shantie thanks to a recommendation from the school district's pre-K program director. When we first met, he was 5 years old and had been diagnosed with Significant Developmental Delay (SDD). According to Heather, due to his "violence towards the other children," the decision was made for Shantie to spend 2 hours each day in a "self-contained" SPED class during the spring semester of the school year. Even though our observation in his pre-K class began two months after this placement decision, we repeatedly observed incidents similar to what was described in Vignette 1 whenever Shantie had to make the transition from his pre-K class to the SPED class. Each transition took 10–15 minutes, during which time both Shantie and his teachers struggled.

Watching these repeated events, we wondered how to make sense of Shantie's consistently negative responses to the transition to the SPED class, which continued throughout our observations in the last two months of his preschool year. From his teachers' perspective, difficulty in transitions and "running away from teachers" were "noncompliant" behaviors symptomatic of ADHD. Yet, what if these actions reflect the only means that Shantie, as a young child, had to communicate his unhappiness and discomfort with having to transition to the SPED class each day?

Taking the latter as a possibility, we draw on Steven Schultz's (1989/2005) notion of young children's resistance. Based on the ideas of the critical theorists, including Martin Carnoy, Henry Giroux, and Paul Willis, Schultz defined children's resistance as "acts which run contrary to the teacher- or school-defined boundaries of acceptable, sanctioned behavior" (p. 7). Emphasizing that these acts are initiated by children, he argued: "Perhaps it is simply the self-initiation of these acts that pits them against some of the more powerful adults and institutions in their lives" (p. 7). Schultz viewed resistance in the early years as a foundation of the adult's ability to organize sociopolitical movements. He wrote:

> [The] comparisons between preschool resistance and later socially rich and organized instances of resistance are comparisons of acts of self-empowerment. If we accept that organized political actions by adults are the descendants of coordinated acts and individual initiative of young children, then we might find an important connection here in terms of self-control. … [Empowerment] cannot be given to them by those in positions of authority. Oppressed groups, clearly, must take that power for themselves. Likewise, if we are to make any comparisons between adult and preschool acts of resistance, we must look at the issue of empowering the lives of our children not only from the standpoint of the ways in which teachers *give* self-direction to them, but also in the ways in which children *take* it for themselves. The simple fact is that many children (and certainly those who number among the many disenfranchised groups) will need to use lessons in learning how to take those rights that are not being freely offered as they enter the adult world. It is in this sense, in an unequal world, that these acts of resistance are more precise sources of empowerment. And perhaps the importance of seeing these connections demands a little stretching. (p. 14; emphasis in original)

Schultz's idea of children's resistance as a source of self-control and empowerment challenges the teacher's perception of a child like Shantie, who is characterized as lacking self-control. When discussing the characteristics of Shantie's behavior, Heather shared: "He enjoys being in control of the class." Reporting a similar pattern, Shantie's SPED class teacher, Claire, elaborated on her observation:

> He is a little impulsive. When he thinks something, he does it. There's not a lot of stopping and thinking. I've noticed that he doesn't regulate himself very well. When he is upset, he is very upset. When he's happy, he's very happy. Modulation issues. And … in the context of the classroom, he has trouble following directions, not because he doesn't understand, but because he doesn't want to. He'd rather do something else. I find he is very, he wants control. Even if something as small as sit down here, and he'll just sit down slightly over this way, you know what I mean? … So he likes to be in control, he likes for things to be his idea. And just certain school readiness skills, sitting and attending and listening are pretty delayed with him. … Like sometimes I feel like he's out of control and he'll knock something over and then he'll remember the next day and tell me sorry. … I know a lot of times he's not in control of what's going on. It's like zero to ten.

Self-control here was conceptualized as the child's ability to regulate his emotions and behaviors and to comply with adult directions. In this context, the child's desire to be in control was not treated as a positive trait. Instead, it was often pathologized as a manifestation of impulsivity and immaturity. Schultz's notion of resistance invites educators to reconsider this prevalent conception of self-control.

In this study, we read Shantie's reactions to the transition to the SPED class not as symptoms of his potential ADHD but as his resistance to a part of the daily routine that he did not like or want. In so doing, this chapter addresses a central research question: What are the aspects of the daily routine in the pre-K and SPED classrooms experienced by Shantie that might have contributed to his resistance to transitioning to the SPED class?

In the remaining sections of this chapter, we provide a brief review of the literature on SPED placement from the perspective of children identified with disabilities. We then describe the research method used for this study. Next, we present three key findings from our data analysis. Finally, we conclude with implications for the education of children with diverse needs and abilities.

Placement from the Perspective of Children with Disabilities

There are few studies of SPED placement from the perspective of children identified with disabilities (Jones, 2005; Klingner, Vaughn, Schumm, Cohen, & Forgan, 1998). Billington (2006) and Humphrey and Lewis (2008) argued that such studies would promote our understanding of these students' lives in school, as they are the experts on their experiences with SPED services and practices. Miller and Fritz (2000) also pointed out that neglecting these children's voices might negatively influence their academic performance due to their disenchantment with school.

Our review of the existing research literature reveals no consensus among students identified with disabilities regarding their SPED placement. For example, several researchers reported that, compared to separate SPED placements (e.g., resource rooms, self-contained SPED classes, and pull-out models), their participants appreciated inclusive settings (e.g., general education classrooms, collaborative classrooms, and in-class support) because those settings allowed them to make friends, learn academic subjects better and more rigorously, and keep positive self-perceptions (e.g., Tetler & Baltzer, 2011; Vaughn & Klingner, 1998; Wiener & Tardif, 2004). On the contrary, other researchers found that the students in their studies preferred separate SPED settings because they were able to receive instruction in a quiet place and at the level and pace appropriate for them with more adult support (Fitch, 2003; Klingner et al., 1998; Padeliadu & Zigmond, 1996; Prunty, Dupont, & McDaid, 2012). Klingner et al. (1998) also noted that a small group of youth with learning disabilities who returned to resource rooms after spending one year in general education settings reported that "the pull-out model was better for learning and making friends" (p. 156). Some researchers found that students tend to positively evaluate their present settings (Norwich & Kelly, 2004; Prunty et al., 2012) and prefer the type of class or school in which they spend the most time (Lovitt, Plavins, & Cushing, 1999).

Meanwhile, some study findings presented more complicated views. For instance, Fitch (2003) conducted a longitudinal study of 11 students labeled "developmentally handicapped" (p. 236) in urban midwestern elementary and middle schools. These students were initially placed in self-contained SPED classes. Over a period of 6 years, during which the researcher conducted interviews with the participating students, different students were placed in different settings, including inclusive classrooms where teachers were willing to work with diverse students, traditional classrooms where teachers were "technically … considered inclusion teachers" but "quietly opposed having any special education students placed in their classes" (p. 237), and separate SPED classes. Fitch found that the participating students' sense of self was significantly different depending on "the nature of their educational placements" (p. 237). The students placed in inclusive classrooms developed confidence and a positive sense of self whereas those in traditional classrooms "often expressed a sense of rejection, resignation, and a desire to escape to the safety of the special education classroom" (p. 237). For the students who experienced inclusive settings and then had to return to separate SPED settings, their "former sense of confidence, hope, and belonging was severely shaken and in some cases all but disappeared" (p. 238). He pointed out: "the longer [students] remained within the special education classroom, the more they took on a kind of deviant subcultural identity as outsiders" (p. 238). Even though the students placed in separate SPED settings preferred "the perceived safety and anonymity of the special education class, they admitted a secret sense of shame, embarrassment, and desire to eventually escape its confines" (pp. 238–289). Nevertheless, not all students placed in separate SPED classes accepted their placement and developed their identity as outsiders. Fitch shared the case of an 8th grade girl who "rejected the idea that she did not belong in the mainstream" (p. 247) when she had to return to the separate SPED class after staying in inclusive settings for several years.

All of these studies have been conducted with elementary, middle, and high school students, and little is known about the perspective of young children who have experienced different SPED placements. In addition, although some researchers (e.g., Fitch, 2003; Prunty et al., 2012) incorporated observation and document analysis into their methods, the existing studies on students' views of inclusive or separate SPED services heavily relied on interviews and surveys (see

Miller, Garriott, & Mershon, 2005). Our study fills these gaps in the research literature by conducting a case study of a preschooler. Graue and Walsh (1998) pointed out that individual interviews with young children cannot provide an adequate understanding of their feelings and perspectives. Thus, we pay close attention to Shantie's verbal and non-verbal expressions recorded in videos during the transitions between his pre-K and SPED classrooms.

Method

Shantie was one of the four participating children in our study of young children who were suspected by their pre-K and kindergarten teachers of having ADHD (see Lee, 2017 for more details on the research method). In this chapter we decided to focus on Shantie because he was the only participating child who experienced the pull-out SPED service due to his behavior during the preschool year.

Settings and Participants

Shantie's pre-K class was located in a southern U.S. town and led by Heather, a European American first-year teacher. The class had 20 children, including 11 African-American, five European-American, three Latinx-American, and one biracial Asian and European-American. Heather explained that nearly all of her classroom's children qualified for free and reduced-price meals. This pre-K class was called a "collab" (i.e., collaborative) classroom due to six children who initially came with Individualized Education Programs (IEPs) requiring collaboration with SPED teachers. Heather collaborated with Katie, a European-American SPED teacher, who came to the class for two days a week and every other Friday. The classroom also had an assistant teacher, Jada, who was African-American.

According to Heather, Shantie did not come to school initially with an IEP. However, his behavior issues were so severe from the beginning of the school year that he was enrolled in the Response to Intervention (RTI) process for the identification of special needs. Shantie quickly moved to Tier 3 of RTI, requiring intensive individualized interventions. In the subsequent evaluation he qualified for SPED services under the category of SDD and began to receive an IEP. The state Department of Education website states that the category of SDD is used for 3 to 9-year-olds who show a delay in "adaptive behavior, cognition, communication, motor development or emotional development to the extent that, if not provided with special intervention, the delay may adversely affect a child's educational performance in age-appropriate activities." Children with SDD are retested before age 9 to change the diagnosis to more specific categories, such as emotional behavioral disorder, learning disability, or other health impairment including ADHD.

The SPED class to and from which Shantie made transitions each day was led by a European-American teacher, Claire, who worked with two to three assistant teachers and a student teacher. In addition to Shantie and an African-American girl, who also spent a part of each day in that classroom, the class had eight children eligible for full-time SPED services. These children included five African-American boys, one European-American boy, one Latino-American boy, and one Asian-American girl. All of these children were 4 to 5 years old and had a variety of diagnoses, such as SDD, Autism spectrum, Down Syndrome, and Pervasive Developmental Disorder Not Otherwise Specified.

Data Collection and Data Analysis

Due to the extensive time spent to identify target children and receive consensus and permission from all parties involved in the larger study, the field work in pre-K was conducted during the last two months (April and May) of the participating children's school year. Heather's pre-K class had Shantie and another participating child, Cody, for the larger study, but activities for these children were often different (e.g., Shantie spent 2 hours a day in the SPED class, whereas Cody stayed in the pre-K class throughout the day). To be able to observe each child carefully, Kyunghwa, who led the larger study, worked with two graduate student videographers. When the two children were in different places, each videographer followed her focal child while Kyunghwa alternated between these children during each visit. She and the student videographers visited Heather's pre-K class weekly, spending two half days and two full days and generating a total of 36 hours of video data on the two children. In addition, Kyunghwa interviewed the teachers in both the pre-K class and the SPED class who worked closely with Shantie and collected a total of 3 hours of audio-recorded interview data.

For this chapter, we focused on analyzing 17 hours of video of Shantie. Throughout the data analysis, we met regularly to carry out "collaborative coding" by reaching "agreement on each code through collaborative discussion rather than independent corroboration" (Smagorinsky, 2008, p. 401). To conduct micro-analysis of the video data (Graue & Walsh, 1998), we watched the videos multiple times and recorded codes with video running times and analytic memos in Excel spreadsheets. To identify patterns and "breaks in patterns" (Graue & Walsh, 1998, p. 163), we made careful notes of time, places, activities, grouping structures, materials, and people involved in the daily routines in which Shantie participated. In what follows, we present what we identified as the aspects of the daily routine in the pre-K and SPED classes that might have contributed to Shantie's resistance to transitioning to the SPED class.

Results

Our analysis revealed that transitions between the two classes led Shantie to (a) experience some repetitive activities and a sense of fragmentation, (b) face difficulties in developing sustained engagement and relationships, and (c) become isolated and invisible in his pre-K class.

Repetitive Activities and Fragmented Days

When examining activities provided for Shantie in his pre-K and SPED classes, we noticed several repetitive activities and frequent transitions that he experienced daily. Table 7.1 presents the daily schedules observed in the two classrooms. Highlighted in gray are the activities Shantie had to repeat in the two classrooms, as he transitioned from the pre-K class to the SPED class and then back to the pre-K class.

As shown, Shantie had to listen to the day's schedule and participate in the calendar and the read-aloud at least twice each day. All of these are teacher-led, whole class activities relevant to math and reading, in which many young children find it challenging to meaningfully engage (Katz & Chard, 2000). At times, Shantie had center activities twice a day (see April 19 and May 2) and was reminded of rules in both classrooms (see May 2). Although children were allowed to choose activities during center time, having to make transitions in the middle of this free choice activity posed another challenge to Shantie, as detailed in a later section.

In addition, we wanted to see how many transitions children in each of these two classrooms had to make. To this end, we compared what Shantie did in the SPED class with what his peers in the pre-K class did during his absence. Table 7.2 presents the results of our comparison.

As highlighted in gray, overall, Shantie's peers in the pre-K class had 2–3 transitions to make each day, while Shantie had to make 4–6 transitions in the SPED class and move between the two classrooms. Heather shared that "transitions were difficult for him." Nevertheless, on average, Shantie had twice as many transitions as his peers in the pre-K class. This practice was contradictory to the intent of the daily 2-hour placement in a self-contained SPED class, which was in part to help reduce transitions, as explained by Claire:

> [For] some students [like Shantie], the distraction of a [general education or collaborative] room … is too much. Too much going on, too many students, too many transitions, … and so they need to be in a room with fewer distractions, at least for now, to get those skills.

Table 7.1. Repetitive Activities Experienced by Shantie in Pre-K and SPED Classes.

Class \ Date	4/19	4/27	5/2	5/10
Pre-K class	Morning announcements		Free play	Morning work
			Moring announcements	
	Morning meeting: Class helpers	Morning meeting: Check the schedule	Morning meeting: Singalong: *Good Morning*	Morning meeting: Singalong: *Good Morning*
	Check the schedule	Review the class rules	Review class rules	Review class rules
				Talk about the ceremony, summer, & kindergarten
		Class helpers	Class helpers	Class helpers
	Calendar: Sing *Months of the Year* Talk about the date Sing *Days of the Week* Talk about the day	Calendar: Talk about the date Sing *Days of the Week*	Calendar: Sing *Months of the year* Talk about the date Sing *Days of the Week* Talk about the day	Calendar: Talk about the date Sing *Days of the Week* Talk about the day
	Weather	Weather	Weather	Weather
			Check the schedule	Check the schedule
	Read aloud: *Look Out Kindergarten Here I come*	Read aloud: *Sharks*	Read aloud: *Cloudy with a Chance of Meatballs*	Read aloud: *Other Goose*
	Talk about a field trip			
	Watch a movie			
	Breakfast			
	Transition to the SPED class			

Special class	Morning meeting: Calendar: Sing *Days of the Week*; Talk about the date Morning message Check the schedule	Morning meeting: Singalong: *Hello to Everyone* Check the schedule Calendar: Sing *Days of the Week*; Talk about the date Morning message Recheck the schedule	Morning meeting: Singalong: *Letter Sounds* Check the schedule Review class rules Calendar: Talk about the season; Sing *Days of the Week*; Talk about the date Singalong: *Happy Birthday*; *I can count to 100*; *Months of the Year*	Morning meeting: Singalong: *Hello to Everyone* Calendar: Sing *Days of the Week*; Talk about the date and day Color patterns Morning message Singalong: *I can count to 100 song* Check the schedule
	Small group: Measurement activity Singalong: *Letter Sounds*	Small group: Play with play dough	Recess	Small group: Play with play dough

(*Continued*)

Table 7.1. (*Continued*)

Special class	Read aloud: *Ducks*	Read aloud: *Cats*	Recess (cont.)	Read aloud: *Under the Big Top*
	Centers	Dance break		Recess
		Read aloud: *Gus the Duck*		
	Read aloud: *Gus the Duck*	Recess	Centers	
		Circle time		
	Transition to the Pre-K class			
Pre-K	Centers	Centers	Centers	Centers
		Singalong: *Alphabet*	Math workshop: Sorting	Dance break
	Lunch	Lunch	Lunch	Lunch
	Nap time	Nap time	Nap time	Nap time

Table 7.2. A Comparison of the Frequencies of Transitions Between Two Classrooms.

4/19		4/27		5/2		5/10	
SPED Class	Pre-K Class	SPED Class	Pre-K Class	SPED Class	Pre-K Class	Special	Pre-K Class
Transition from the pre-k class		**Transition from the pre-k class**		**Transition from the pre-k class**		**Transition from the pre-k class**	
Morning meeting		Morning meeting		Morning meeting		Morning meeting	
Calendar: Sing *Days of the Week* Talk about the date	Writer's workshop: Write about a kindergarten	Singalong: *Hello to Everyone*	Writer's workshop: Write about the field trip yesterday	Singalong: *Letter sounds*	Writer's workshop: Write words with a white crayon	Singalong: *Hello to everyone*	Writer's workshop: Write words
Morning message		Check the schedule		Check the schedule		Calendar: Sing *Days of the Week* song Talk about the date	
Check the schedule		Calendar: Sing *Days of the Week* Talk about the date		Review the class rules		Color patterns	
		Morning message		Calendar: Talk about the season Sing *Days of the Week* Talk about the date		Morning message	
		Check the schedule		Singalong: *Happy Birthday* *I Can Count to 100*		Singalong: *I Can Count to 100*	
						Check the schedule	

(*Continued*)

Table 7.2. (*Continued*)

Transition to a small group activity	Writer's workshop (cont.)	*Transition to a small group activity*	Writer's workshop (cont.)	*Transition to recess*	Writer's workshop (cont.)	*Transition to a small group activity*	Writer's workshop (cont.)
Small group: Measurement activity	*Transition to the whole group*	Small group: Play with play dough	*Transition to recess*	Recess	*Transition to Recess*	Small group: Play with play dough	*Transition to the whole group*
Transition to the whole group	Whole group: Write a story together	*Transition to the whole group*	Recess	Clean up	Recess	*Transition to the whole group*	Whole group: Watch a video
Singalong: *Letter Sounds*	Singalong: *Alphabet, Finger Families, & Nursery*	Read aloud: *Cats*	Clean up		Clean up	Read aloud: *Under the Big Top*	*Transition to a small group activity*
Reading aloud: *Ducks*	*Transition to P.E.*	Dance break			*Transition to centers*	*Transition to recess*	Small group: Doing diverse activities through centers
Transition to centers		Read aloud: *Gus the Duck*				Recess	
Centers: Free choice		*Transition to recess*					
		Recess					

(*Continued*)

<table>
<tr>
<td>Centers (cont.): Individual work with the SPED teacher
Free choice</td>
<td>P.E.
Transition to the classroom</td>
<td>Recess (cont.)</td>
<td>Transition to the classroom
Math: Put paper clips according to the numbers
Transition to centers</td>
<td rowspan="2">Transition to centers
Centers: Free choice
Individual work with the SPED teacher
Transition to the pre-k class</td>
<td rowspan="2">Centers</td>
<td rowspan="2">Recess (cont.)
Clean up
Transition to the pre-k class</td>
<td rowspan="2">Small group (cont.)
Transition to centers</td>
</tr>
<tr>
<td>Clean up
Transition to the whole group
Singalong: Letter Sounds
Transition to the pre-k class</td>
<td>Centers</td>
<td>Clean up
Transition to the classroom
Whole group
Transition to the pre-k class</td>
<td>Centers</td>
</tr>
</table>

Difficulties in Developing Sustained Engagement and Relationships

The fragmented daily schedule seemed to lead Shantie to face difficulties in developing both sustained engagement in an activity and relationships with his peers.

Too many activities

As presented above in Table 7.1, Shantie and his peers in both classes participated in many activities in their daily routines. For example, the list below shows a typical morning meeting Shantie and his classmates in the pre-K class took part in:

May 10, 2012 (Pre-K Video Segments, 00:24:12–00:38:36)

00:24:12–00:24:54	Morning Song
00:24:55–00:25:37	Reviewing Classroom Rules
00:25:38–00:29:14	Talking about the Graduation Ceremony, Summer, Kindergarten
00:29:15–00:29:39	Announcing Today's Classroom Helpers
00:29:40–00:31:33	Calendar
00:31:34–00:32:04	Weather
00:32:05–00:32:39	Today's Schedule
00:32:40–00:38:00	Reading Aloud (on the Smartboard)
00:38:01–00:38:36	Transition to Breakfast

This morning meeting, which took less than 15 minutes total, consisted of nine activities. And, as discussed in the previous section, Shantie had to join in this sort of morning meeting again when he transitioned to the SPED class each day.

Claire talked about why short activities with quick transitions were critical to Shantie:

> You know … typical children at this age in pre-K in May would be able to sit and attend for now up to twenty minutes on the rug … or fifteen minutes in a small group. … [At] this time I don't see that his skills are there yet. … [We] need quick transitions, don't have to sit too long here or there, unless something is on the smart board that he likes. And then he can focus.

In fact, due to their concern about children's short attention span, many teachers of young children with and without disability labels tend to design and implement short, discrete, and often disengaging activities (Katz & Chard, 2000). However, this practice seems to result in cramming many activities into the daily routine and, as discussed above, requiring children in general and those like Shantie who are considered to have issues with attention in particular to make frequent transitions.

Struggles with entry into peers' ongoing play

Frequent transitions further challenged Shantie when attempting to play and build relationships with his peers. Each day he transitioned to the pre-K class during center time when his pre-K classmates had been engaged in free choice activities (see Table 7.1 again). Corsaro (1985) discussed how gaining entry into peers' ongoing play is difficult for young children. Shantie had to face this challenge daily due to the transitions between the two classes.

The following vignette illustrates a sequence of struggles Shantie experienced as he returned to his pre-K class and tried to gain access to his peers' ongoing play activities:

Vignette 2

> It is center time in Heather's pre-K class. Returning from the SPED class, Shantie looks around the room and watches his peers' play activities. He then goes to the water table where two boys and one girl are playing. When he splashes the water, one of the boys in that group raises his voice and says, "Hey!" while the girl calls the teacher. Shantie walks backward and mumbles, "I want to play water." He goes to Heather and says that he wants to play water. Looking over at the water table, she asks, "How many people are over there?" Shantie counts three, but she cuts him as if she has just realized something: "No. Remember? The other day you put water in your mouth and spit it out. So, no more water." Shantie softly says sorry. Heather responds, "I know you are sorry, but no more water." Then Shantie goes to a table where three boys are playing with blocks. He quickly grabs two of the blocks placed in front of Cody. "No!" Cody whines. Heather comes and takes the blocks back to Cody, telling Shantie, "You cannot take that from Cody." The assistant teacher, Jada, comes and asks Heather, "Is he allowed at water now?" While Heather says no and explains the reason, Shantie cries out, jumps up and down, squats down, and hits a trash can with his hand. Jada goes, "Oh, no!" and tells him to pick up the trash and put it back in the trash can.

Corsaro (1985) explained that gaining entry into peers' ongoing play is challenging because those involved in play try to protect the space and theme of their play. Thus, the entry requires "a variety of access strategies" (p. 123) combined with verbal and non-verbal negotiation skills in much the same way that we as adults feel challenged when trying to join in other people's ongoing conversation at a social gathering. Developing these negotiation skills takes time and requires experience.

However, the teachers tended to immediately intervene in real and potential conflicts between Shantie and his peers, not giving them enough time to negotiate with each other, but often treating Shantie as if he was a trouble maker.

Being Alone and Becoming Invisible

We noted that in the pre-K class Shantie was involved in many solo activities and often became invisible.

A lone learner

Shantie's interactions with his peers were quite limited in both classes, as he was placed in situations requiring more interactions with teachers than with children. In the pre-K class, upon his arrival on the morning, his teachers let him play with a computer while his peers worked on writing letters at their tables. As described in Vignette 1, he had to leave the cafeteria early for the transition to the SPED class when his pre-K classmates were still having breakfast. In addition, when these peers were still engaged in a classroom activity, he was taken to the cafeteria to have early lunch alone. Then, his teacher brought him back to the pre-K classroom and put him to sleep by cuddling him before his peers came back from lunch for the naptime. His teachers explained that they had to do this with Shantie in order to keep him from disrupting other children's activities or sleep.

Despite his limited peer interactions, Shantie seemed to have a strong sense of affiliation with his pre-K class. Over time, we heard him calling his pre-K class "my class," but he never referred the SPED class in the same manner. Instead, in the SPED class he frequently asked, "Am I going back to my class now?" While his use of the words "my class" seemed to reflect his sense of belonging and identity, the words "your class" said to him by his teachers seemed to mean just the place where he should be at a particular moment based on the schedule. This difference often created conflicts between Shantie and his teachers, as described in the following vignette:

Vignette 3

> Shantie is with the SPED class, and they are having recess on the playground. Soon, the pre-K class joins them for recess. Riding a bike, Shantie talks to and interacts with some of his pre-K class peers. After a while, Heather calls out, "Ms. Heather's class, line up please!" Hearing the announcement, Shantie runs to get in line. … Heather gives each child in the line a token and says, "Thank you for lining up." When it comes to Shantie's turn, she tells him, "Go back to *your* class." In a whining voice, Shantie

> says, "No! I don't want to." He folds his arms and crouches down at a corner by the entrance. … Looking at his pre-K classmates going inside the building with Heather, Shantie begins to run around the playground. … Then, he finds Jada, the assistant teacher of the pre-K class, gathering the kids left out. Shantie runs to her and hugs her. Not realizing that Shantie is currently in the SPED class, she tells him, "Go ahead and clean up. Look at that scooter. Bring it back here [in the storage]." Smiling, he runs to the scooter and says, "Thank goodness!" He puts the scooter back in the storage and comes to Jada, saying, "I'm done. I'm going *my* class now?"

From the teacher's perspective, referring to the SPED class as "your class" might be a simple reminder of his individualized class schedule. However, for Shantie, the words could be heard as a rejection or denial of his membership in the pre-K class.

Becoming invisible

The teachers' frequent intervention in Shantie's interactions with his peers and the many solo activities that he engaged in seemed to affect the way his peers interacted with him. In what follows, we present a series of vignettes involving his pre-K classmates' interactions with Shantie. We would like to direct the reader's attention to how the teachers' suggestion for ignoring Shantie's inappropriate words was eventually taken by his peers as ignoring Shantie himself.

Vignette 4

> Shantie, Cody, and two other boys in Heather's pre-K class are playing with blocks at a table. Shantie goes to the container of blocks, which is placed in front of Cody, and takes some blocks out of the container. Cody looks up to Heather, who stands behind him, and complains in an inaudible voice.

Heather:	(Looking down at Cody) No, he can. No, he can get stuff out of there.
Shantie:	(Coming back to his seat and putting his blocks together) I really hate Cody.
Cody:	(Turning his body to Heather) He said he hated me.
Heather:	What should you do?
Cody:	Ignore.
Heather:	*Ignore it.*
	(Cody says some inaudible words to Shantie.)
Shantie:	Shut up!
Cody:	(Turning his body to Heather and raising his voice) He said a bad word to me, too!
Heather:	(Putting one hand on her ear) Remember, we don't listen to that stuff.

Vignette 5

It's lunchtime in the pre-K class. Today is a special day, as the class has a pizza party to celebrate the end of the school year. Shantie and five other children, including Devon, are sitting at a table, eating pizza, and drinking juice.

Shantie:	(Turning around and shouting at someone across the room) Hey look, buddy! Aren't you gonna bad ass?
Other children:	Woo!
Shantie:	(Turning back to eat his pizza) Yes!
Devon:	(Pointing his finger to Shantie and in a surprising tone) Hey fellow, what? (Shantie does not respond to Devon. Instead, he gets up and falls out of his chair.)
Devon:	(To Jada, who is busy putting mats on the floor near Shantie's table to get ready for naptime) Ms. Jada, Shantie is saying in your face. Shantie is saying it in your face.
Shantie:	(Getting up and then sitting down) I'm not saying a word!
Jada:	(Continuing to take mats out of the closet nearby Shantie's table) What are we supposed to do when our friends say stuff like that?
Devon:	Ignore!
Jada:	Okay, then.
Child across room:	Ignore him!

Vignette 6

In the dramatic play area of Heather's classroom, Shantie is playing with a toy cell phone. He sits in a corner of the dramatic play area, touching a board separating the dramatic play area from the block play area. Isabella and Lucas stand by the stove in the dramatic play area.

Isabella:	(Looking at Lucas and raising her voice) Where is my food?
Shantie:	(Turning back and looking at Isabella) Mommy! Mommy! (Not responding to Shantie, Isabella and Lucas continue to play by the stove.)
Shantie:	(Raising his voice and continuing to touch the board without looking at Isabella) Mommy! Mommy! Take me out to work! Mommy! Mommy! (Not looking at Shantie, Isabella and Lucas continue their play by the stove.)
Shantie:	(Turning around to see Isabella and waving at her) Mommy! Mommy! (Although Isabella continues to avoid eye contact with Shantie, Lucas looks at Shantie.)

Shantie: (Getting up and walking toward Isabella) Mommy! Mommy! Mommy! (He goes to Isabella and touches some materials that Isabella has been playing with.)

(Isabella neither looks at nor responds to Shantie. Instead, she continues to put some toys in a cabinet with which she has been playing. Lucas does not say a word to Shantie either and goes to pick up a toy tool box.)

Shantie: (Going to Lucas) Daddy, I need some of that.

(Lucas does not respond to Shantie. Instead, he walks around the dramatic play area, avoiding eye contact with Shantie.)

Shantie: (Following Lucas) Daddy! I need some, I need some of that.

(Lucas does not respond to Shantie and quickly goes back to where Isabella is.)

Many teachers encourage children to ignore inappropriate words and behaviors they hear or observe from peers as a positive behavior intervention strategy (Carr et al., 2002). Yet, distinguishing between ignoring peers' words and behaviors and ignoring and rejecting the peers themselves must be challenging for young children. This might be also true for adults, and perhaps that is why it is hard to practice the wisdom "hate the sin, but love the sinner."

Discussion

In this study, we attempted to understand what made Shantie, our 5-year-old focus child, resistant to transitioning to the SPED class. We found that transitions between the two classes led him to experience some repetitive activities and a disjointed schedule, to face difficulties in developing sustained engagement with activities and peers, and to become isolated and invisible in his pre-K homeroom class despite the strong desire he expressed for membership in the class. Thus, from Shantie's perspective, the transition to the SPED class could be a source of boredom, fragmentation, and alienation. Given his strong sense of affiliation with the pre-K class rather than with the SPED class, we also think that his resistance to transitioning to the SPED class could be read as his refusal to identify himself as a child with disability and special needs, as defined by the school.

Schultz (1989/2005) noted:

> Resistance is most successful by the children who are skilled in combining "inside" and "outside" elements—or some behaviors which are a part of the given activity with other behaviors outside it. These children are able to operate on a more subtle-level—a level that includes a certain degree of sophistication about the culture of the school, and one where they have already attached school-defined meanings to their own behaviors. (p. 9)

This statement reminds us that all children, not just a child like Shantie who is considered hyperactive, impulsive, and violent, resist certain parts of their experience in school to some extent. Unlike his peers who resist in a more subtle and sophisticated manner, Shantie's resistance tends to be too direct (e.g., running away from the teacher), too physical (e.g., hitting a trash can), and too vulgar (e.g., calling a friend a "bad ass" in public), and thus does not conform to the school's norms for appropriate behavior and expression. Schultz's perspective encourages us to think about seemingly defiant behaviors demonstrated by a young child like Shantie not necessarily as symptoms of a disorder requiring a separate placement and treatment, but as unsophisticated and unsuccessful resistance with and around which *any* competent teachers, not just those trained in special education, should be able to work.

Although Shantie's "violence towards the other children" was given as the main reason for the daily 2-hour placement in the self-contained SPED class, at least during our observation we could not find any moment when Shantie posed a physical threat to his peers. According to Schultz (1989/2005), "Successful individual resistance has varying effects upon the group. Some of these events result in individual children's simply being able to do things that other children do not or cannot do as part of the activities of the group" (p. 10). In light of that observation, is it possible that Shantie's "violence" might not be his threats to other children, but rather his threats to the teachers' authority and the classroom order through his explicit violation of classroom norms, which might provoke his peers' non-compliance?

Schultz (1989/2005) pointed out that successful resistance does not result only from an individual initiator. Instead, it often involves "coordinated group actions (CGA)" which require "a readiness on the part of the group" (p. 11). However, CGAs might be challenging for a child like Shantie, who is often separated from his peers. Or might the teacher's fear of Shantie's (albeit unintended) instigation of a CGA be a reason why he was given more solo activities or activities requiring more interactions with adults than with his peers? Schultz wrote:

> When young children assume an independent power through their coordinated group acts, even when there appears to be no purpose to them, they are often interpreted by the teacher as threatening *simply because they are not within her control.* … The creation of a breach in normal classroom relations is a disruptive act in and of itself. (p. 11; emphasis in original)

If we read Shantie's actions not as the manifestation of his potential ADHD but as normal (though unsuccessful) resistance that many students attempt to exercise, how should we respond to such actions? Expanding Schultz's Marxist approach to resistance to de Certeau's (1984) notion of "tactics" and Bakhtin's (1984) conception of the "carnivalesque," Tobin (2005) suggests viewing children's non-compliant behaviors as "acts of disagreement with our classroom policies and with the fairness of our leadership" (p. 36). Considering that Schultz perceived young children's resistance in preschool as "a rehearsal or training ground for resisting authority later in life" (Tobin, 2005, p. 32), Tobin encourages us to "expect and respect our students to express a diversity of opinions about classroom rules and expectations" (p. 37). He proposes acknowledging rather than ignoring, suppressing, or endorsing children's disagreement expressed through their resistance.

Schultz (1989/2005) valued children's resistance as a way to exercise their empowerment, emphasizing that resistance is critical, particularly for those from marginalized groups. Considering many documented accounts of the way the behaviors of African-American boys from economically disadvantaged families are perceived and treated negatively (e.g., Ferguson, 2001; Harry & Klingner, 2014; Laura, 2014), we believe that the resistance exercised by a young student like Shantie, an African-American boy from a working-class family, at the very beginning of his schooling demands a thoughtful and ethical response. To further empower a child like Shantie, we argue for including his voice in the decision making about his placement. Discussing "person-centered planning," O'Brien and O'Brien (1999) advocated for "honoring the voices of the person and those who know the person best" (p. 14) when serving an individual with a disability label. To practice person-centered planning, meetings to discuss and determine the placement of children with disabilities need to be conducted in a manner and in a language that is both family- and child-friendly by involving not only school personnel but also the children who need service, family members, friends, and community people who can talk about both the needs and the strengths of the children on their behalf. Such meetings require changing the power dynamics prevalent in typical IEP meetings where the knowledge and perspectives of professionals from the school are privileged, while the voices of the children and their families in general and those from marginalized groups in particular tend to be neglected.

We believe that framing our discussion about the implications for practice in the simple binary of inclusive and exclusive settings is not going to be very useful. We also hope that our chapter is not read as a critique of individual teachers, especially preschool teachers who have not received the respect they deserve from our society. Instead, we would like to end this chapter by inviting early childhood educators to critically examine some of the taken-for-granted conditions and systems in schools that contribute to making the schooling experience of many children like Shantie unpleasant, unfair, and alienating. Those conditions and systems include rigid age- and grade-segregated grouping, assigning students to an individual teacher and classroom, and designing daily routines with many activities focused on discrete academic skills and with frequent transitions. Instead, as many international early childhood programs, including the much-acclaimed Reggio Emilia Approach in Italy (Edwards, Gandini, & Forman, 1998) have done, we need to seriously consider implementing mixed-age grouping and allowing children to engage in the investigation of phenomena that is interesting and meaningful to them over a period of time they need (Katz & Chard, 2000) as alternative conditions. Boldt and Valente (2016) also introduced a fascinating model, L'école Gulliver, a preschool in Paris that is operated based on the notion of a "group-subject" conceptualized by the French social theorist and psychotherapist Felix Guattari (see Chapter 11, this volume). In this preschool, children with and without disability labels are integrated and not assigned to an individual teacher, classroom, or age group. Instead, "the children are moved throughout the day, changing activities, educators, classroom spaces and groups of children" (p. 328). Gulliver encourages us to acknowledge how inclusion is emotionally difficult work not only for children but also for teachers. This model also inspires us to move beyond our focus on the individual child or teacher and toward appreciating the collective construction of subjectivities. Certainly, creating new cultures and conditions that embrace and respect difference in schools requires collective responsibilities beyond the individual child or teacher.

Note

1. The names of places and people in this chapter are pseudonyms.

References

Bakhtin, M. M. (1984). *Rabelais and his world* (H. Iswolsky, Trans.). Cambridge, MA: MIT Press.

Billington, T. (2006). Working with autistic children and young people: Sense, experience and the challenges for services, policies and practices. *Disability & Society, 21*(1), 1–13.

Boldt, G., & Valente, J. M. (2016). L'école Gulliver and La Borde: An ethnographic account of collectivist integration and institutional psychotherapy. *Curriculum Inquiry, 46*(3), 321–341.

Carr, E. G., Dunlap, G., Horner, R. H., Koegel, R. L., Turnbull, A. P., Sailor, W., Anderson, J. L., Albin, R. W., Koegel, L. K., & Fox, L. (2002). Positive behavior support: Evolution of an applied science. *Journal of Positive Behavioral Intervention*, 4(1), 4–16.

Corsaro, W. (1985). *Friendship and peer culture in the early years.* Norwood, NJ: Ablex Publishing.

De Certeau, M. (1984). *The practice of everyday life.* Berkeley, CA: University of California Press.

Edwards, C., Gandini, L., & Forman, G. (Eds.). (1998). *The hundred languages of children: The Reggio Emilia approach—Advanced reflections* (2nd ed.). Westport, CT: Ablex Publishing.

Ferguson, A. A. (2001). *Bad boys: Public schools in the making of black masculinity.* Ann Arbor, MI: University of Michigan Press.

Fitch, F. (2003). Inclusion, exclusion, and ideology: Special education students' changing sense of self. *The Urban Review, 35*(3), 233–252.

Graue, M. E., & Walsh, D. J. (1998). *Studying children in context: Theories, methods, and ethics.* Thousand Oaks, CA: Sage.

Harry, B., & Klingner, J. (2014). *Why are so many minority students in special education? Understanding race & disability in schools* (2nd ed.). New York, NY: Teachers College Press.

Humphrey, N., & Lewis, S. (2008). Make me normal: The views and experiences of pupils on the autistic spectrum in mainstream secondary schools. *Autism*, *12*(1), 23–46.

Jones, P. (2005). Inclusion: Lessons from the children. *British Journal of Special Education*, *32*(2), 60–66.

Katz, L. G., & Chard, S. C. (2000). *Engaging children's minds: The project approach* (2nd ed.). Stamford, CT: Ablex.

Klingner, J. K., Vaughn, S., Schumm, J. S., Cohen, P., & Forgan, J. W. (1998). Inclusion or pull-out: Which do students prefer? *Journal of Learning Disabilities*, *31*(2), 148–158.

Laura, C. T. (2014). *Being bad: My baby brother and the school-to-prison pipeline.* New York, NY: Teachers College Press.

Lee, K. (2017). Making the body ready for school: ADHD and early schooling in the era of accountability. *Teachers College Record*, *119*(9), 1–38.

Lovitt, T. C., Plavins, M., & Cushing, S. (1999). What do pupils with disabilities have to say about their experience in high school? *Remedial and Special Education*, *20*(2), 67–83.

Miller, M., & Fritz, M. F. (2000). *What do special education students think of school placements?* Terre Haute, IN: Indiana State University. (ERIC Document Reproduction Service No. ED439562).

Miller, M., Garriott, P., & Mershon, D. (2005). Special education students' placement preferences as shown in special education journals. *Electronic Journal for Inclusive Education*, *1*(9), 1–19. Retrieved from https://corescholar.libraries.wright.edu/cgi/viewcontent.cgi?article=1064&context=ejie

Norwich, B., & Kelly, N. (2004). Pupils' views on inclusion: Moderate learning difficulties and bullying in mainstream and special schools. *British Educational Research Journal*, *30*(1), 43–65.

O'Brien, C. L., & O'Brien, J. (1999). *The origins of person-centered planning: A community of practice perspective.* Lithonia, GA: Responsive Systems Associates. Retrieved from https://files.eric.ed.gov/fulltext/ED456599.pdf

Padeliadu, S., & Zigmond, N. (1996). Perspectives of students with learning disabilities about special education placement. *Learning Disabilities Research & Practice*, *11*(1), 15–23.

Prunty, A., Dupont, M., & McDaid, R. (2012). Voices of students with special educational needs (SEN): Views on schooling. *Support for Learning*, *27*(1), 29–36.

Schultz, S. (1989/2005). Finding meaning in the resistance of preschool children: Critical theory takes an interpretive look. *Bank Street Occasional Paper Series*, *14*, 6–15.

Smagorinsky, P. (2008). The method section as conceptual epicenter in constructing social science research reports. *Written Communication*, *25*(3), 389–411.

Tetler, S., & Baltzer, K. (2011). The climate of inclusive classrooms: The pupil perspective. *London Review of Education*, *9*(3), 333–344.

Tobin, J. (2005). Everyday tactics and the carnivalesque: New lenses for viewing resistance in preschool. *Bank Street Occasional Paper Series*, *14*, 32–38.

Vaughn, S., & Klingner, J. K. (1998). Students' perceptions of inclusion and resource room settings. *The Journal of Special Education*, *32*(2), 79–88.

Wiener, J., & Tardif, C. Y. (2004). Social and emotional functioning of children with learning disabilities: Does special education placement make a difference? *Learning Disabilities Research & Practice*, *19*(1), 20–32.

CHAPTER EIGHT

Negotiating the Culture of Expertise

Experiences of Families of Children with Mild Autism and Other Sensory/Behavioral Differences

MELISSA SHERFINSKI AND SERA MATHEW

High-stakes testing and the intensification of schooling over the past decade have formed a "culture of expertise" (Novinger, O' Brien, & Sweigman, 2005) in which the knowledge of many experts is needed to develop the competencies in children that are recognized in high stakes schooling. The culture of expertise is fueled by an increasingly globalized orientation toward testing and accountability driven by international competition (Apple, Kenway, & Singh, 2005). The culture of expertise affects relationships between homes and schools. The potential democratic nature of schooling that incorporates the participation of children, teachers, and parents has become co-opted (Dahlberg, Moss, & Pence, 2007). Structures, roles, and practices for schools, teachers, families, and children have shifted, and this change has affected children and families who are marginalized: those on the "borders" of education. In this essay, the borders we explore are the experiences of families of young children (preschool-elementary) with mild autism and other sensory/behavioral differences.

Families of children with mild autism and other sensory/behavioral differences must continually negotiate educational culture and (re)make their identities in the process. We focus on families of children who identify with diagnoses of and/or evaluation for autism spectrum disorder (ASD) presenting in its "milder" forms, Asperger's syndrome, Pervasive Developmental Disorder (PDD), sensory disorders, and other related and concomitant diagnoses. Because the interviews were completed in 2012–2013, on the cusp of a new iteration of the American Psychiatric Association's

Diagnostic and Statistical Manual (DSM) (American Psychiatric Association, 2013), there was both flux and anxiety shown by interviewees around labels, diagnoses, and their meanings. While this clustering of labels used in the chapter is somewhat messy, it also recognizes the multiplicity of conditions that may present for individuals. We refer to this group as "neuro-atypical"[1] (Smagorinsky, 2011), a play on the term "neurotypical," which is used by those on the autism spectrum to refer to those who do not share their makeup. Our interest is in young children because there is increased impetus to now diagnose and label children early and intervene, whereas in the past many people were not diagnosed until later in life (Fountain, King, & Bearman, 2011).

In the culture of expertise, there is intense pressure to bear the burden of being "special" (Naraian, 2013). Neuro-atypical children and their families often seek out inclusive education, an environment in which their rights to participate are supported (Purdue, Gordon-Burns, Gunn, Madden, & Surtees, 2009). In a culture premised on creating proficiency for each individual, disability is believed to reside within the child, and the child is constructed as negatively different and thus in need of adult expertise (Purdue, 2009). The culture of expertise promotes the idea that the problems that children with disabilities face are caused only by their impairment(s) and not by an education system that can be disabling (Purdue, 2009). In response to their positioning, families take on "chooser" identities as they seek appropriate settings and services, sometimes private and/or virtual (Molnar, 2014). More families are taking the education of their neuro-atypical children into their own hands through homeschooling (McDonald & Lopes, 2014; Murphy, 2012). Given this context affecting children and families, we considered the following research question: How do contemporary families of children with neuro-atypicalities navigate the culture of expertise in early childhood and elementary schooling?

In this chapter, we follow the journeys of seven families as they navigate the borderlands constructed by a society deeply uncomfortable with atypical cognitive and sensory presentations. In the context of society and school choice prevalent in U.S. schools, we see these families as nomads in search of fertile ground for their children's education. We organize this essay by explaining our poststructuralist framework and case study method, and then present the data organized by themes of identities, emotions, and pedagogies. We end by touching on possibilities for inclusive education.

Neuro-atypicalities

As mentioned, the autism spectrum consists of a group of complex neurodevelopmental conditions including autism, Asperger's syndrome, and Pervasive Developmental Disorder (PDD) (Blumberg et al., 2013). The condition is characterized by different levels of challenges regarding social behaviors, communication, rituals, and stereotypes (Matson & Kozlowski, 2011; Worley & Matson, 2012). Common to nearly all individuals on these spectra are atypical behavioral responses to sensory information (Marco, Hinkley, Hill, & Nagarajan, 2011). Because of the behavioral nature of the autism spectrum, it is time-consuming and complicated to diagnose (Blumberg et al., 2013). Although guidelines have suggested that children on the autism spectrum should have symptoms appearing by 18–24 months, increasingly children are not diagnosed until school age, when parents and teachers notice social issues. At school age, formal diagnoses are likely to occur because they are needed to obtain special education supports under the Individuals with Disabilities Education Act (IDEA). School age diagnoses are more common for children with mild forms and/or children from socially disadvantaged groups (Leonard et al., 2010).

Recently, many researchers have inquired into the question of how and why dramatic increases in the prevalence of autism spectrum diagnoses have emerged (Matson & Kozlowski, 2011). The global occurrence of autism has increased from the reported numbers in the 1960s and 1970s (Centers for Disease Control, 2014b). In the U.S. in 2014, 1 in 68 children had been diagnosed with ASD (Centers for Disease Control, 2014a). The prevalence of typical autism in the U.S. was recently found to be 7.1/10,000 children, whereas for the full autism spectrum including Asperger's and PDD, the rate was 20.0/10,000, indicating that the majority of autistic children have milder forms (Riby, Hancock, Jones, & Hanley, 2013; Williams, Higgins, & Brayne, 2006). This finding is supported by the recent National Survey of Children's Health, in which 58.3% of parents reported their child's autism as mild, 34.8% as moderate, and only 6.9% as severe (Blumberg et al., 2013).

For decades, controversy about the criteria for autism has been sparked by revisions of disease classification manuals (Leonard et al., 2010). The 2013 widening of the American Psychiatric Association's criteria of autism—in their parlance, Autism Spectrum Disorder (ASD)—has implications for the number of diagnoses. In the new DSM-V, separate diagnoses for Autistic Disorder, Asperger's Syndrome, and PDD are placed under a unified diagnosis of autism. The unified diagnosis of autism combines individuals with milder symptoms and those with moderate or severe autism symptoms. The re-categorization was done to maintain the sensitivity of autism diagnoses while increasing the specificity; however, "distinctions between the disorders comprising the autism spectrum remain controversial and research findings regarding the differences tend to contradict each other" (Worley & Matson, 2012, p. 965). The shifting nature of autism diagnosis causes many discomforts and challenges for families and their children, and for educational and medical communities.

There is an "invisible nature" to mild forms of autism that affects negotiation within the culture of expertise. The child and family may or may not see themselves as disabled, and society may deny any differences that they see as disability (MacLeod, Lewis, & Robertson, 2013). Without clear visible "disabilities," children and families may experience claims of "faking" a disability, while they may also have the luxury of when to disclose (Lindgren, 2011). At the same time, some of these children may be "twice exceptional"; that is, talented in some ways yet also needing extra support in others, a context that causes unique challenges that are not always addressed by school policies and practices (Nielsen & Higgins, 2005). This shifting ground occurs within a broader educational context in which the resources that children diagnosed with disabilities need are not considered to be a right. Rather, parents and teachers are positioned to push forward through "special pleading" (Purdue, Gordon-Burns, Rarere-Briggs, Stark, & Turnock, 2011, p. 101). This need for vociferous advocacy, we have found, creates a painful tension for children and families with neuro-atypicalities that may prohibit inclusivity and make these conditions some of the hardest for teachers to understand and support in the classroom (Hurlbutt, 2011).

The Culture of Expertise

There are multiple lenses through which to view the culture of expertise and its effects on families. Standardized test-oriented schooling is structured through long-standing policies such as No Child Left Behind (NCLB) and Race to the Top (RTTT). Within such policies, the organizing language of programming, implementation, engagement, controls, and maintenance structure a vocabulary "marked by precision, regularity, and standardization to the interpretation of human activities" (Danforth & Naraian, 2007, p. 279) and promoting ability-normativity (Collins & Valente, 2010). The preoccupation with high-stakes testing structures a complex web of educational triage (Connor & Ferri, 2007) as childhoods are bound in ecologies of social networks, professional support, managerial trainers, policy-makers, and science (Keenan, Dillenburger, Doherty, Byrne, & Gallagher, 2010). Expert knowledge is often valued over the knowledge of parents, students, community advocates, general educators, and students themselves (Slee, 2001). This context affects educational relationships at school and at home, by shaping roles and identities for parents, children, and teachers in complex ways (Sherfinski, Weekley, & Mathew, 2015).

Our first examples from the literature deal with the context of power among various actors in school classrooms. Purdue (2009) found in her study of inclusion in New Zealand preschools that the type of disability, the teacher's identity, concern for all children's learning, and available resources shaped teachers' attitudes about the notion of disability. Children diagnosed with disabilities were seen as "too different" to contribute to classroom learning. They were discussed by parents of children without diagnoses as a force that subtracted time, money, and attention from their "normal" children. Zindler (2009), in her in-depth case study of an early elementary classroom, noted complex social relations among mixed groups of children such that those children with IEPs in the context of inclusion-oriented pedagogy still experienced lower levels of social inclusion than their nondisabled peers. This research points out the complicated challenges of bridging current theory and practice for the purpose of creating inclusive heterogeneous classrooms because of the effects of power in these settings.

The next examples deal with the goals of education and the associated pedagogical processes in which differences are labeled and remediated. Most often in contemporary education, differences are not viewed as assets for teaching and learning (Connor & Gabel, 2010). For example, in classroom discourses, talk of "disabilities" can be silenced in a way similar to racial/ethnic silencing (e.g., Bonilla-Silva, 2006). But maintaining the status quo in classrooms is more complicated than only a silencing phenomenon. It actually involves the "both/and" of pointing out and intervening in various neuro-atypical conditions and silencing other differences (Smagorinsky, 2014). More specifically, for most children with neuro-atypicalities, graduating from a formal IEP and special services and therapies is an important goal (Broderick, 2009). But as Valle (2014) states, some teachers recognize the violence involved in "fixing" students who are different. These kinds of tensions among and within school, medical, and home logics and goals of education can result in challenges for children and families, as we have found in our research.

Our final set of examples from the literature addresses the family context. Because the culture of expertise sets up a hierarchy of knowledge between experts and others, it is difficult to engage in more democratic conversations and actions toward inclusive practice that draw on the strengths of teachers, families, and children (Novinger et al., 2005; Schofield, 2004; Whitaker, 2007). Two studies, by Woodgate, Ateah, and Secco (2008) and by Trainor (2010), show the specific mechanisms by which this process occurs. They found that with limited support, families grapple with the deficit perspectives of their children, uncertainty about possibilities for inclusive experiences, and difficulties in understanding legalistic program structures and technical jargon. This view has been supported by researchers who have noted disproportionate representation of African American groups labeled with cognitive and externalizing behavioral disabilities, learning disabilities, and neuro-atypicalities such as Asperger's syndrome and mild autism (e.g., Blanchett, 2006; Connor & Ferri, 2007; Heilker, 2012). Although research highlighting group experiences is vital, there has not been much research that looks at the intersectionality of identities and the roles of culture and context in constructing experiences for children, families, and teachers. This oversight is especially problematic because homogenizing narratives may reinforce the idea of a static and impenetrable culture of expertise. Addressing these issues, we report on families with diverse racial/ethnic, class, and gender backgrounds using a variety of school contexts. Table 8.1 below introduces the characteristics of our participants.

Table 8.1: Identifying Study Participants.

Family name	Class/race or ethnicity/ national origin	Parents' employment M = Mother, F = Father	Ages of children	Child with disability	School history
Pereira	Middle class/ Latinx & White/USA	M & F: Group home managers	9, 8	Isabel (9)	Private (Pre-K, K) > Homeschool (1) > Public (1) > Private (2) > Public (3, 4)
Franken-burg-Chavez	Poor/Latinx & White/ USA & Caribbean	M & F: SSI	10, 3	Puritee (3)	Birth-Three > Homeschool (Pre-K 3)
Gross	Middle class/ White/USA	Sister (23) has custody: Homemaker	26, 24, 23, 21, 18, 8, 2	Gino (2)	Birth-Three
Jorgenson	Middle class/ White/USA	M: Homemaker F: Hairdresser	11	Lily (11)	Private (Pre-K 4, K, 1, 2, 3) > Homes-chool (4, 5, 6)
Kant	Upper middle class/White/ Scandinavia & USA	M: Professor F: Veterinarian	6, 4	Rory (6)	Public (Pre-K 4) > Private (Pre-K 4, K)
King	Working class/ White/USA	M: Administra-tive assistant F: Warehouse foreman	6, 1	Jude (6)	Birth-Three > Public/Some Private (Pre-K 3, Pre-K 4) > Public (K)
Liu	Middle class/ Asian/USA	M: Homemaker F: Car salesman	6, 4	Jonathan (6)	Birth-Three > Public (Pre-K 3, Pre-K 4, K)

Theory

Smagorinsky (2011) has used the work of Vygotsky (1993) to illustrate the cultural nature of the *secondary disability* that is constructed when disability is viewed as a defect that is organic and developmental, one that must be only intervened in and recovered from. This process of constructing people of difference as in need of pity or as objects of scorn produces feelings of inferiority, the secondary disability that Vygotsky finds much more debilitating than the source of difference. Whereas organic and developmental facets of disability do exist, the conceptualization is problematic. Individuals and groups use cultural tools such as arts and technology to construct new cultural worlds that reconceptualize people of difference such that more inclusive environments mitigate against the secondary disability of internalizing the feeling of low social stature. Because of the ages of children addressed in this sample (3–11), we also consider the roles of age and development relative to pedagogy and education.

In our framework, we build on cultural understandings of (dis)ability to analyze the connections with the power of language that individuals use to position others in various ways. This language and positioning offer inroads or barriers on the path to the kinds of inclusive agency that is possible for children and families. Because we are concerned with navigation of the culture of expertise, we sought a framework to analyze how families used, interpreted, and resisted discourses that positioned them in particular ways that did and did not support inclusive possibilities. We chose post-structuralist tools to examine participants' experiences. These allowed us to explore subject positioning as a mechanism that shapes educational journeys.

Sabat (2003) has used positioning theory (Harre & van Langenhove, 1999) to show how narratives of individuals, caregivers, and professionals can construct sub-human identities. This kind of positioning can inhibit agency and inclusive settings. People take up, impose on others, accept, and reject particular social interactions through talk. These processes can be interactive as people position each other in dialogue, or reflexive as individuals position themselves. Explicit positioning occurs through blunt, blanket statements made about identities, such as "The parents are creating the problem, there is nothing wrong with that child." Implicit positioning occurs when individuals do the "benign" work of being surprised that normativity is shown by people known to have particular, inherent deficits. Professionals then validate both explicit and implicit positioning statements by rearticulating them as commonsense within the field. In our data, friends and family members also contributed to the context of positioning that "boxed in" individuals with neuro-atypicalities, labeling them in stereotypical ways and/or silencing the challenges.

One form of positioning that we draw upon in our analyses is called "slippage." This term comes from the world of cultural studies and film analysis. Ellsworth (1997) discusses how films target particular audiences, such that those outside the demographic in which the film is written may experience "slippage" (p. 24), a sense that the film is not meant for them and doesn't speak to their circumstances. Similarly, in education policy, families are expected to be in a place where the policy can be "pitched to" to capture benefits and resources. But based on their multiple and shifting realities in and out of this center, families experience different effects. This outcome may follow when the policy attacks the distinct challenges associated with the (dis)ability, for example, by stripping access to social supports through increased testing, or in the example of Asperger's syndrome, by ignoring the difference in presentation at school that often occurs between boys and girls by focusing on the majority, that is the boys (see Jack, 2014). Two competing modes of address can be present in the same storyline (Ellsworth, 1997). For example, families can be expected to engage with schools in multiple ways that can be in tension.

Pedagogies can potentially reposition problematic discourses. Following from studies with Maori populations in New Zealand, Purdue and her colleagues (2009) have theorized poststructuralist educational moves that we call "border pedagogies" because their purpose is to open up possibilities for children and families at the margins. Some of these strategies include de-centering hegemonic discourses (for example, about (dis)ability and race) in the classroom and reconceptualizing difference as not a deficit, but rather a necessity. Border pedagogies can best be understood as working in nested contexts. The physical educational space of a school or home is an important variable in analyzing how families interrelate with and make decisions about education, because "in architectural spaces, bodies have 'affective somatic responses'" (Gross & Eisenman, 2003, p. xiv). This impact of material spaces on human relationships is especially true for children with neuro-atypicalities and their families. The structures of schooling (time spent, transitions, class size, etc.) and different cultures present within a classroom and the cultures created in the classroom and school all matter regarding teaching/learning relationships among teachers, students, and educational content (Gonzalez & Mulligan, 2014), and contribute to a setting in which border pedagogies can work to both de-marginalize and actively support children.

Methodology

We compiled a case study (Stake, 2006) of the education experiences of families of children with neuro-atypicalities in the early childhood and elementary school years. We use pseudonyms for all people and place names. The purpose of the case study was to explore families' experiences relative to the "culture of expertise" described in the introduction to this article. The analysis combines data from two larger studies: Finding Care and Homeschooling Perspectives.

Data and Participants

The data included are the in-depth interview transcripts of 9 parents (and one case an adult sibling) from 7 families who had children diagnosed with autism (mild), Asperger's syndrome, pervasive developmental disorder (PDD), or sensory integration disorder, or those who were seeking diagnosis or counseled by a school to seek evaluation based on issues in line with neuro-atypicalities. The interviews were done by the first author and lasted from 45 minutes to 2 hours in length. Because these interviews were part of broader research undertaken since 2011 and currently ongoing, the first author obtained a solid understanding of the educational contexts in the participants' communities in the Midwest and Mid-Atlantic regions of the U.S. While neuro-atypicalities are often thought of as White, middle class phenomena, 3 of our participants were low income, and 3 were from minoritized racial groups (2 Latinx and 1 Asian). One of the low income families has a Latino father and White mother, and the other low income families were White. In two of the families, one parent had immigrated to the U.S. from the Caribbean and Scandinavia and so likely carried somewhat different understandings regarding (dis)abilities and schooling (Tobin, Arzubiaga, & Adair, 2013). The interview designs supported participants' narrative telling regarding their experiences (Kvale & Brinkmann, 2009). The interview questions centered on life history, family context, community context, medical and school experiences, relations between home and school, and the parents' educational roles.

Analysis

We read the interview transcripts many times and saw several narrative constellations across the narratives (Craig, 2003). Primarily, they showed overlap and a storyline around the culture of expertise. Families' narratives of (dis)engagement with the culture of expertise revealed that they were situated in the material circumstances in which they found themselves. They often could not acquire resources when they were really needed. And there was sometimes the reverse issue as well—resources were offered that families felt might create limited agency. Their agency was defined in many cases by their abilities to choose schooling forms and supplementary therapies. This choice was connected with their knowledge of educational and medical systems, their social networks, and their insurance/financial situations as well as the resources available in the states and communities in which they lived. These "constellations" of storyline across participants became our general themes through which we organize our findings. Our postructuralist framework and the specific discursive tools of positioning, slippage, and border pedagogies helped us to articulate the processes through which inclusive education is created and resisted.

Findings

In this section, we describe and analyze our findings. "Travel" is a defining metaphor in this section. For families, travel is a search for comfort, acceptance, and normalcy sought by families. We describe the identities that families took up on their journeys, the school environments that inter-related with families' identities, and the pedagogies that were created.

Nomads and Choosers

Six of the seven families moved their young children between school sites, sometimes changing schools many times. In the literature, researchers have discussed the "loss of the perfect child" that parents must grapple with when their children present atypical behaviors and are diagnosed with disabilities (Ellis, 1989). We found parents who, although they likely were experiencing grief and distress to a degree, were also active and grappling for action that would support and remediate their children with neuro-atypicalities. In our analysis, we originally saw the participants as "nomadic," continually moving to find sustaining education when the meager resources got used up or did not pan out as hoped. They searched for nurturing and appropriate education. But the families characterized themselves as "choosers," fitting in with identities pitched in the media, local education policies, and neighborhood and church discourses. However, at a closer look, there was complexity in how identities of "nomad" and "chooser" were embodied and enacted.

The Pereira family demonstrates the role of positioning (Harré & van Langenhoeve, 1999) between the mother and father. Positioning is important to consider as a mechanism for de-stabilizing family identities as choice-makers for schooling. In this family the father and mother played different roles in negotiating the culture of expertise:

> This is where we kind of vary, Mrs. Pereira and I. Mrs. Pereira is very into the high-autism spectrum and Isabel with her disabilities. I am like a little bit but not really confident about that … I think [Isabel] had a lot of problems as much as I did.

> So I can relate to Isabel in terms of her behaviors. But I didn't want to put a title on it, and I didn't want to say, "Well it's because of autism, or it's because of this." So Mrs. Pereira and I fought back and forth a lot about that, and Mrs. Pereira pushed to get a specialist out there, and as a father and as a husband I'd say, "Yeah, OK, go ahead." Although I didn't agree with her 100% on some of those things. (Mr. Pereira, Father of Isabel, age 9)

The difference between Mr. Pereira and Mrs. Pereira involved personal experience with disability as well as different advocacy expectations from the mother versus father roles. Their case illustrates "slippage" between the individual parents and broader discourses of choice and expertise. Similar "slippage" was seen in the Kant family, in which the mother and father had very different educational experiences, with Mrs. Kant growing up in Scandinavia and her husband in the US. Like the Pereiras' daughter, their eldest child was faced with problems at school. Mr. Kant was more aware of the presence of the culture of expertise and the need to actively negotiate like Mrs. Pereira. However as the mother, Mrs. Kant eventually took that on as her role. These forms of slippage were prominent in early childhood because there was so much societal pressure put on intervention and success at that juncture, and multiple scripts were available within the discourse of choice.

During Isabel's IEP meeting at the public school in second grade, she was denied services even with the medical diagnoses of Asperger's syndrome and sensory integration disorder. A specialist claimed that because there were too many children with needs, and Isabel's academics were OK, she would not receive school-based services. A similar situation at the preschool level affected the Frankenberg-Chavez family: Puritee, 3, was facing assessment for a sensory/behavioral issue and could not currently access school support. In the Liu family, Jonathan, age 6, "graduated" from his IEP for mild autism. His parents were told that their son had strong academics, but his performance was coupled with shrinking resources for school support. In these cases, experts' performances and the realities of neuro-atypicality were two "lines of address" that did not work together compatibly (Ellsworth, 1997). The experts' claims that services were not needed solidified what counted as "real" autism at school (Sabat, 2003). This slippage amongst discourses of real autism resulted in several families not obtaining adequate education for their children, and pushing them to move on to other forms of schooling.

Mrs. King was a low income, single mother when her son was diagnosed with autism as a toddler. Not unlike what happened in the Frankenburg-Chavez and Liu families, her first experiences with the early intervention system were marked with shifts between different learning centers and home care as she tried to cobble together a coherent program of intervention. Her greatest concern was for the agency of her son, Jude, at preschool:

> He was sitting on the floor staring … you had to really engage Jude, because he would just … space out. … And I went over and he was just standing there staring … in the mirror. Just like a zombie. … [The teacher] was like, "Yeah, he's just been sitting there like that." And I thought to myself, "What? So you guys are like, "Great, he's not bothering you, we'll just leave him sitting there."' So in the back of my mind I'm like, "OK. This just isn't a good fit for me." I ended up finding Lucky Charms Learning Center and they did periodic assessments … they were focusing on his development. (Mrs. King, Mother of Jude, age 6)

When Mrs. King was connected to an integrated learning center offering a range of therapies and caregiving, things changed for her son: "So he got the diagnosis, and that really helped because then he could get all this extra support like the OT and stuff. And he's actually doing really well now … I had great experiences with those people because I was there to try to help him, and they were there to try to help him. So it was really good engaging. And I have to say that it made all the difference" (Mrs. King, Mother of Jude, age 6).

While Mrs. King saw the relationship with early childhood experts as productive, there were other challenges related to identity. For example, the moms in Mrs. King's neighborhood and peer group circles discussed Jude as not *really* being different:

> Because Jude, he's quirky but he makes a lot better eye contact, his socialness is … you know, everyone when I use the word "autism," they're going, "I don't think Jude is autistic." And I'm like, "Yeah, we've worked really hard to get him to where he is, and it's like, he's still really quirky, but I deal with him every day so that's how I know." (Mrs. King, Mother of Jude, age 6)

In the case of the King family, implicit positioning occurs when individuals do the "benign" work of being surprised that normativity can present for a child officially labeled as neuro-atypical. In this case, the mother was the placeholder between the discourse of autism and the discourse of recovery, bridging the gap between varied audiences within the culture of expertise. This role was particularly painful for Mrs. King, who needed to work and be an advocate while most of her friends were stay-at-home moms who did not have children with diagnoses of disabilities. Mrs. Liu (mother of Jonathan, age 6) had very similar experiences.

Support as Mirage

The participants searched for educational settings in which inclusive participation and academic learning could occur. This section shows how families experienced and rationalized support in different settings. The lack of trust and support at school was disturbing to Mr. and Mrs. Pereira. Similar problems with trust were experienced over the years by all of the families in the study except for the Grosses, but never quite to the same intensity as the Pereiras endured. The trust issue was exacerbated for the Pereiras when school people accused the family of fabricating a disability in order to receive state aid:

> The occupational therapist said to me, and the classroom teacher, "You know you're not going to get any money from Medicaid if she gets a school diagnosis, right?" … Because they know we take care of people with special needs. And I was like, "Who would want their child to have a disability? Who would rightfully want their child to be signed off as having any problems?" And I was just dumbfounded. I was [thinking], "Why would you even say that to a parent?" It was asinine. (Mrs. Pereira. Mother of Isabel, age 9)

When the first author probed Mr. Pereira in an interview as to whether he viewed race as a potential factor in how the family was treated, he said that although he and his children look Euro, his Latin surname made a negative difference. In this example, experts cemented their position as "the knowers" of not only clinical and educational knowledge, but of parents' moral and ethical intentions. After switching schools four times in four years, Mr. and Mrs. Pereira finally found a public school and classroom teacher who recognized and supported Isabel's participation:

> We were able to switch schools, to a public school, and the teachers there listened to us about her needs and they just worked with her, and she had no anxiety problems. I think through the therapy too, all of those combined interventions, she started to really turn around, and is an amazing young lady now, but without those interventions, I don't know where we would be today. I'm sorry, it's a long story, a frustrating story. It really made an impact on our marriage, stressed it out, just because we had no support. (Mrs. Pereira, Mother of Isabel, Age 9)

In this "happy ending" there is an interesting discourse at play. Mrs. Pereira saw the early intervention as the reason for Isabel's positive adjustment finally at the third grade, rather than the shift to a welcoming, knowledgeable, and better resourced school environment—which was the case. Although Mrs. Pereira wanted inclusive education, she foregrounded the parents' roles as choosers in securing therapies and choosing a workable school setting. She attributed a large portion of the inclusive outcomes to the child's personal ability to overcome her atypical behaviors rather than the workable context that they finally landed upon.

For the Jorgenson family, choosing homeschooling was a "security measure." Like Mrs. Pereira, Mr. Jorgenson discussed quite a bit the importance of the child being able to control her own emotions and thus mediate her educational activities as an elementary student:

> My daughter likes to know what she has to do for the entire day, and then she likes to strategize her day around her emotions, basing it on, "I'm tired right now," "I'm not ready to do math," what have you. So we allow her to choose the structure and the flow of her day the way she wants it to go ... because it allows her to have control. When your child has more choices and more control ... things go better for them. If they're forced to do things they don't want to do, they tend to resist. And with resistance comes anti-learning. They don't want to learn at that moment. So we allow her to choose the pace, the class, the time, everything that she does on her own at this point. And it actually has helped her willingness to do all of her work. If she's not, let's say she doesn't want to do English that day, she's allowed to take that assignment and put it into the next day. And come back to it tomorrow if she's just not feeling like studying literature, or doing this or doing that. We allow her to do that. But with that responsibility, she has to take the responsibility that the next day she's going to have twice the work. (Mr. Jorgenson, Father of Lily, age 11)

Different from the Pereira family, though, the Jorgensons saw the both/and of educational setting (the home in their case) and the private and individual therapeutic techniques they and other interventionists had used as important. As Mr. Jorgenson alluded, home education delivers the "luxury" of time. It stretches the possibilities of self-regulation. These possibilities are available because in homeschooling, nights and weekends are open for instruction by parents. This shift in environment and teacher from school to private home was not a perfect solution for the Jorgensons, and neither was it for our other participants.

We noticed in our analysis of the interviews that families of children who were a bit older (the Jorgensons and the Pereiras specifically) were concerned about developmental effects on their children's self-concepts as their children grew up and became more aware of what other children and adults in their environments were thinking of them. The Pereiras explained that Isabel (age 9) dwelled on how children at school reacted to her, and that she needed instruction in coping strategies. Mr. Jorgenson explained that even though they had removed their only child from peers to a large degree by homeschooling, Lily (age 11) still was affected by peers in other settings:

> She's realizing, being around children her age and older children, that she is different. Her hand flapping, her toe walking. She looks around and no one else is doing it, and it's making her insecure. And it was creating digestive problems, sleeping problems. She has terrible insomnia. She's a very sensitive girl. And these deficits, what she assumes is a deficit, is affecting her ability to function. And so today she has a [group] counseling session ... with other children like herself ... and she's able to talk to somebody. (Mr. Jorgenson, Father of Lily, age 11)

Lily's inclusion was complicated in both school and home settings, although the family was hopeful that building affiliation with children experiencing similar challenges would help. Most of the children in the study experienced oral communication delays when they were young, and so the kind of group therapy that Lily experienced may be easier for older children, although there are certainly individual differences.

The Lius, due to Jonathan's diagnosis at age 2, found the interventions that some others in the study craved (i.e., the Pereiras and Frankenburg-Chavezes). However, they too experienced difficulties. For example there was a long-term substitute in the classroom for a semester who was trying but struggling to meet the children's needs. The Lius worked around this challenge by meeting with a private developmental specialist outside school and tutoring Jonathan (age 6) in the evening at home. In the data, "support" was sometimes a mirage, obfuscating inclusive education. The performances of teachers, children, families, and specialists could be more and less oriented toward inclusivity in public, private, and home settings. The continual choice-making of parents did not yield perfect outcomes for any child in this study. What seemed to be the promise of support-through-wise-choice-making often ended up as a "mirage." The values and meanings of "student," "parent," "teacher," and "specialist" positioned families to choose while at the same time prevented choices from being made (Chang, 1996). There were "oases" that created learning, inclusive relationships, trust, and relief. Support was a multicultural issue involving intersectional identities. Because of the role of Latinx identity shown, our data challenge the notion that neuro-atypicality is simply a form of Whiteness (e.g., Heilker, 2012).

Border Pedagogies

Pedagogical languages can serve as bridges between homes and schools. These are pedagogies that work around the idea of typical notions of dialogue as a smooth pathway to learning and change (Ellsworth, 1997). Lily Jorgenson enjoyed virtual activities at home because her family allowed a space for her to become comfortable with her products before she shared them. The eldest child in our study, she was able to experience a more coherent identity through virtual and electronic means:

> [Lily] plays the Sims, they're called sandbox games. … you get to make it the way that you want it to be. So these games … allow her to express the way that she would like her life to be. … Her Sims are a way to express her own emotions, and her own expressions of herself. … She loves to sing, but she won't sing in front of people. But she'll take her iPad downstairs and sing in front of that and then show it to us. … she

> can go and edit what the end result is. … And she has the confidence in her almost alter ego. (Mr. Jorgenson, Father of Lily, age 11)

The use of technology as a device to mediate uncomfortable interpersonal interactions is a kind of border pedagogy. It allowed her to tinker and refine her product before it was made visible, a very different process from the linear expectations of a test-driven school culture. Although border pedagogies were often absent from the school lives of children in this study, Lily's example shows potential that could be expanded in multiple school settings and might benefit all children whether or not they are neuro-atypical.

The Jorgensons often went *with* the grain of their daughter's disability. The Lius also struggled with their autistic son's sensitivity, but this condition was more of an issue at school. He was released from his IEP at age six because of his solid academic performance and high I.Q. But this bureaucratic change did not mean that he could easily control his behaviors and edit his responses. In Kindergarten he experienced social and emotional challenges related to the classroom management system:

> [Jonathan] had to pull a stick in Kindergarten [a classroom management program]. Oh dear God. … He's only had to pull one, and it was one of those circumstances where the teacher said, "The next person who opens their mouth is going to be in trouble." So he happened to be the next one, normally she would have just overlooked it and kept on going, but it was one of the moments where the whole class is looking to see if the teacher is going to follow through. And she felt bad, and she told me that day, she said, "If he's upset … this is why he's bent out of shape when he gets home." (Mrs. Liu, Mother of Jonathan, age 6)

Although we see problems with the behaviorist management system used by the teacher, we present this example to show how border pedagogies could alternatively be used. Instead of a focus on classroom standardization and equality aimed at making all children proficient behaviorally and academically, a more individualized system could be a workable alternative. Along with this shift, there could be explicit instruction at an appropriate level for young children to help them understand that difference in communication styles and behaviors is reasonable and can be expressed and supported in multiple, equitable ways (Gonzalez & Mulligan, 2014).

This pedagogy involves a social justice perspective that includes (dis)ability as a difference that is seen, discussed, and taken into account rather than silenced in the "pitch" of a standard system to a classroom of six-year-olds. Importantly, though, the teacher recognized that Jonathan had a difficult time communicating verbally about any frustration and sadness related to the incident. She called

Mrs. Liu right away, and they talked about what happened, allowing the Lius to follow up more at home. Mrs. Liu saw this outreach as extremely important, a step that other teachers had not taken, causing severe emotional and physical issues for Jonathan related to preschool. The slippage here between the classroom management system and Jonathan's needs may have caused Mrs. Gray, the teacher, to reflect on her practice and tweak her social pedagogy; it is hard to say. The culture of expertise requires ongoing control of even very young bodies so that their minds might be made ready for learning facts and skills. This pressure provides a strong force on teachers, shaping their decision-making and relationships with parents (Lee, 2010). Border pedagogies, as shown by our data, were used by few. This area represents a common problem in classrooms and is a crucial area for teacher education and professional development (Brown, 2009; Connor & Gabel, 2010; Purdue et al., 2009).

The families in this study varied widely in the types of provisions they were afforded and in their experiences with inclusive participation, professional support, and care. All seven of the families in our study strived to find the supports that allowed their children to feel comfortable in their own skin, to make choices, and to communicate and be with others. The process of how they worked toward these ends varied, but technology and social scaffolds tended to support education positively, albeit differently in different settings. All seven families in the study experienced fragmented constellations of tools and supports, and all negotiated intensively at multiple levels to locate, choose, and support better experiences for their children.

Discussion and Conclusion

> Travel, in both its metaphorical and physical reaches, can no longer be considered as something that confirms the premises of our initial departure, and thus concludes in a confirmation, a domestication of the difference and detour, the homecoming.
>
> —Chambers (1994, p. 245)

Grosz and Eisenmann (2001) have said that life's potentialities can be released only through movement into and within the messy intervals of space and time between the "things" people already know and between the "beings" they have already made of themselves and others. Indeed, negotiating the culture of expertise is no straightforward trip for families, children, and educators because goals and desires "should" but do not always fit within the culture of expertise that is so pervasive in early education. Some of the families in our study are learning through difficult experiences that they must find spaces to just be and to use their strengths to create new spaces for positive educational change. Identities, emotions, and pedagogies were at play in these journeys.

The cultures and contexts shaping education and the relative lack of resources provided to professionals and schools for developing responsive environments and pedagogies exacerbated the challenges of inclusive education. Indeed, this context contributed to families grappling with, avoiding, and even moving away from schools to educate in their homes. Because the children often fit well with the culture of expertise in some ways but not others, the identities of both the children and the parents were destabilized. Because the children aligned with the expectations of test taking much better than children with other disabilities, their needs for support were sometimes silenced, and their internal tensions leaked out into their homes. Because the culture of expertise involves parents in pre-defined ways and the context of neuro-atypicality worked both for and against the expectations of expertise, there was often friction as well as new possibilities.

Conceptual Implications

The spaces that limit potentials and support the status quo can be reconceptualized, although not easily, by opening up new educational cultures that use school and home resources to support learning for all students. As illustrated by the Pereira and Liu families, their IEP support was contingent on academic functioning rather than on social relations. The culture of expertise may push children out of classrooms and schools because of a narrow focus on testing and a lack of inclusive education and support for teachers and specialists, as well as a complicated relationship between special/therapeutic and general education that is not easily understood by parents, and sometimes the professionals themselves.

This problem plays out uniquely in early education, as parents themselves are just beginning to understanding schooling and their children's (dis)abilities. The recent shift to the new ASD labeling system has added tension and complexity. As "rigor" has increasingly been required of schools, often through standardized curriculum, instruction, and assessment, it becomes even more important that compassion be developed as a resource to speak back to the exclusion of the college and career focused system. Equity in this context means building more empathic environments for children with neuro-atypicalities and their families. This affective emphasis requires combining what the field understands about inclusive education and expanding the tools and pedagogies used to achieve it. It is important that school people ask parents and children what they need for success, as well as engage in professional growth opportunities that empower them to support children and families guided by appropriate skills and information. This emphasis on relationships in turn should strengthen communities, because then children and families will want to stay and become part of the school community. Although sometimes moving between non-responsive schools and programs was necessary for individual families, continual choice-making may add to the stress and problems children and families experience even while the process of choosing may provide a sense of agency and sometimes educational improvements. Indeed, going through educational transitions is particularly problematic for children and for families with neuro-atypicalities.

Sometimes public schools, private schools, and home schools are pitted against one another as being able/not able to support children well. Instead of arguing for more policy to support parents' decision making, it seems most sensible to strengthen the environments that can address inclusive education at both individual and societal levels. Public schools generally offer the best platforms through which to potentially break down some of the isolation that often accompanies neuro-atypicality, as the Pererias and Lius experienced when they encountered schools with well-developed intervention teams. As homeschooling becomes an increasingly popular school option, some may think that this alternative is the answer for children with neuro-atypicalities. But as the Jorgensons' experience suggests, Lily was more anxious at home than she had been at school, although her parents continued to favor homeschooling. And the Pereira family found that homeschooling did not work, because Isabel had difficulty separating the roles of mother and teacher, a function of her neuro-atypical makeup. While the contexts of expertise and choice are complex and inter-related, there are many reasons for further developing the resource contexts of public schools to support all students.

Practical Implications

Given the uneven distribution of resources to schools and professional development for teachers seen in our research, it is crucial that pre-service and in-service teacher development be addressed. Training and ongoing professional development for administrators and teachers in creating inclusive environments for all students is needed. Teachers and administrators should understand their own cultural makeups, including their racial/ethnic positioning and the contexts of Whiteness and neoliberalism that permeate society. However, they also need to critically examine their neuro-atypicality and how that makeup serves to position themselves and the children and families that they work with. This area has rarely been broached in teacher education, a problem that Disability Studies in Education might help to address.

While neuro-atypicalities have been associated in the literature with Whiteness, in this research complicated racial/ethnic texts played out. These racial/ethnic texts contributed to how school supports were provided for students. Stereotypically, the two Latinx families in the study pushed and struggled to receive a diagnosis and support, whereas the Chinese American boy, Jonathan, was quickly deemed "recovered" by his teacher and school professionals. More research is needed on neuro-atypicalities as they relate with Whiteness and race/ethnicity as well as other intersections such as gender, a factor that we did not emphasize in this chapter.

Given our findings, it is clear that school life and education need to be broadened to incorporate engagement with difference through the expansion of border pedagogies. Morton (2015) argues that educators must not only look at pedagogy in building inclusive education, but also assessment. Given our findings, assessment is one of many variables to address in constructing inclusive classrooms. Educators must also assess the broader contexts of schooling such as climate in the school and classroom, particularly the context of inclusivity. In fact, reconceptualizing how assessment matters can be a tool for destabilizing the culture of expertise. This attention is especially crucial as researchers (e.g.,Wiebe Berry, 2006; Zindler, 2009) have found that even "best practice" pedagogies for inclusion do not necessarily translate to inclusive outcomes. That is why border pedagogies cannot be defined and delimited, but rather must be created/assessed by teachers, children, and their families, ongoing and in context. Other school-level changes could also improve education for children with neuro-atypicalities, and perhaps for all children. For example, classroom looping, in which the child remains with the same classroom, teacher, and classmates for multiple years, serves to alleviate or smooth transitions that can be especially disruptive for children with neuro-atypicalities, assuming that these settings are accommodating to begin with. Year-round schooling might serve a similar purpose. More research is clearly needed to better understand how these possibilities could work in various contexts.

Our research has found that the journey is ongoing for families, as well as for educational professionals and other stakeholders. We hope that our participants' examples have inspired our readers to continue to re-work cultural scripts and actions to (re)claim resources while expanding visions of difference, knowledge, and care.

Note

1. Smagorinsky actually uses *neuroatypical*, without the hyphen, but the hyphen improves readability when both neurotypical and neuro-atypical appear in conjunction with each other.

References

American Psychiatric Association. (2013). *Highlights of changes from DSM-IV-TR to DSM-5.* Arlington, VA: Author. Retrieved April 5, 2016 from http://www.dsm5.org/Documents/changes%20from%20dsm-iv-tr%20to%20dsm-5.pdf

Apple, M. W., Kenway, J., & Singh, M. (Eds.) (2005). *Globalizing education: Policies, pedagogies, & politics.* New York, NY: Peter Lang.

Blanchett, W. J. (2006). Disproportionate representation of African American students in special education: Acknowledging the role of White privilege and racism. *Educational Researcher, 35*(6), 24–28.

Blumberg, S. J., Bramlett, M. D., Kogan, M. D., Schieve, L. A., Jones, J. R., & Lu, M. C. (2013, March 20). Changes in prevalence of parent-reported Autism Spectrum Disorder in school-aged U.S. children: 2007 to 2011–2012. *National Health Statistics Reports, 65*, 1–11.

Bonilla-Silva, E. (2006). *Racism without racists: Color-blind racism and the persistence of racial inequality in the United States* (2nd ed.). New York, NY: Rowman & Littlefield.

Brinkmann, S., & Kvale, S. (2014). *InterViews: Learning the craft of qualitative research interviewing* (3rd ed.). Thousand Oaks, CA: Sage.

Broderick, A. (2009). Autism, "recovery [to normalcy]," and the politics of hope. *Intellectual and Developmental Disability, 47*(2), 263–281.

Brown, C. P. (2009). Confronting the contradictions: A case study of early childhood teacher development in neoliberal times. *Contemporary Issues in Early Childhood, 10*(3), 240–259.

Centers for Disease Control and Prevention. (2014a, March 28). Prevalence of Autism Spectrum Disorder among children aged 8 years: Autism and Developmental Disabilities Monitoring Network, 11 sites, United States, 2010. *Morbidity and Mortality Weekly Report*, 1–21.

Centers for Disease Control and Prevention. (2014b). *Community report on autism.* Atlanta, GA: National Center on Birth Defects and Developmental Disabilities, Centers for Disease Control and Prevention. Retrieved from http://www.cdc.gov/ncbddd/autism/states/comm_report_autism_2014.pdf

Chambers, I. (1994). Leaky habitats and broken grammar. In G. Robertson, M. Mash, L. Tickner, J. Bird, B. Curtis, & T. Putnam (Eds.), *Travellers' tales: Narratives of home and displacement* (pp. 243–247). New York, NY: Routledge.

Chang, B. G. (1996). *Deconstructing communication: Representation, subject, and economies of exchange.* Minneapolis, MN: University of Minnesota Press.

Collins, K. M., & Valente, J. (2010, June 17). (Dis)abling the race to the top. *Teachers College Record*, Retrieved February 21, 2019 from http://www.tcrecord.org/Content.asp?ContentId=16020

Connor, D. J., & Ferri, B. A. (2007). The conflict within: Resistance to inclusion and other paradoxes in special education. *Disability & Society, 22*(1), 63–77.

Connor, D. J., & Gabel, S. L. (2010). Welcoming the unwelcome: Disability as diversity. In T. K. Chapman & N. Hobbel (Eds.), *Social justice pedagogy across the curriculum* (pp. 201–220). New York, NY: Routledge.

Craig, C. J. (2003). Story constellations: A way to characterize reforming school contexts and contextualize teacher knowledge. *Curriculum and Teaching Dialogue, 5*(5), 31–41.

Dahlberg, G., Moss, P., & Pence, A. (2007). *Beyond quality in early childhood education and care: Languages of evaluation* (2nd ed.). New York, NY: Routledge.

Danforth, S., & Naraian, S. (2007). Use of the machine metaphor within autism research. *Journal of Physical Disabilities, 19*, 273–290.

Ellsworth, E. (1997). *Teaching positions: Difference, pedagogy, and the power of address.* New York, NY: Teachers College Press.

Fountain, C., King, M. D., & Bearman, P. S. (2011). Age of diagnosis for autism: Individual and community factors across 10 birth cohorts. *Journal of Epidemiology and Community Health, 65*(6), 503–510.

Gonzalez, T., & Mulligan, E. (2014). Creating classrooms for all learners. In E. B. Kozleski & K. K. Thorius (Eds.), *Ability, equity, & culture: Sustaining inclusive urban education reform* (pp. 107–133). New York, NY: Teachers College Press.

Grosz, E. A., & Eisenman, P. (2001). *Architecture from the outside: Essays on virtual and real space.* Cambridge, MA: MIT Press.

Harré, R., & van Langenhove, L. (Eds.). (1999). *Positioning theory: Moral contexts of intentional action.* Oxford, UK: Blackwell.

Heilker, P. (2012). Autism, rhetoric, and whiteness. *Disability Studies Quarterly, 32*(4). Retrieved April 6, 2016 from http://dsq-sds.org/article/view/1756/3181

Hurlbutt, K. S. (2011). Experiences of parents who homeschool their children with autism spectrum disorders. *Developmental Disabilities, 26*(4), 239–249.

Jack, J. (2014). *Autism and gender: From refrigerator mothers to computer geeks.* Urbana, IL: University of Illinois Press.

Keenan, M., Dillenburger, K., Doherty, A., Byrne, T., & Gallagher, S. (2010). The experiences of parents during diagnosis and forward planning for children with autism spectrum disorder. *Journal of Applied Research in Intellectual Disabilities, 23*(4), 390–397.

Lee, K. (2010). Who is normal? Who is abnormal? Rethinking child development from a cultural psychological perspective. In K. Lee & M. Vagle (Eds.), *Developmentalism in early childhood and middle grades education: Critical conversations on readiness and responsiveness* (pp. 35–58). New York, NY: Palgrave Macmillan.

Leonard, H., Dixon, G., Whitehouse, A. J. O., Bourke, J., Aiberti, K., Nassar, N., Bower, C., & Glasson, E. J. (2010). Unpacking the complex nature of the autism epidemic. *Research in Autism Spectrum Disorders, 4*, 548–554.

MacLeod, A., Lewis, A., & Robertson, C. (2013). "Why should I be like bloody Rain Man?!" Navigating the autistic identity. *British Journal of Special Education, 40*(1), 41–49.

Marco, E. J., Hinkley, L. B., Hill, S. S., & Nagarajan, S. S. (2011). Sensory processing in autism: A review of neurophysiologic findings. *Pediatric Research, 69*(5, Pt. 2), 48R–54R.

Matson, J. L., & Kozlowski, A. M. (2011). The increasing prevalence of autism spectrum disorders. *Research in Autism Spectrum Disorders, 5*, 418–425.

McDonald, J., & Lopes, E. (2014). How parents home educate their children with an autism spectrum disorder with the support of the schools of isolated and distance education. *International Journal of Inclusive Education, 18*(1), 1–17.

Molnar, A. (Ed.). (2014). *Virtual schools in the U.S. 2014: Politics, performance, policy, and research evidence.* Boulder, CO: National Education Policy Center. Retrieved April 8, 2016 from https://carde.gsehd.gwu.edu/sites/carde.gsehd.gwu.edu/files/downloads/report NEPC2014.pdf

Morton, M. (2015). Using disability studies in education to recognize, resist, and reshape policy and practices in Aotearoa, New Zealand. In D. J. Connor, J. W. Valle, & C. Hale (Eds.), *Practicing disability studies in education: Acting toward social change* (pp. 197–216). New York, NY: Peter Lang.

Murphy, J. (2012). *Homeschooling in America: Capturing and assessing the movement.* Thousand Oaks, CA: Corwin.

Naraian, S. (2013). Dis/ability, agency, and context: A differential consciousness for doing inclusive education. *Curriculum Inquiry, 43*(3), 360–387.

Nielsen, M. E., & Higgins, L. D. (2005). The eye of the storm: Services and programs for twice-exceptional learners. *Teaching Exceptional Children, 38*(1), 8–15.

Novinger, S., O' Brien, L., & Sweigman, L. (2005). Challenging the culture of expertise: Moving beyond training the always, already failing early childhood educator. In S. Ryan & S. Grieshaber (Eds.), *Practical transformations and transformational practices: Globalization, postmodernism, and early childhood education* (pp. 217–241). Amsterdam, NL: Elsevier.

Purdue, K. (2009). Barriers to and facilitators of inclusion for children with disabilities in early childhood education. *Contemporary Issues in Early Childhood, 10*(2), 133–143.

Purdue, K., Gordon-Burns, D., Gunn, A., Madden, B., & Surtees, N. (2009). Supporting inclusion in early childhood settings: Some possibilities and problems for teacher education. *International Journal of Inclusive Education, 13*(8), 805–815.

Purdue, K., Gordon-Burns, D., Rarere-Briggs, B., Stark, R., & Turnock, K. (2011). The exclusion of children with disabilities in early childhood education in New Zealand: Issues and implications for inclusion. *Australasian Journal of Early Childhood, 36*(2), 95–103. Retrieved April 6, 2016 from http://search.informit.com.au/documentSummary;dn=052987465682207;res=IELHSS.

Riby, D. M., Hancock, P. J. B., Jones, N., & Hanley, M. (2013). Spontaneous and cued gaze-following in autism and Williams syndrome. *Journal of Neurodevelopmental Disorders, 5*(1). Retrieved December 24, 2018 from https://www.ncbi.nlm.nih.gov/pmc/articles/PMC3766200/

Sabat, S. R. (2003). Malignant positioning and the predicament of people with Alzheimer's disease. In R. Harré & F. Moghaddam (Eds.), *The self and others: Positioning individuals and groups in personal, political, and cultural contexts* (pp. 85–98). Westport, CT: Praeger.

Schofield, J. W. (2004). Improving intergroup relations among students. In J. A. Banks & C. A. M. Banks (Eds.), *Handbook of research on multicultural education*, 2nd ed. (pp. 799–812). San Francisco, CA: Jossey Bass.

Sherfinski, M., & Chesanko, M. (2014). Disturbing the data: Looking into gender and family size matters with U.S. evangelical homeschoolers. *Gender, Place & Culture: A Journal of Feminist Geography, 7*(14), 1–18.

Sherfinski, M., Weekley, B. S., & Mathew, S. (2015). Reconceptualizing advocacy: Creating inclusive education in U.S. universal pre-kindergarten. *International Journal of Inclusive Education*, *19*(12), 1213–1228.

Slee, R. (2001). Social justice and the changing directions in educational research: The case of inclusive education. *International Journal of Inclusive Education*, *5*(2–3), 167–177.

Smagorinsky, P. (2011). Confessions of a mad professor: An autoethnographic consideration of neurotypicality, extranormativity, and education. *Teachers College Record*, *113*(8), 1700–1732. Retrieved April 5, 2016 from http://www.petersmagorinsky.net/About/PDF/TCR/TCR2011.pdf

Smagorinsky, P. (2014, November 26). Taking the diss out of disability. *Teachers College Record*. Retrieved April 5, 2016 from http://www.petersmagorinsky.net/About/PDF/TCR/TCR2014.html

Stake, R. E. (2006). *Multiple case study analysis*. New York, NY: Guilford Press.

Tobin, J., Arzubiaga, A. E., & Adair, J. K. (2013). *Children crossing borders: Immigrant parent and teacher perspectives on preschool*. New York, NY: Russell Sage.

Trainor, A. A. (2010). Reexamining the promise of parent participation in special education: An analysis of cultural and social capital. *Anthropology & Education Quarterly*, *41*(3), 245–263.

Valle, J. W. (2014). Enacting research: Disability studies in education and performative inquiry. In D. J. Connor, J. W. Valle, & C. Hale (Eds.), *Practicing disability studies in education: Acting toward social change* (pp. 65–82). New York, NY: Peter Lang.

Vygotsky, L. S. (1993). *The collected works of L. S. Vygotsky. Volume 2: The fundamentals of defectology (abnormal psychology and learning disabilities)* (R. W. Rieber & A. S. Carton, Eds.; J. E. Knox & C. B. Stevens, Trans.). New York, NY: Plenum.

Whitaker, P. (2007). Provision for youngsters with autistic spectrum disorders in mainstream schools: What parents say—and what parents want. *British Journal of Special Education*, *34*(3), 170–178.

Wiebe Berry, R. A. (2006). Inclusion, power, and community: Teachers and students interpret the language of community in an inclusion classroom. *American Educational Research Journal*, *43*(3), 489–529.

Williams, J. G., Higgins, J. P., & Brayne, C. E. (2006). Systematic review of prevalence studies of autism spectrum disorders. *Archives of Disease in Childhood*, *91*(1), 8–15.

Woodgate, R., Ateah, C., & Secco, M. L. (2008). Living in a world of our own: The experience of parents who have a child with autism. *Qualitative Health Research*, *18*(8), 1075–1083.

Worley, J. A., & Matson, J. L. (2012). Comparing symptoms of autism spectrum disorders using the current DSM-IV-TR diagnostic criteria and the proposed DSM-V diagnostic criteria. *Research in Autism Spectrum Disorders*, *6*, 965–970.

Zindler, R. (2009). Trouble in paradise: A study of who is included in an inclusion classroom. *Teachers College Record*, *111*(8), 1971–1996.

CHAPTER NINE

Learning from Deaf Education

JENNIFER HENSLEY, PATRICK GRAHAM, AND JOSEPH TOBIN

For most deaf children, early education begins either with them being mainstreamed in general preschool classrooms where they may be given extra-services (speech therapy, an aide), or in an oral methods program for deaf children designed to transition them, as soon as possible, into mainstreamed, hearing-based elementary classrooms. A fortunate minority of deaf children get the opportunity to attend a preschool based on Deaf culture principles, where the primary medium of communication is ASL or another national sign language.

Educators working in these culturally and linguistically Deaf early childhood settings over time have developed pedagogical approaches and spatial arrangements that support deaf children's social, cognitive, and academic development. These Deaf spaces have evolved outside of and, therefore, to some extent free from the taken-for-grantedness of mainstream (audist) educational practices. This development has led to what a World Federation for the Deaf position statement rightly refers to as "the diversity [that] deaf culture adds to our world." In this paper we draw on a study our research team conducted in signing preschool classrooms in France, Japan, and the U.S. to describe characteristically Deaf early childhood educational approaches and to argue that these approaches can add to our world by informing educational practice in hearing settings.

There has been a history (which we see as on the whole unfortunate) of practices developed in special education settings trickling up into mainstream education.

Examples include breaking content up into discrete packets of knowledge and skill, and reward-and-punishment-oriented classroom management systems. Viewing Deaf signing education not as a domain of special education, but instead as a unique cultural approach to education, our project here is in the tradition of educational anthropologists whose ethnographic studies of educational approaches in other countries work to question the taken-for-grantedness of familiar educational approaches and expand the repertoire of the possible. Anthropologists have an adage: "As ethnography makes the strange familiar, the familiar becomes strange." Or to suggest a queer metaphor for this paper, we can call it "Deaf Eye for the Hearing Educator." If this paper were to take the form of a reality television show the concept would be: What if a team of talented Deaf early childhood educators could give your hearing preschool an educational make-over?

Deaf World and the Uneasy Relationship of Deaf Culture and Disability

Before going further, we need to provide some definitions and key concepts and locate our project in the larger context of Deaf studies and Deaf politics. In Deaf Cultural Studies, little "d" deaf denotes a physical construction of deafness, while big "D" Deaf signals a kinship to Deaf culture, community, and sign language (Christiansen & Leigh, 2002; Woodward, 1972). The study we conducted that informs this paper had as its central research question how, in three countries, little "d" deaf children come to be enculturated into big "D" Deaf culture, or what members of this culture often call the "Deaf World" (Lane, Hoffmeister, & Bahan, 1996). As Lane (2005) explains: "The members of this group have a collective name in their manual-visual language by which they refer to themselves. We refer to them by that name in adopting the English gloss of their compound sign: the *Deaf-World*" (p. 292; emphasis in original). Deaf-World includes Deaf Epistemology and Deaf Pedagogy (Ladd, 2003; Lane, 2005). Deaf educational researchers have identified Deaf ways of making and communicating meaning (see, for example Hauser et al., 2010) and Deaf ways of teaching and learning (for example, Calderon & Greenberg, 2003).

Our project has some affinities with but also some differences from Universal Design, which has the central goal of creating shared environments that are as accessible as possible for everyone. For example, Conn-Powers, Conn-Powers, Traub, and Hutter-Pishgahi (2006) published a piece that presented seven principles that can make early childhood education and care settings more accessible for all children. We share with advocates of Universal Design the idea that architectural and program features developed in response to the needs of a specific group can be beneficial for others. As Conn-Powers et al. write:

> At first these design applications may seem solely intended for people with disabilities. But developers of the universal design framework recognized that usability would increase as special needs features began to serve all. People who use wheelchairs benefit from curb cuts and ramps, but so do bicycle riders, parents pushing strollers, and travelers pulling wheeled luggage. Elevators that announce floor numbers assist individuals with impaired sight along with shorter people who may not be able to see the light indicators when the elevator is crowded with riders. Doors that open automatically aid those not strong enough to open them as well as individuals whose arms hold packages or young children. (p. 2)

Consistent with this logic, we will suggest in this paper that some key pedagogical and spatial features of Deaf early childhood education can also enrich classrooms serving hearing children. On the other hand, we need to keep in mind that the central goal of the Deaf Space and allied Deaf movements is creating spaces that are ideal for Deaf people, a goal that, as Edwards and Harrold (2014) argue, is in tension with the ethic of inclusion that informs the Universal Design movement. To date, most Universal Design projects have been more focused on creating environments that remove barriers to mobility than on the needs of Deaf people, who process the world visually and generally do not define themselves as having a disability.

Deafness has an uneasy relationship not only with Universal Design, but also with the fields of special education and Disability Studies (Hoffmeister 2007). The core of the tension arises from the fact that while Deaf people define themselves as a language and cultural minority group, in most countries their access to services falls under disability legislation and funding. As the 2018 World Federation of the Deaf position paper on "Situating Deaf Communities within 'disability' vs 'cultural and linguistic minority' constructs" states:

> Deaf people consider themselves as a linguistic and cultural group, with highly complex natural languages but the rights of deaf people are however assured through disability policy, legislation and international instruments. … Disability is defined according to a human rights model of disability. Under the social model of disability that precedes the human rights model, it is the interaction between an individual's "impairment" and barriers in society that creates "disability." In other words, it is the environment that is disabling, not the "impairment" itself. (p. 1)

Even under a social definition of disability, the Deaf Community at times finds itself at odds with their counterparts in the disability rights community, as the WFD position paper goes on to explain:

> The Deaf Community's primary language of communication is a non-dominant and often marginalised language within the broader national community. Language difference and lack of equity with communication has often created multiple layers of negative impact, which is greatest in the sphere of education. This difference. ... creates a friction between the Deaf community and other disability groups. Foundational to this difference is why the concept of "inclusion" focused on educational placement in mainstream settings is so devastating for deaf children. Inclusion presumes an important fact—that the person with the disability shares the use of the dominant language in the community and education. Inclusion and language immersion are not synonymous in their impact on the Deaf Community. This understanding is key to WFD's advocacy for the right to deaf culture, and its celebration, shared by many, of the diversity deaf culture adds to our world. (p. 3)

The Deaf Kindergarten in Three Countries Project

Before turning to presenting some of our research findings, we should say something about our own backgrounds and subjectivities that informed this research. Patrick Graham, who is d/Deaf, is an assistant professor of Deaf Education and early childhood education at Western Oregon University. Jennifer Scarboro Hensley, who is a "Coda" (child of deaf adults), is the Director of Deaf Programs at the Arizona State Schools for the Deaf and the Blind. Joseph Tobin, who is hearing, is an educational anthropologist and a professor of early childhood education at The University of Georgia. Graham and Hensley wrote their Ph.D. dissertations, under Tobin's direction, on aspects of a larger ethnographic study our team conducted on how Deaf preschools in Japan, France, and the United States approach the task of introducing deaf children to the Deaf World and sign language. This paper reflects ideas that emerged over years of doing research together and reflecting on the findings of the research from our different experiences and perspectives.

The project we worked on together was called "Deaf Kindergartens in Three Countries." Our team studied Deaf early childhood education from an ethnographic and international comparative perspective. Our heterogeneous research team, which was led by Joseph Valente of Pennsylvania State University, Thomas Horejes of Gallaudet University, and Tobin included Deaf, Coda, and hearing researchers from the U.S., Japan, and France. The team made videotapes of typical days in preschools in each country where signing was the primary language and then used edited versions of these videos to interview teachers, administrators, parents, children at schools for the Deaf, as well as Deaf education experts. Other researchers have studied Deaf culture in various locations around the world (e.g., Ladd, 2003; Nakamura, 2006; Padden & Humphries, 1988; Sacks, 1989; Stokoe,

1980; Woodward, 1983), but this was the first international comparative study of Deaf early childhood education.

Method

The research method we used was a new application of the "video-cued multivocal ethnography" method developed by Joseph Tobin and his colleagues in *Preschool in Three Cultures* (1989) and subsequent projects (Tobin et al., 2009; Tobin, forthcoming). The core idea of this version of stimulated recall is that an edited video showing a typical day in a classroom can function as a rich and provocative cue for discussions. The specific steps of this method are to: (1) video one day in one kindergarten in a school for the Deaf in each country; (2) edit the video down to 20 minutes; (3) have focus group discussions of the video with parents, teachers, and children of the classroom where we filmed, as well as school staff and administrators in this school; (4) have focus-group discussions of the videos shot in each country in multiple other schools for the Deaf within each country; and (5) have focus-groups discussions in each of the countries of the videos made in the other two countries. The dialogic nature of these discussions allows participants to share with each other and with us how their beliefs about deafness and Deaf culture inform school and language choices. In this chapter we present scenes from the videos we shot in Deaf preschool classrooms in Japan, France, and the United States, combined with some reflections of Deaf educators on these scenes, to illustrate key principles of Deaf early childhood education.

Findings

Lines of Sight

While "circle time" is a common feature of morning opening in many preschools, Deaf signing preschools give more explicit attention to organizing spaces and routines throughout the day that maximize children's ability to see each other's faces, hands, and bodies. Optimizing lines of sight in a preschool classroom for hearing as well as deaf children requires a combination of attention to architecture, furniture, and routines. And even when they are attending classrooms in which spaces, things, and time are optimally arranged, young children need systematic guidance from adults on how to situate themselves and direct their attention, a meta-cognitive skill that Jenny Singleton and other researchers conceptualize as "joint attention" (for example, see Singleton & Morgan, 2005; Singleton & Supalla, 2010). We find many examples of facilitating lines of sight and joint attention in the classroom arrangements and pedagogical practices of the Deaf early childhood educators we videotaped and interviewed in deaf schools in Japan, France, and the U.S..

For example, when we first videotaped in the preschool classroom at Meisei Gakuen in Tokyo, Tobin, a hearing member of the research team who that day was tasked with filming the children from a vantage point next to the teacher, repositioned the children's chairs before morning opening, moving them from an arc to a straight line. His goal was to make it easier to film each child head-on. Sitting in a line rather than their usual arc allowed the children to see and be seen by the video camera and by the person leading the morning opening, but the children's views of each other's faces and hands were blocked, forcing them to stand up and come to the front of the room to sign to each other. As Ikeda later explained when she watched the video: "When I was about to start morning opening I was surprised to see the chairs in a straight row. I didn't move them into an arc as I normally would because I didn't want to mess up your videotaping. But it made the morning opening a little awkward, because the children couldn't easily communicate with each other."

Figure 1. Facing the speaker

Once morning opening began, Ikeda-sensei took a seat behind the row of children, facing Reiko, that day's designated morning opening leader (Figure 1). When one of the seated children wanted to respond to a question posed by the morning leader, such as "What day is it today?" the student would stand up and walk over to face the seated children and Ikeda-sensei. When Ikeda-sensei wanted to make a point, she would get up from her seat in the back and come around the row of chairs to face the children. When a child, like Satoshi, wanted to respond to a question of Ikeda's, such as why one child left school that morning, he would join Ikeda in the front of the class (Figure 1d). To hearing educators, so much moving around each time there is a change in speaker might seem unnecessary or distracting. However, we would argue that the benefits in terms of allowing for face-to-face embodied communication and introducing and reinforcing earnest speaking and attentive listening outweigh the drawbacks.

Deaf people continually adjust their location and sometimes the locations of others to make sure all communication is visible. In a scene in the video we shot in a Deaf classroom in Toulouse, France, we see an example of a teacher calling her students' attention to the importance of locating themselves so as to not block the view of others and of moving their location when their view is blocked. In a scene in this video, one of the classroom teachers, Sophie, leads the children in a lesson on how to recite French sign language (LSF) deaf poetry. Before the children arrived, Sophie recorded a short video of herself reciting a simple poem. Later in the morning Sophie gathered five of the children around her to watch the video and then take turns reciting the poem.

When Henri volunteered to perform the poem, Sophie changed her location to a seat that would allow Henri to be able to see the computer and her while still being visible to his classmates. Sophie motioned for him to move back a little bit, so that everyone could see. When she noticed that Zoe still could not see, she motioned for Zoe to move to another seat, the one previously used by Henri. Henri protested, saying, "That's my place!" Sophie then responded, in a matter of fact way, "She can't see you from over there" (Figure 2).

When we asked Sophie about this interaction, she said: "I always ask people to move over for me to see. It is automatic. If I don't see, I need to make the person bothering me move, and I do the same for the children." Here Sophie emphasizes a normative behavior of Deaf culture. She interrupts the flow of her poetry activity to have the children adjust their positions to allow for better sight lines. She points out that because she had grown up Deaf, insisting on such spatial adjustments before proceeding with a conversation or lesson is "automatic." An implication is that for hearing teachers, who grew up not needing a clear line of sight to follow a conversation, such a break in the flow of a lesson to re-arrange sight lines would be less automatic and therefore perhaps less likely.

Sophie: Move over a little

(points to Zoe)

Sophie: Come here….

Henri: Hey!

Henri: That's my place!

Sophie: She can't see…

Figure 2. Adjusting seat positions

The Deaf preschool teachers we filmed in the United States were similarly directive about sight lines. And they, like Sophie, not only adjusted their students' locations, but also provided meta-level explanations for doing so. For example, in a scene we filmed in the preschool classroom at the Maryland School for the Deaf, we see teacher Bonnie preparing her students to listen to a story about a truck that delivers flowers. Bonnie asked the students to get their chairs and sit in a semicircle. The students stood up, moved their chairs, and sat down in a semicircle, giving them a clear view of both their teacher and each other. Except, that is, for Emma, who this morning decided it would be fun to sit next to Bonnie instead of with the group. Bonnie asked Emma to change location and join her classmates, so she could follow the story. Emma moved her chair alongside those of her classmates, but then, to be funny, scooted further and further away. Bonnie asked Emma to stop, explaining that she wants her students to sit in a small semicircle close to her so they can see each other well. Bonnie relaxed her facial expression as a form of comfort while discussing her desire for close proximity with her students, signifying that if the students were to sit close, she would not have to work hard to see them. She also stressed with her facial expressions that if the students sat too far away, it would be difficult for her to see the students, and she would have to work harder, which could cause some strain (Figure 3). Bonnie's way of dealing with Emma here reflects Deaf educators' commitment to helping their students understand the rationale for how they position their bodies vis-à-vis others.

Bonnie: If you sit up close, I can see you all just fine.

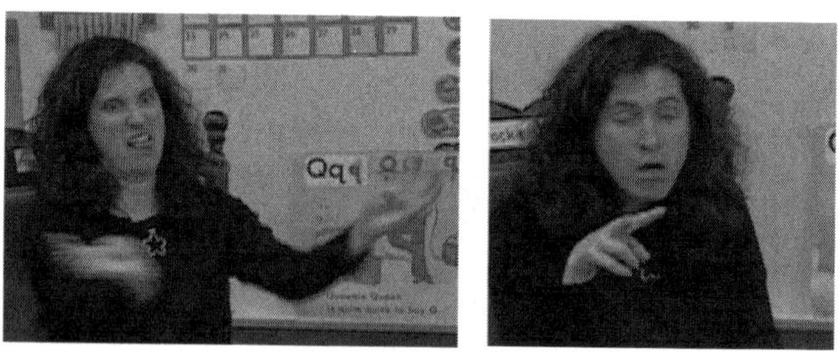

Bonnie: If you sit far away, then it will be hard for me to see.

Figure 3. Lines of sight

We suggest that the logic Ikeda, Sophie, and Bonnie presented for attending to the location of children during group sharing times would apply for hearing as well as deaf children. Hearing children in a classroom can hear their classmates' words even if they are not oriented face-to-face. But the addition of seeing their classmates' facial expressions, gestures, and body language can facilitate their receptive language development.

Deaf preschools give a great deal of attention to their architecture and arrangement of furniture to facilitate lines of sight. In U.S. preschools, classrooms are often divided up into "centers" or "areas" defined by movable furniture that is low enough to allow teachers to see everyone in the room, but high enough to keep children from being distracted by seeing classmates who are in other centers. In the Deaf preschools where we videotaped, in contrast, the classrooms were open, allowing children at all times to see their classmates, teacher, and the whole room. At Meisei, the classrooms were open even to the hallways. "Open plan" classrooms were popular in the U.S. for a time (the 1970s) and then fell out of favor. The Deaf Spaces (Edwards & Harold, 2014) of Deaf preschools remind us of the advantages of a more visually open environment.

In hearing preschool classrooms, which are often noisy, children must learn to screen out background noise and focus auditorily on people addressing them, while at the same time being able to hear and respond to the call of a teacher across the room. Similarly, in Deaf classrooms, which are generally arranged to allow for children to have a wide open field of vision, teachers emphasize the need for children to learn to focus their visual attention on those with whom they are interacting, while at the same time being aware of what is going on across the room and on their periphery. An implication for non-deaf settings is that classrooms can be more open visually, with teachers giving more emphasis to helping children become intentional in their visual as well as auditory attention.

Embodied Expression

It is time for a story at Meisei Gakuen School for the Deaf. Akiko Ikeda, seated in front of her students, starts telling a story about a donkey who is making backpacks for his friends. The story goes: When Donkey gives his friends their new backpacks, his friends thank him profusely, and make plans to take their lunches in their new backpacks. They invite Donkey along, and this is when he realizes he had forgotten to make a backpack for himself. He goes back home, and works all night making a backpack for himself. In the end, they all enjoy their new backpacks.

During this story, Ikeda used a variety of linguistic and emotive facial expressions to tell the story. She showed happiness with her face, body, and a JSL sign while Donkey's friends thank him for the wonderful backpacks, and she showed a serious working facial expression while Donkey is making his backpacks. She also raised her eyebrows to indicate when she was asking students questions (Figure 4).

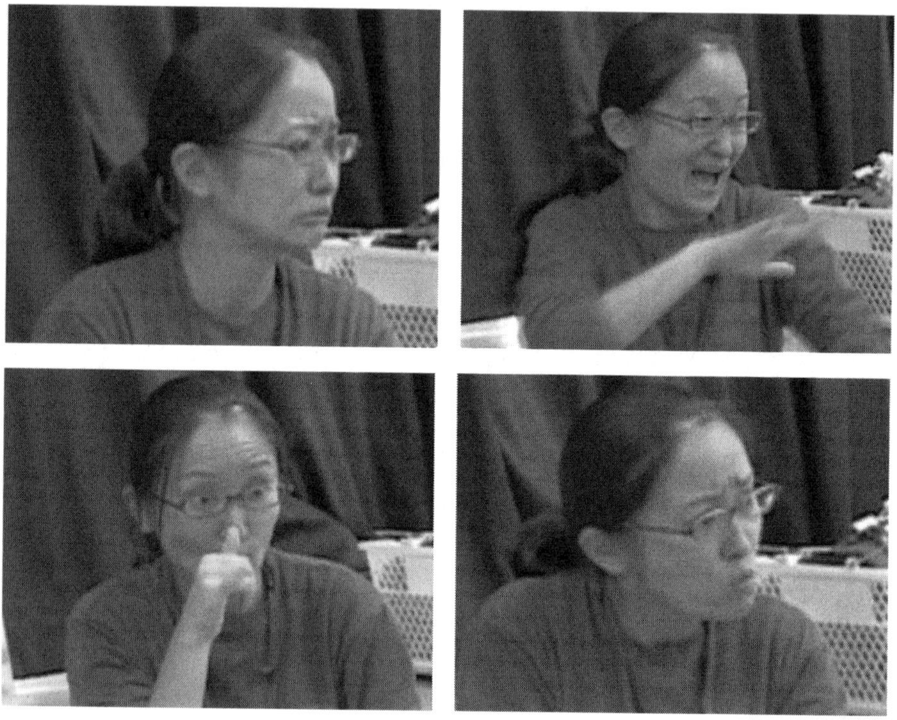

Figure 4. Displaying emotion

We find a similar example in the scene we filmed in France of Sophie leading a poem exercise that was an explicit lesson on how the children should communicate by using not just their French Sign Language but also their faces, gestures, and posture (Figure 5). The poem she recorded on her computer and then had each of the students recite one-by-one went:

> Monday we walk, walk, walk to school
> Tuesday we paint, paint, paint
> Wednesday we take care of the duck
> Thursday we play, play, play doll
> Friday we ride, ride, ride the horses
> Saturday we wash, wash, wash the car
> Sunday we rest!

As they watched for the second time the video of her reciting the poem, Sophie periodically froze the screen to point out how she used her body to communicate the appropriate emotional state to match the words. For example, noticing that the children's faces registered little emotion when reciting the lines about working hard on Saturday washing the car and then resting on Sunday, Sophie rewound the video to that point in her recitation of the poem and explained, with sign and gestures:

> Wash … Look there. Wash.
> With your mouth like this. And then,
> Why did I blow out air here? Like this?
> Yes. Really Tired

Imitating her teacher

Pointing out a facial expression

"Look at my face."

"I am working hard washing the car".

Performing fatigue

Figure 5. Matching facial expressions with words

When we showed this scene to Jenny Singleton, who studies how young deaf children acquire communicative competence, she commented: "She's using mouth morphemes. She's expanded meaning by asking them why it's important to puff out the cheeks. Does it mean a different thing if you sign without puffing your cheeks? She's giving them a meta-analysis of what goes along with the signs. That's good practice." When we asked Sophie about her reasons for doing this video-based lesson, she explained:

> This is something typically Deaf. You need to say "tired" with a tired facial expression, you cannot say it while smiling. Most of the time the children disconnect their signs from their facial expressions, they do not completely have the knowledge of the inseparable link between both. There, I ask them, "Why do I blow out like that?" A person who masters LSF completely but nothing more, a hearing person for instance, will not think of questioning the children about this facial expression. The person will think that the children are already aware of the fact that blowing out that way is linked to the "tired" sign. But children don't have this awareness, and so they smile while signing "tired." They need to be taught that facial expressions give a specific meaning. These are little details we need to emphasize.

An experienced Deaf teacher in Poitiers, France commented on this scene: "The teacher here dissects the language. She goes deeper in the details of what she's doing with facial expressions, hand-shapes, space, movement, everything. Grammar. In short, all the parameters of the language." This teacher and Sophie make a strong case for the value of giving deaf children explicit instruction in facial expressions to be able to communicate and understand emotion. This reasoning can be transposed to hearing classrooms, where teachers could give similar attention to children synchronizing their verbal and embodied communication. Some courtroom lawyers and sales people participate in workshops where they are taught to more effectively employ facial expressions and gesture in their verbal presentations. Why not provide similar opportunities to young children?

Conversational Conventions

Another feature of Deaf pedagogy is systematically teaching and reinforcing appropriate norms of conversational participation, norms that include ways of seeking help, getting a teacher's or classmate's attention, and entering into a conversation without interrupting. For example, a boy runs over to Sophie on the playground to report on a dispute in the sand box and pushes her from behind to get her attention. Sophie turns to him and signs, with a facial expression that

Figure 6. Appropriating tapping

mixes pain and anger, "Ow, that hurt. Don't push me so hard. Tap on the shoulder. Yes, that's better" (Figure 6).

In the Meisei video there is a scene of children playing tug of war on the playground (Figure 7). A cluster of five children holds one end of a rope, the assistant teacher, Kurihara, stands alone on the other side, holding the other end, and the head teacher, Ikeda, stands in the middle, ready to announce the beginning of the contest. A four-year-old girl, Mika, approaches Kurihara-sensei, takes the end of the rope from her, throws it on the ground, and stomps away.

Mika:	It's not fair. My team will lose. The other team has more players on their side. (Satoshi, a five-year-old boy holding on to the other end of the rope, comes over to Mika and vigorously disagrees with her assessment.)
Satoshi:	But your team has Kurihara-sensei. She is big and strong. And my team has many girls, who are weak.

As this argument continues for five minutes or so, another four-year-old girl, Chika, approaches to say something to Mika. Satoshi pushes her away and angrily tells her not to interrupt. Chika, with tears in her eyes, walks away, and then signs, "I'm sad." Towards the end of Mika and Satoshi's heated discussion, Ikeda sits on a bench, ten meters away from the argument. Chika eventually comes over and stands near her. Ikeda explains to Chika that Satoshi has a tendency to dominate conversations.

Finally, the tug of war began and, as Satoshi predicted, Kurihara's team wins. Mika and Satoshi then debrief what transpired.

Satoshi:	Now how do you feel?
Mika:	I see now that you are right that the red team sometimes wins and I shouldn't quit.
Satoshi:	I am sorry.
Mika:	I am sorry.

The children begin the tug of war.

Mika and Satoshi argue.

Chika approaches Mika.

Satoshi tells Chika not to interrupt.

Figure 7. Embodied conversation

The tug of war scene includes discussion by both Ikeda and the children on rules and norms of Deaf sociolinguistics. Satoshi at several points told Chika, in no uncertain terms, that it is inappropriate to interrupt while he and Mika were having a discussion. When Chika attempts to interrupt by tapping Mika on the shoulder, and then turning her face with her hand, Satoshi criticizes her and pushes her away. As Mika and Satoshi continues their discussion, Chika comes over to Ikeda, who uses the opportunity to point out some shortcoming of Satoshi's conversational style:

> Satoshi's talking is very long. It's better to talk more briefly. Satoshi keeps talking so Mika keeps quiet. This is not a good way. They should talk with each other, to listen to what the other person is saying and to tell their opinion. Yes. Mika keeps quiet. This is not a good way. It's better to not only tell your opinions, but also to talk with each other, right. (Figure 8)

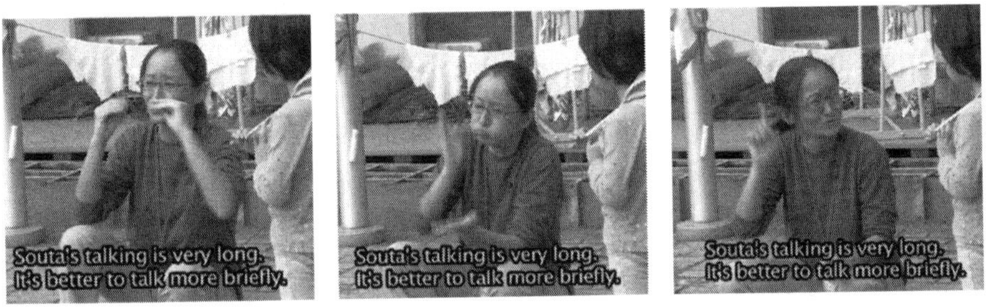

Figure 8. Conversational turn-taking

After Satoshi and Mika finish their discussion and apologize to each other, Satoshi says to Mika: "I did a bad thing to Chika by saying 'It's our business.'" This statement implies that he intended to apologize, either for his gruffness or for not letting Chika interrupt the conversation to say something to Mika. But when he reaches Chika, instead of apologizing, he reiterates his meta-level point about conversational rules: "It's not OK to intervene when two of us are talking. It's our problem. It's fine to talk after that conversation." Chika's response acknowledges the general principle Satoshi is making, but argues that her interruption would have been so short as to not harm their conversation: "I knew you two were talking, but I wanted to say just one little thing." Satoshi refuses to accept this exception to the new interruption rule: "I told you, 'Please wait because we are talking now,' when you interrupted."

Different cultures have different implicit rules for what constitutes appropriate and inappropriate forms of conversational turn taking for a third party to enter into or interrupt a conversation. In Deaf communities, due to the need for interlocutors to face each other, there is generally more hesitation than in hearing communities to interrupt a dyadic conversation. Waving or tapping on the shoulder someone involved in a conversation to get her attention is more acceptable than grabbing the face of someone whom you want to talk with and turning it toward you and away from a co-conversationalist, as Chika does with Mika. Many hearing and some deaf viewers of the tug of war scene saw Chika as a victim and Satoshi as a bully. In contrast many Deaf viewers pointed out that while his manner was unnecessarily abrasive, Satoshi was right to tell Chika that she should wait until a conversation is over before starting a new one.

Meta-level Discussions of Conversational Routines

We would argue, again, that there are implications here for educators working with hearing children. Conversational routines are conventional. We shouldn't assume that young children come to school already knowing how to enter conversations, interrupt appropriately, and take conversational turns of appropriate length, across different contexts (for example, during circle time, on the playground, or during a teacher-led activity). The need for explicit discussion of conversational norms is especially true when a classroom is home to children from different backgrounds. Because the usually unstated rules of school conversation tend to reflect the way conversations are conducted more in White middle class than in other communities (Tobin, 1995), not making conversational routines explicit disproportionately disadvantages children who come from immigrant, working class, and other non-White middle-class families. Because their deaf students usually come from homes where there are no Deaf, signing adults, teachers in Deaf early childhood education settings know that they have to spend a good deal of time and energy teaching not just how to sign (including the use of accompanying gestures and facial expressions) but also conversational conventions. These pedagogical strategies for providing young children with skills and meta-level awareness for how to engage with others can be transposed to hearing classrooms.

Conclusion/Implications

Preschool classrooms across the U.S. look and function very much alike because they are based on widely shared assumptions and habits. Engaging with educational practices from other cultures is one effective way to question the taken-for-grantedness of familiar approaches and expand the repertoire of what is possible and desirable to do in classrooms. Our argument in this chapter has been that just as U.S. educators can learn from educational approaches in other countries, so too can they learn from Deaf culture and Deaf education. Deaf pedagogy developed largely apart from mainstream (hearing) education, and therefore, like flora and fauna on an isolated island, it developed some unique characteristics, characteristics that can be adapted to hearing educational settings.

In the case of learning from Deaf early childhood education, the transposition from Deaf to hearing preschool classrooms may not be all that difficult because many of the core principles of progressive early childhood education share with Deaf pedagogy a focus on embodied teaching and learning. Core practices we documented in the videos we made in signing Deaf preschool classrooms in Japan, France, and the U.S. include an emphasis on lines of sight, embodied expression, joint attention, and explicit discussion of conversational routines. While each of these topics is addressed to some extent in most hearing preschool classrooms, we believe that learning about how experienced Deaf educators organize their classrooms and teaching can help teachers in hearing settings to modify some of their practices and reconceptualize some of their notions of teaching and learning. If early childhood educators in hearing settings were to embrace these Deaf practices and principles, their classrooms would become more accessible to a wider range of children. And yet, without signing, these classrooms still would not be ideal settings for deaf children.

Our larger argument is that engaging with insights from non-typically abled communities can enrich "regular" education. There are things Deaf preschool teachers and other educators who operate outside of the educational mainstream know that educators in the mainstream can learn from. And we can expand this argument to other categories of difference. Educators who have grown up differently abled can share with their more typically abled colleagues sensibilities and practices that can be beneficial for all young children. The Universal Design movement has created new classroom designs by drawing on the experiences and wisdom of people with conditions that make it difficult for them to navigate environments that assume that everyone is ambulatory. Similarly, pedagogical strategies that are effective for neurologically atypical learners can inform practices in early childhood educational settings serving a general population. The field of early childhood education has been hampered by the taken-for-grantedness of beliefs and practices that are unreflectively audist and ableist.

References

Calderon, R., & Greenberg, M. (2003). Social and emotional development of deaf children. In M. Marschark & P. E. Spencer (Eds.), *Oxford handbook of deaf studies, language, and education* (pp. 177–189). New York, NY: Oxford University Press.

Christiansen, J. B., & Leigh, I. W. (2002). *Cochlear implants in children: Ethics and choices.* Washington, DC: Gallaudet University Press.

Conn-Powers, M., Conn-Powers, A. F., Traub, E. K., & Hutter-Pishgahi L. (2006). The universal design of early education. *Young Children on the Web*, 1–9.

Edwards, C., & Harold, G. (2014). Deaf Space and the principles of universal design. *Disability and Rehabilitation*, *36*(16), 1350–1359.

Hauser, P. C., O'Hearn, A., McKee, M., Steider, A., & Thew, D. (2010). Deaf epistemology: Deafhood and deafness. *American Annals of the Deaf, 154*(5), 486–492.

Hoffmeister, R. (2007). Language and the deaf world: Difference not disability. In M. Brisk & P. Mattai (Eds.), *Culturally responsive teacher education: Language, curriculum & community*. Mahwah, NJ: Lawrence Erlbaum Associates.

Jacobs, R. L., & Park, Y. (2009). A proposed conceptual framework of workplace learning: Implications for theory development and research in human resource development. *Human Resource Development Review, 8*(2), 133–150.

Nakamura, K. (2006). *Deaf in Japan: Signing and the politics of identity*. Ithaca, NY: Cornell University Press.

Ladd, P. (2003). *Understanding deaf culture in search of deafhood*. Clevedon, UK: Multilingual Matters.

Ladd, P. (2008). Colonialism and resistance: A brief history of deafhood. In D. L. Bauman (Ed.), *Open your eyes: Deaf studies talking* (pp. 42–59). Minneapolis, MN: University of Minnesota Press.

Lane, H. (2005). Ethnicity, ethics, and the deaf-world. *The Journal of Deaf Studies and Deaf Education, 10*(3), 291–310.

Lane, H., Hoffmeister, R., & Bahan, B. (1996). *A journey into the deaf-world*. San Diego, CA: Dawn Sign Press.

Singleton, J., & Morgan, D. (2005). Natural signed language acquisition within the social context of the classroom. In B. Schick, M. Marschark, & P. E. Spencer (Eds.), *Advances in the sign language development of deaf children* (pp. 344–376). New York, NY: Oxford University Press.

Singleton, J., & Supalla, S. (2010). Assessing children's proficiency in natural signed languages. In M. Marschark & P. E. Spencer (Eds.), *The Oxford handbook of deaf studies, language, and education*, Volume 1. 2nd ed. (pp. 306–320). New York, NY: Oxford University Press.

Tobin, J. (1995). The irony of self-expression. *American Journal of Education, 103*(3), 233–258.

Tobin J., Wu, D. Y. H., & Davidson, D. H. (1989). *Preschool in three cultures: Japan, China, and the United States*. New Haven, CT: Yale University Press.

Tobin, J., Hsueh, Y., & Karasawa, M. (2009). *Preschool in three cultures revisited: China, Japan, and the United States*. Chicago, IL: University of Chicago Press.

Tobin, J. (forthcoming). The origins of the method. *Anthropology and Education Quarterly*.

Woodward, J. (1972). Implications for sociolinguistic research among the deaf. *Sign Language Studies, 1*, 1–7.

World Federation of the Deaf. (2018, May 11). *Situating Deaf communities within 'disability' vs 'cultural and linguistic minority'*. Helsinki, FI: Author.

CHAPTER TEN

Schools as Asylums

A Case Study of a Girl with OCD

XIAOYING ZHAO

In this chapter I present a case study of Julia, a 10-year-old, bi-racial girl diagnosed with Obsessive-Compulsive Disorder (OCD). Using Bakhtinian discourse analysis of her descriptions of her divergent school experiences at two school spaces, I locate the discourses of difference that contribute to her OCD.

My analysis is consistent with the Critical Disability framework used by the other contributors to this volume. A shortcoming of both Critical Disability studies and special education is the lack of including the voices of children with special needs (Bailey, Boddy, Briscoe, & Morris, 2015; Davis & Watson, 2001). This chapter is a response to Peters's (2010) call for educators to listen to student voices and to use children's perspectives to help us rethink how we think about such issues as inclusion, equity, and least restrictive environments. Embodied life stories, like the story I tell in this paper of ten-year-old Julia's experiences in two very different school settings, can help to unravel the complex interactions of social, racial, biological, and political factors that contribute to the educational experiences of neurologically atypical students.

As a conceptual framework I draw on two Russian theorists, Mikhail Bakhtin and Lev Vygotsky. From Bakhtin (1981) I take the idea that "The ideological becoming of a human being … is the process of selectively assimilating the words of others" (p. 341). Bakhtin believes that discourse, which he defines as chains of spoken and written language, is socio-ideological and constitutive. Subjects come into being through their engagement with the authoritative and internally persuasive discourses that swirl around them. Among these are discourses about what it means to be normal and how differences are categorized and evaluated. I see Vygotsky's understanding of disability as consistent with this Bakhtinian perspective. Vygotsky (1993) recognized the damage of negative social responses to disability, which he called "secondary disabilities." He argues that preventing secondary disabilities is at least as important as compensating for biological disabilities.

Methods

This chapter came out of research I conducted at a private alternative school, School of Joy (SOJ), in the Southeastern U.S. At the time of the study, 17 children from age six to thirteen were enrolled. All of them had transferred from local public and private schools. SOJ was designed to be a learning community where students steered their own education. Two teachers created a project-based curriculum that catered to children's interests. Learning was assessed through portfolios, instead of standardized tests. Each day students had about two hours of free choice activities. This is a case study of one of these SOJ students, Julia, a 10-year-old, working-class, biracial girl (White mother and Black father). Julia attended a public school before her transfer to SOJ. At the time of the research Julia had been at SOJ for fifteen months. Julia had been diagnosed with mild Obsessive-Compulsive Disorder (OCD), a condition in which people have uncontrollable, reoccurring thoughts and behaviors (National Institute of Mental Health, 2016). She was obsessed with things to be in order, in her way, and perfect. She had a difficult time dealing with people and conditions that were out of her control.

I used participant observation and videotaped semi-structured interviews. I observed Julia at SOJ from 8:30 am to 3:00 pm (a full school day) once every other week over three months. I paid attention to her interactions with teachers, the other students, and learning materials. I interviewed Julia about her experiences at two school settings, the former public school and SOJ. I also interviewed Julia's mother, and asked her to respond to selected video clips from Julia's interview for corroboration. I encouraged Julia to share her knowledge and speak for herself. I listened to and observed her attentively. Luckily, Julia seemed to be comfortable with this positioning. She permitted my presence when hanging out with friends and working on projects at SOJ, and she willingly answered my questions. Moreover, Julia seemed to have a sense of control over how the research proceeded. She reserved her right to have private conversations with her friends by respectfully asking me to leave for a moment. She also took initiative during the interview. For example, Julia compared SOJ with her former public school without being asked to.

I believe and am moved by what Julia had to say about her the hardships she experienced at her former public school. Childhood hardships may seem petty and trivial from adults' perspectives, but they are painful for the children at that moment and may even have lasting consequences (Miller, 1991; Waksler, 1996). This is particularly true for children with emotional disorders, which are likely to be interpreted as character weakness or social maladjustment. As adults and educators, we should take a child's emotional interpretation of her experience seriously and acknowledge its validity and value. Bakhtin (1990) sees the ethical imperative to answer the utterances of another. When our research participants share parts of their lives with us, they deserve responses. I tried to do this during my interactions with Julia by showing empathy and asking follow-up questions that communicated my interest and understanding of what she was telling me. Now, long after my face-to-face interactions with Julia are over, and I have spent many hours reading and thinking about what she told me, I answer again with writing this chapter.

After transcribing the interviews and proofreading the fieldnotes, I read the transcripts line by line and analyzed them using Bakhtinian discourse analysis. Bakhtin (1981) suggested that our speech is cobbled together out of the already uttered "words of others":

> Every conversation is full of transmissions and interpretations of other people's words. At every step one meets a "quotation" or a "reference" to something that a particular person said, a reference to "people say" or "everyone says," to the words of the person one is talking with, or to one's own previous words, to a newspaper, an official decree, a document, a book and so forth. (p. 338)

We cite discourses that circulate around us, adding our own inflections. These inflections reflect what Bakhtin calls our "ideological evaluations." These take the form of our attitude towards the topics we talk about, attitudes that range from respect to ridicule to bitterness. To understand her ideological evaluations of her two schools, I paid attention to the descriptive and evaluative phrases Julia used to describe her school experiences, phrases such as "I don't like ...," "I felt happy ...," and "They made me upset." I used the transcript of my interview with Julia's mother to corroborate my emerging interpretations.

A Bakhtinian interpretive method suggests that an individual's utterances can be used to read the larger dominant discourses and ideologies of a community. In this way Julia's words and body language can be read as reflecting the discursive and ideological worlds of the two schools she attended. Julia's emotional descriptions of these two schools' pedagogical approaches and social order articulate the profound contrast between the dominant discourses of differences at these schools. Her former public school is a site of hierarchical power differences between teachers and students and where differences among peers are harshly judged. In contrast, at her alternative school, differences were accepted as facts, and differences in status among peers and between students, and teachers were minimized. Julia's depictions of these two educational worlds led me to a new understanding of what the experience of being mainstreamed in a public school can be like for a student like Julia and of the sense of relief and asylum such students can find in an alternative setting.

Findings

School Power Hierarchies

Julia described the power difference between children and teachers at her former public school. She described her feelings of being subjugated, as students had little control over recess time, learning, and decision-making. I suggest that while feelings of lack of control and agency are frustrating for many or even most students in public schools, these dynamics are especially hard on a student like Julia with OCD. When asked about her experience at her former school, Julia sighed deeply and audibly, with closed eyes. Just my mentioning her former school triggered some negative emotion. Then Julia slightly shook her head, rested it on her right hand, and said: "Public school is like … Kids should not be locked in a cage for eight hours a day, learning the same old stuff that they would never ever use." Julia's metaphor of the school as a "cage" works to capture both her view of the teachers as guards and of her as a prisoner. Julia went on, "Sometimes I get upset with Michelle Obama for being like 'Sixty hours [minutes] a day. Eat healthy food. Blah, blah, blah.' It's like you just make it seem so fun and happy. …" Julia used a high-pitched, upbeat voice, and a stiff smile to parody Michelle Obama's initiative of promoting children's physical activity. She pointed out the hypocrisy of adults who encourage children to be active and then limit recess to fifteen minutes a day.

Julia criticized teachers' control over student learning. She complained about having to "learn the same old stuff that they would never ever use." She also found the teaching too challenging:

> I was in the gifted education program. Our challenge teacher expected us to be in college. He didn't say it, but just gave us that look, "This is what we expected out of you."

> I am like, "We are eight! We are not developed yet. Our brains (right index finger pointed at her temple) are not even functioning right yet." It's ridiculous.

Julia's mother interpreted this complaint as reflecting Julia's preference to learn at her own pace. Even for children in the gifted program, her public school's structured curriculum failed to respond to children's diverse learning styles and needs. Julia continued:

> If you want these children to live a happy life, don't stick them in the cage and expect them to be perfect! Because kids have so much more meaning than people think they do. Kids are (sigh) so underestimated. It's ridiculous (frown). Every single kid has worth. Every kid out there should know that!

Julia's right palm was up above the table as she spoke, and her fingers hit the table when she said "don't" to stress her emotions. Instead of demanding students to have excellent academic performance, Julia suggested teachers and adults in general should get to know children and acknowledge their worth in multiple aspects.

Julia was particularly bothered by the absolute power teachers hold over students:

> If you had leadership place in your life, if the plan for your life was to be a leader, you wouldn't get that in public school because there are leaders and they are adults. And if you are not an adult, you are not a leader. And that kills me because (paused 1.5 seconds, took a breath out, and looked bitter), there are so many kid leaders out there that proves those public school teachers are wrong.

Julia added that she would be too scared to speak up for her peers in front of teachers. She felt subjugated by the teachers and the school. Julia was constantly aware of and frustrated about the imbalanced power relations and the unfairness.

From Julia's perspective, students are oppressed because their physical activity, learning, and participation in decision-making processes are dominated by teachers and the school. I would argue, again, that while many elementary students resent their lack of agency, Julia's OCD led her to being extremely frustrated about being constrained and by her lack of control. As she described the power dynamics in her public school, the tone of her voice, facial expressions, and body language communicated how this hierarchical positioning generated stress, frustration, and fear.

Difference as Deviance

In her public school, Julia found her peers as frustrating as her teachers. She told me that peer interactions at her former public school were dominated by policing difference, and viewing and treating anyone who was deemed different as deviant. This positioning drove Julia to feel compelled to appear to be as similar to the other children as she could for fear of exclusion. Julia said that she contributed to her social isolation, because her OCD made it hard for her to relate to classmates who had perspectives different from hers. Julia related a sad story of becoming friends with a girl who seemed most like her, but then losing this friendship when they began to compete with each other.

Julia was stressed by being teased by her peers for being different. Classmates made fun of her for wearing glasses, for the way she laughed, and for her flamboyant hair styles. On the day I interviewed her at SOJ, she wore her hair in three walnut-sized buns on the left, middle, and right sides of her head. She also wore a headband with a black bow. Julia contrasted how this hairstyle was accepted by her classmates at SOJ with how it would have been received at her public school:

> If I would have gone to my former public school with this hair, everybody would be like, "Eww! That looks dumb!" And I would be like, "No!" But here [SOJ] I don't care what people think about my hair, who I am, what my style is, or how I talk.

Julia's imagining here of how her former classmates would have ridiculed and ostracized her for her appearance suggests a level of social anxiety that made the her classmates' taunts unbearable to her.

What Julia described as "drama" characterized her daily interactions with peers in her public school:

> Public school was not fun (sighed, took a breath deep, and shook her head). There was lots of drama. … If I wouldn't have gone to public school, I would have a better life right off the bat. There are [sic] so much drama. I have so many friends that turned on me.

As examples of drama, Julia told of getting caught in the middle of arguments among classmates: "If you try to stick up for one kid, sides would be picked. Consequences would be told and given."

Julia had a best friend with whom she had a lot in common. The need they felt to be alike led to intense competition that ruined their friendship and left Julia further isolated:

> We had everything in common. We both liked pink. So when she would get a new pink outfit, I would get really jealous, and I would go get a pink outfit. When I wore a special necklace, she would get really jealous, and she would wear a special necklace the next day. When she got straight hair, I wanted straight hair so I straightened my hair. And we went on and on and on until I was done. She ended up playing me and

> shared all my secrets [with other people] and stuff like that. And that's ridiculous. She was one of the most unloyal friends that I have ever had. I don't want to be her friend ever again.

Competition with this friend brought out the worst in her. Julia admitted that she was rude and aggressive. Such interactions with a peer might seem routine and trivial, but it was brutal and consequential for Julia. Her mother described this as a "bad divorce" that contributed significantly to her eventual decision to change schools.

Julia's OCD led to her having uncontrollable, reoccurring thoughts about her troubles with peers and teachers during her fourth-grade year. We could say that Julia's condition led to her failure at her public school. However, I would argue that the school failed her. Although Julia was not formally excluded for her condition, she suffered in addition to her OCD from the "secondary disabilities" (Vygotsky, 1993) caused by the school's structures and social dynamics. The hierarchical power positioning of teachers, the constraints on her freedom of movement and attention, and her peers' discourse of difference as deviancy combined to present Julia with more stress than she could handle. This positioning led by the end of fourth grade to her difference becoming a formal disorder. As she told me: "I had developed OCD, and really bad anxiety. Over the summer, I was a little depressed." Rather than embracing diverse learning styles and being a space for all children, the school implicitly expected standardized, obedient students. Consequently, Julia was overwhelmed by the frustration and stress in her daily interactions with teachers and peers. When Julia transferred to SOJ the next fall, within the first week, according to Julia's mother, Julia's stress level lowered significantly and her ways of engaging with others changed.

The Enabling Effects of Viewing Difference as Fact without Judgment

When talking about her experiences at SOJ, Julia emphasized that the biggest change from her public school was that at her new school difference was just a fact to be accepted, without judgment. At SOJ teachers didn't seem to dominate over students. They trusted students' autonomy and used community rules, such as "Freedom and Responsibility" and "Community Agreements" to let students regulate themselves. Students participated in making and applying communal rules. Hence, they understood that to enjoy the freedom, each and every one of them should abide by the agreements as their responsibilities. Julia described this accountability as: "When a train is coming, you have to be responsible [by] not playing on the train tracks. … But you are free to learn new things, make mistakes, and learn from those mistakes." Understanding that the school's structures were for her best interests, she didn't feel constrained. In her words: "That's basically the only rule we have." Students disciplined themselves and one another since they were responsible for one another. Teachers only offered support when needed.

Students shared leadership roles with teachers. They resolved conflicts by themselves through conflict resolution procedures. Julia explained:

> We do our best to communicate and understand how each other feels. If the same situation keeps re-occurring, we come up with agreements to put into place. … There's never a conflict that leaves people sad for a long time. It always ends up getting solved.

Students trusted the procedures and one another, and teachers would intervene only when the conflicts persisted. Last but not least, teachers provided resources and led learning activities that were project-based and related to students' interests. They did not force students to learn certain content at a certain pace to meet standards. Students' learning progress was assessed through portfolios, instead of paper-and-pencil tests. Hence, the learning was more relaxed and less stressful. Students had more than one-hour recess for free play and to explore their interests. The teachers' role was to be more helpers, resource providers, facilitators, and co-leaders with students. In Julia's mother's words, the teachers were friends and mentors to Julia.

At SOJ, with individual variation among peers positively recognized, Julia started getting used to the fact that everyone was different and unique. The teachers emphasized that people have different ways of communicating, and that they were at "different levels," and that was okay. Julia described how the students and teachers recognized and accepted each others' communication styles and abilities by referring to these differences as "levels":

> Level one is [that] you are not very direct. You are very afraid of hurting people's feelings. It's not easy for you to open up about how you feel. … You never actually get to explain how you feel until someone pushes you to do that. Level two is [that] you are not very good at. … My best friend is at level one or level two. It takes her a while to warm up. She likes writing notes. She can be very open but not face to face. So that's what we do. I am level three. Level three is very direct about how you feel. Once there is a problem you want to solve it, and you want to make sure everybody gets their points across.

In this way, diversity at SOJ was acknowledged and incorporated into modes of interacting. Students didn't need to be like one another to be accepted. In Julia's words, "It's really diverse here. Everyone is welcome. It doesn't matter how old you are, your religion, race, you are always welcome here. And you can be your own unique style." Julia dressed however she wanted because she knew her peers would not put her down. For example, the hairstyle Julia thought her former classmates would have laughed at would be complimented on by her peers at SOJ.

Julia did not transform overnight. It was a process to shift her understanding of difference. It took a while for her to get past the negative meaning attached to difference in her former school and to learn to view difference positively. She gradually learned to accept differences as fact, as something to cope with and even benefit from. Julia said: "There are different types of people here. So for a while it's hard for me to communicate with people with different religion. … And it's really hard to communicate with people of another communication levels. But it always seems to work out."

Julia readily acknowledged her OCD condition, telling me about it in the first minute of the interview. She said frankly: "I am really into art and it's one of my passions. It helps me to let go a little bit because I have OCD. It's really hard for me for something not to be perfect," followed by laughter. Julia did not seem ashamed of her special condition. Instead, she seemed to regard it as her uniqueness. At SOJ Julia quickly developed a close friendship with another girl whose personality, communication style, and racial background were different from hers. They did not compete against each other perhaps because at SOJ they felt confident in and comfortable with their own uniqueness. According to Julia's mom, Julia felt she was one of a kind at SOJ. She came to accept that peer conflicts and disagreements were an inevitable part of life and she felt well-equipped in the context of SOJ to deal with them. Hence, Julia felt happy and supported most of the time.

All in all, at SOJ Julia learned to accept differences in others and to feel comfortable being different herself. As Julia's differences were embraced at SOJ, she came to recognize the new roles that could be played by teachers and students. Julia also acquired news ways to cope with and even benefit from her diversity. She remained obsessive and compulsive, but she was freed from the secondary defects. In this milieu, Julia transformed into an abled student.

Discussion: The Enabling Effects of Asylum

This study has emphasized the value of listening to the voices of children (or, in this case, one child) to better understand the intersection of the discourses of difference, school structures and experiences, and disability. It's not my intention to demonize public schools and public school teachers or to draw an idealized picture of private alternative schools. I have not intended to perpetuate the tendency of progressive researchers to depict struggling, unhappy students in public schools as heroic or pitiable characters unwilling to put up with the regimentation, boredom, and authoritarianism of the public schools. Nor has it been my intention to suggest that all students with disabilities cannot take advantage of what a public school has to offer students. In Julia's case, the public school didn't work for her, and her private school did. Julia attributed her unhappiness at her public school to the way her OCD and distinctive personality (mis)matched with the school's structures and her peers' modes of interaction. In this context, difference produced secondary disabling effects.

Boldt and Valenti (2014) argue that for some students the least restrictive environment is to be found not in mainstreaming, but in a school set up as an asylum. Different from traditional asylums such as tuberculosis sanatoriums and mental hospitals that were established for the purpose of segregation, there can be institutions that are asylums more in the sense of political asylum, places established to offer safe harbor to those suffering in the larger world (Masschelein & Verstraete, 2012). This notion of schools as asylums rejects psychological, psychiatric diagnoses, and other reified linguistic evaluations (Boldt & Valente, 2014). Test scores, clinical labels, and IEPs too often attach normalizing, disabling judgements to children's differences. They divide students into categories of "the abled," "the disabled," "high performers," and "the falling-behind." Under the pressure to assess and diagnose, educators focus on student deficits (Adair, 2014). At schools set up as asylums, teachers help students explore their multiple capabilities. Julia thrived when she was allowed to learn at her own pace. Her differences were acknowledged, but not invidiously. In these ways asylums can protect students from secondary disabilities caused by negative interactions under the ontology of sameness. Aligning with Adair (2014), I suggest policy makers consider a holistic understanding of learning and schooling. The difficulties of teaching against the grain (Cochran-Smith, 1991) are formidable, but I encourage my fellow educators to focus more on students' unique experiences, abilities, and not their shortcomings.

More importantly, in this notion of schools as asylums, differences and disabilities are considered as ontological facts to be accepted, accommodated, and lived with. The epistemological interstices allow teachers and students to suspend judgment, center the relationship between self and other, and be curious about the possibilities the students embody. Hence, students live in the whole presence of one another, instead of living in hierarchical relations and with oppositional roles. The teachers and students at SOJ did not think in terms of what was "wrong" with Julia. Instead, she was embraced as who she was and offered tools to accept and cope with individual variation in her daily school life. To construct asylums in public as well as private schools for all students, educators need to instill the idea that differences are to be accepted and coped with, not judged. It is important to institute daily practices to reinforce this understanding. For instance, teachers and students need to be reminded to recognize and accept one another's differences and to practice respectful communication methods. Asylums should be not places reserved for people identified with a particular disability, but instead open to all students who for any reason cannot thrive in the usual classroom settings.

References

Adair, J. K. (2014). Agency and expanding capabilities in early grade classrooms: What it could mean for young children. *Harvard Educational Review*, *84*(2), 217–242.

Bailey, S., Boddy K., Briscoe, S., & Morris C. (2015). Involving disabled children and young people as partners in research: A systematic review. *Child: Care, Health & Development*, *41*(4), 505–514.

Bakhtin, M. M. (1981). *The dialogic imagination: Four essays by M. M. Bakhtin*. (M. Holquist, Ed.; C. Emerson & M. Holquist, Trans.). Austin, TX: University of Texas Press.

Bakhtin, M. M. (1990). *Art and answerability: Early philosophical essays by M. M. Bakhtin*. (M. Holquist & V. Liapunov, Eds.; V. Liapunov & K. Brostrom, Trans.). Austin, TX: University of Texas Press. (Original work written ca. 1920–1923).

Boldt, G., & Valente, J. M. (2014). Bring back the asylum: Reimagining inclusion in the presence of others. In M. N. Bloch, B. B. Swadener, & G. S. Cannella (Eds.), *Reconceptualizing early childhood care and education: Critical questions, new imaginaries and social activism* (pp. 201–213). New York, NY: Peter Lang.

Cochran-Smith, M. (1991). Learning to teach against the grain. *Harvard Educational Review*, *61*(3), 279–311.

Davis, J. M., & Watson, N. (2001). Where are the children's experiences? Analysing social and cultural exclusion in "special" and "mainstream" schools. *Disability & Society*, *16*(5), 671–687.

Masschelein, J., & Verstraete, P. (2012). Living in the presence of others: Towards a reconfiguration of space, asylum and inclusion. *International Journal of Inclusive Education*, *16*(11), 1189–1202.

Miller, A. (1991). *Breaking down the wall of silence: The liberating experience of facing painful truth*. New York, NY: Dutton.

National Institute of Mental Health. (2016). *Obsessive-Compulsive Disorder*. Retrieved from https://www.nimh.nih.gov/health/topics/obsessive-compulsive-disorder-ocd/index.shtml

Peters, S. J. (2010). The heterodoxy of student voice: Challenges to identity in the sociology of disability and education. *British Journal of Sociology of Education*, *31*(5), 591–602.

Vygotsky, L. S. (1993). *The collected works of L. S. Vygotsky. Volume 2: The fundamentals of defectology (abnormal psychology and learning disabilities)*. (R. W. Rieber & A. S. Carton, Eds.; J. E. Knox & C. B. Stevens, Trans.). New York, NY: Plenum.

Waksler, F. C. (1996). *The little trials of childhood and children's strategies for dealing with them*. London, UK: Falmer Press.

CHAPTER ELEVEN

The Emotional Work of Inclusion

Living within Difference at L'Ecole Gulliver

GAIL BOLDT AND JOSEPH MICHAEL VALENTE

An Introduction to A.P.A.T.E. and the Landscape of Special Education in France

Although laws and policies supporting inclusive education have been implemented and revised worldwide across the past four decades, the accomplishment of inclusion has been partial at best. A multitude of research studies have demonstrated many challenges to inclusion, from funding of inclusion programs and curriculum development, to preparation of teachers able to work successfully in inclusive classrooms, to meeting legal requirements for accommodations and meaningful participation of students and their families, to shifting attitudes from integration (mainstreaming) to inclusive classroom practices, and more (e.g., Armstrong, Armstrong, & Barton, 2016; Artiles, Kozleski, & Waitoller, 2011; Haug, 2016; Kanter, Damiani, & Ferri, 2014; Valente & Danforth, 2016; Watermeyer, McKenzie, & Swartz, 2018). In this chapter, we draw on our research at L'Ecole Gulliver, one of four preschools overseen by the community-based organization A.P.A.T.E. (*Association Pour l'Accueil de Tous le Enfants* [Association for the Reception of All Children]) in Paris, France, to call attention to a challenging facet of inclusion that is rarely commented upon: the emotional struggles, resistances, difficulties, and aggressions that arise when working across differences that are marked as "disability."

A.P.A.T.E is nationally recognized by the French government and news media as a model program for its pioneering approach to and critical advocacy of inclusive education. The A.P.A.T.E. preschools were the first in France to unconditionally accept children regardless of the nature or severity of their disability condition or chronic illness. Since its inception, A.P.A.T.E. has adhered to a reverse-inclusion admissions policy, which requires that at least 30% of the children in each preschool have identified disabilities. We visited L'Ecole Gulliver, the A.P.A.T.E. preschool we chose as our research site, in 2013 and 2015 for a week each time. Drawing from video ethnographic methods pioneered by Tobin, Wu, and Davidson (1989), during our time at Gulliver we filmed for two days; edited the films into "typical days"; revised the films based on feedback from teachers and administrators during a film viewing; and finally, used the films as prompts when we interviewed volunteer teachers and Gulliver's director, Ghada Ouba, and Cécile Herrou, who is General Manager of all of the A.P.A.T.E. schools.

Even for people who choose to work in inclusive settings, work across the differences can put into play a range of difficult emotions that, if ignored, can result in defensive and even aggressive forms of interaction, hardening distinctions between those understood as having or not having a disability. In our interviews, administrators and teachers at Gulliver freely acknowledged the emotional challenges of their work. In fact, they argued that being open in their acknowledgement of difficulties and having institutionalized mechanisms designed to address these stressors are key factors in the success of their efforts. In this chapter, we focus on how the institution itself is understood as a site where difference is produced and where deliberate practices are put in place for acknowledging and responding to feelings of anger, aggression, and defensiveness that arise in response to difference. At Gulliver, these deliberate practices are understood as essential to the accomplishment of inclusion.

That differences named as disability give rise to anxiety, distress, and aggression in school settings (and beyond) is demonstrated over and over in the research literature. In the U.S., Office of Civil Rights data (2012) reveal that special education students are subject to physical and emotional aggression, seclusion and isolation, and suspension and expulsion at rates far exceeding children not identified with disabilities. Although we do not have data on physical and emotional aggression against children identified with disabilities in France, we do have data on their exclusion from schools. In 2010, a troubling sign of the exclusions experienced by French students with disabilities came to light after France ratified the United Nations Convention on the Rights of Persons with Disabilities, and subsequently the European Commission authorized a status report on the capacity of the current French system of special education to meet the CRPD's requirements for transitioning to an inclusive education system. The Academic Network of European Disability (ANED) estimates that between 20,000 to 28,000 French school-aged children and youth with disabilities were being denied access to public school (Barral & Velche, 2010; Fage, Moullet, Consel, & Sauzeon, 2017; Senate Report, 2012).

ANED's report called attention not only to how much more widespread, but also how systemic the issue of children and youth being denied access to school was in France. Critics argued that students with disabilities who are denied access to public school continue to be forced to stay at home or to be warehoused in medico-educational institutions with little or no academic benefit. Further complicating matters, ANED also warned that the circumstances of French children and youth with disabilities could be even more fraught as researchers' efforts to collect data on instructional hours for students were especially limited by data that were either unavailable, incomplete, or unclear. These data limitations suggested great uncertainty about whether the 330,200 students with disabilities officially counted as registered in public schools (75% of total population of students in special education) or in medico-educational institutions (25% of total population). It remains unclear if they were in segregated or non-segregated settings with non-disabled peers, enrolled in part- or full-day programs, or attended a program only a few days per week or all week (Barral & Velche, 2010; Fage et al., 2017).

The European Agency for Special Needs and Inclusive Education (2016) found that the challenges greatly complicating France's transition from a special education system to an inclusive educational model follow from the entrenched bureaucratic structures of the field of special education. In France, special education is divided into two systems, with the Ministry of National Education overseeing public schools and the Ministry of Health and Solidarity administering medico-educational institutions, with its focus on caretaking and therapy, not schooling.

The 1975 Law no. 75–534, Policy for People with Disabilities, shifted policy toward "mandatory schooling" (*obligation scolaire*) and "school integration" for children and youth with disabilities (European Agency for Special Needs and Inclusive Education, 2016). However, the legislative and regulatory provisions of "mandatory schooling" *(obligation scolaire)* for all French children were considered too ambiguous, leading to the widespread misinterpretation and misapplication of the 1975 law to be "mandatory education" *(obligation éducative)* for children and youth with disabilities (Barral & Velche, 2010). Importantly, the ANED report points out that the distinction between the term "education" in English versus French is that in English "education" refers to "teaching and learning," whereas in French the term means "training in and adaptation to all aspects of life" (Barral & Velche, 2010).

As a result, "mandatory education" (*obligation éducative*) was widely understood to mean that institutions working with children with disabilities were legally mandated to attend to the children's caretaking but not necessarily their academic needs. Barral and Velche (2010) argue that "'mandatory education' did not imply that children provided for in special institutions should be taught and should learn in the academic sense" (pp. 6–7). The ANED report authors describe how even after the passage of the 1975 law, many special institutions either minimally, inadequately, or did not at all provide students with disabilities access to the official national school curriculum (Barral & Velche, 2010). The French laws of 1975 and subsequent policies of "school integration" and "mandatory schooling" (*obligation scolaire*) led to a separate but unequal system of education for students with disabilities.

Critics have argued that the lack of access to the national curriculum inevitably led to further academic delays and made the possibility of students with disabilities joining mainstream school settings with non-disabled peers nearly impossible. Likewise, critics argue, the ambiguity surrounding the legal definition of "*obligation scolaire*" versus "*obligation éducative*" effectively served as a pipeline for forcing students with disabilities into special education pathways that limited their academic possibilities and further justified the need for special segregated institutions (Barral & Velche, 2010; Ebersold, Plaisance, & Zander, 2016; Plaisance, 2009). This ambiguity created by the distinction between "mandatory schooling" and "mandatory education" would not be legislatively addressed until the law of February 11, 2005, which stipulated that parents of students with disabilities are legally obligated to register their children in public schools and that these schools are legally obligated to provide an academic course plan regardless of their disability condition and accommodation needs (Barral & Velche, 2010).

A.P.A.T.E.'s progressive policy and practices of inclusion are especially significant when considering the fact that in France (and elsewhere around the world), children and youth with disabilities deemed uneducable or too burdensome have historically been and continue to be denied access to public school.[1] A.P.A.T.E. was founded in 1992 by two social workers, Cécile Herrou and Janine Lévy, in response to the difficulties Herrou experienced as a social case worker trying to place children with disabilities in community-based nurseries and preschools. In our interviews with her, Herrou described "unbearable problems," with placements unavailable or of such low quality that

> it turns into exclusion even in the name of integration. The child is physically present … but very often, neither he nor his parents are truly welcomed. Many children are

> excluded from the outset from communities for young children, and their parents do not even plan to apply for a place, because both attitudes are closed to living together.

Herrou's vision for A.P.A.T.E. was to bring together children with and without identified disabilities, their parents and families, and educators of many backgrounds in a deliberate practice of "living together." Herrou understood that a central problem with how inclusion was conceptualized and undertaken was that children with disabilities were always already foreign to the group (Plaisance, 2007), that the child is the one who bears the difference in contrast to the assumed normality of the rest of the group. Her goal was to expand the notion of difference, to foster in all the ability to adapt to the other, and to learn to not be fearful of differences, including those associated with disability, nationality, income, religion, and personal experience (http://www.apate.fr/historique.html).

At A.P.A.T.E, Herrou set out to develop a "collectivist integration" approach in which inclusion is understood to be, she said in an interview, "everybody's inclusion." Collectivist integration stands in contrast to mainstream French approaches to special education because it views "difference" as not being a characteristic of the individual with markers of difference, but that "difference" is produced as an effect of a group coming together. A central principle of A.P.A.T.E.'s collectivist integration approach is that difference ought not be an individual's burden, but the group's collective responsibility. Rather than imagine that disability is something that everyone else has to make room for, Herrou wanted to build the case for an approach to education in which the unique differences of every person are understood as creating both the particular potential and the particular challenges of a given setting. The expectation at A.P.A.T.E. preschools is that children with and without identified disabilities, and their teachers, will learn to live inclusively by dealing with the inevitable complexities of inclusion collectively in their daily work and play together (Boldt & Valente, 2014, 2016).

In a collectivist integration approach, difference is understood as a property of a group. A specific group of individuals comes together, and in relation to one another, difference becomes apparent. For example, the fact that one person does not walk only has meaning because that individual is in a world wherein most people do walk. The difference is created in the juxtaposition of walking and not walking; the difference exists as a property of sets of relationships. These differences are given further weight through all of the structures and systems that assume walking as the norm. Likewise with differences in temperament, preference, modes of communication, prejudices, and other means of departure. Each of us becomes unique and different only as a result of being with others and being enmeshed in systems, institutions, and practices that assume certain norms. Herrou made clear to us that the differences labeled as "disability" can create all sorts of difficulties, but these differences are not necessarily or automatically more difficult than other kinds of differences that characterize all people within groups. In this perspective, the group is both the singularity or unique nature of each participant and the unique nature of the particular group that emerges.

Difference creates conflict and difficulty. Whether it is the need to install a ramp or the need to accommodate deaf participants and their sign language interpreters or the need to negotiate with those who are implacable in demanding their own way or to engage someone who is shy and rarely speaks (as just a few examples among an infinite number of possible differences), the challenge in any setting is how to acknowledge, accommodate, confront, accept, adapt, and/or grow while necessarily functioning in relationships. As we will describe in what follows, institutions can be sites where failures to work productively within difference can lead to breakdowns of communication that cause highly segregated and stereotypical roles. Conversely, institutions can provide opportunities and structures to use the inevitable differences that arise in struggles to live together to generate movement and change. This version of working within difference gives rise to creativity, new possibilities, movement, and energy. As Herrou describes on the A.P.A.T.E. website, "[E]veryone finds, in this experience of living together with respect for singularities, an exciting feeling of meeting the other in a diverse society" (https://www.apate.fr/blank-cfvg). Collectivist integration means, quite simply, the coming together of a group in a way that is functional and adaptive, that is deliberately self-aware and engages in practices intended to focus on how the life of the group supports the well-being of every member.

Importantly, Herrou insists that there is "nothing altruistic" in the work of A.P.A.T.E teachers and administrators. Understanding working with children with disabilities as altruistic or self-sacrificial denies the reality that we do such work for reasons of our own, and it positions the children as recipients of our charity. In fact, it is work that might best be understood as selfish. Calling this work "selfish" brings to the fore the conviction that learning to find the possibility and richness that is inherent in any institutional setting can be understood as a self-interested effort to live in a way that we experience as meaningful and connected. For Herrou, the task is not about what teachers do for children. It is finding ways to live together in a preschool that allows each participant—child and adult—to maximize the potential for creativity, growth, happiness, and love that is present as a result of coming together. Both Herrou and the Gulliver teachers we interviewed testify that teachers are dependent upon the children to learn how to be good teachers for each child. The opportunity to voice frustrations and anger is a necessary part of a bigger process of coming into relationship with children for teachers, who for reasons of their own both want to work with children with disabilities and find it difficult at times.

This work is best thought of as not altruistic because it requires deliberate practices that allow for the acknowledgement and working through of the difficulties. On the A.P.A.T.E. website, Herrou says (translated from French),

> There is nothing altruistic in the proposal. Welcoming all children without discrimination supposes a team functioning based on the decompartmentalization of functions, … a relay work, and a continuous institutional analysis, similar to Institutional Psychotherapy, allowing a diversification of responses to needs. The compartmentalization of functions and the rigidity of hierarchical status can prevent the emergence of knowledge and create incompetence. There is no longer any who are supposed to know and therefore those who are reputed to be ignorant. (https://www.apate.fr/blank-cfvg)

Work with difference, regardless of the kind of difference, is often hard and gives rise to strong emotions. Collectivist integration at A.PA.T.E requires deliberate institutional practices. Above, Herrou names these:

- Decompartmentalization of functions
- Continual institutional analysis
- Relay work

She also acknowledges that these concepts came from "Institutional Psychotherapy." In what follows, we will provide a brief overview of Institutional Psychotherapy in order to give context to A.P.A.T.E's practices of work within difference. We will then describe the practices named above as a way of considering how an institution can develop deliberate ways of working that realistically support the emergent potentials and emotionally challenging work of inclusion as collectivist integration.

Institutional Psychotherapy

Institutional psychotherapy is the name given to a practice of inpatient psychotherapy developed by François Tosquelles at the Saint-Alban Psychiatric Hospital as a result of the Nazi occupation of France. After the war, it was developed further by Jean Oury and Felix Guattari at the La Borde Psychiatric Clinic. During the war, psychiatric clinics throughout France were denied food provisions, and 48,000 psychiatric patients died of starvation and related diseases (Lemoine, 1998; cited in Birley, 2002). The exception to this was Saint-Alban, where no deaths related to starvation occurred (Polack, 2011). Geographically isolated, the hospital was able to function as a refuge and a base of operations for Resistance fighters as well as dissident artists and intellectuals who hid by living among the patients and were often employed as staff. The hospital had an open-door policy, allowing free movement of Resistance fighters and patients among the local population, who supplied food to the hospital. During his earlier service as a captain in the Spanish Republican Army fighting the Franco Fascists, Tosquelles came to believe that many psychoses were cured when the person became involved in useful and meaningful pro-social activity. At Saint-Alban, the integration of Resistance fighters, artists and intellectuals, patients, staff, and the surrounding community proved intellectually, artistically, and psychically productive for all (James, 2014).

Following the war, French youth and hostel movements produced many young activist interns who flocked to Saint-Alban to participate in this transformation of psychiatric care. Among them was Jean Oury, who arrived in 1947. In 1953, Oury purchased a run-down chateau called La Borde and moved there with most of his staff and patients (Dosse, 2010). Felix Guattari came to La Borde in 1955 and worked there until his death in 1992. Although Oury's death in 2014 was a painful loss, La Borde continues to operate and practice Institutional Psychotherapy today, and we were fortunate to visit and conduct informal interviews there in 2015.

Unlike most psychiatric hospitals that are ordered through routines dictated by the staff, insurance companies, and/or regulatory agencies, at La Borde, boarders (the name given to the voluntary inpatients) are actively involved in the daily organization of their communal life. Boarders and staff participate together each day in a democratically run meeting called the Daily Activities Commission that oversees the review, discussion, and revision of planned activities and policies. Daily activities are organized by what became known as "the grid," a chart that includes the name of every staff and boarder, the time of day, and the assigned activity, including chores, workshops, meetings, committees, and individual or group therapy times. Assignments constantly rotate, with doctors assigned to the garden or chicken coop and cooks assigned to the therapy group or ceramics studio. The creation of the grid plays an essential role in enabling the development of new forms of subjectivity through meaningful pro-social activity. At the Daily Activities Committee meetings, boarders and staff debate and vote on particular assignments and policies. This is a deliberate practice of living within difference, as participants need to work toward understanding the perspectives of others and engaging others as allies as they work to gain support for their position (Dosse, 2010). Guattari called the Daily Activities Committee "the mainspring of boarders' local resocialization" (Guattari, 1957; cited in Dosse, 2010, p. 55).

At La Borde, roles are constantly disassembled and reassembled. Doctors, nurses, secretaries, support staff, and boarders are assigned through the grid to a rotating list of tasks, including housekeeping, therapeutic and medical care, the production of bread and other cooking and cleaning chores, the production of the clinic newspaper, and work in creative activities. La Borde is known for its tradition of staff and boarders staging a play each summer that draws audiences from across France.[2] Staff and boarders maintain the singularities of their training and experiences, but these activities are put into constant relation with different people, locations (the kitchen, the garden, the workshop, the toilets, the dispensary, the stage, etc.), materials, and ways of doing and being, thereby opening doors to new ways of thinking about and feeling difference. Additionally, many of the staff live on the grounds of La Borde, send their children to a nursery on the La Borde grounds, and do not separate the daily life of La Borde from their own daily lives. This is intentional living together, using the institution as an opportunity for creating a setting in which all involved will experience new subjectivities as a result of living and working together, arguing, planning, voting, adapting, and creating new and unexpected ways and configurations.

A central part of the philosophy at La Borde involves the need to be intentional in acknowledging and working to eliminate the problem of staff and boarders getting locked into prescribed roles in which no real communication takes place. Institutions often become sites where separate, hierarchical roles cause the hardening of defensive positions in which difference exists as the problem to be defeated. Doctors are the bearers of authority and expertise; patients are infantilized, pathologized, assumed to be ignorant about their own well-being, and stripped of opportunities for efficacy and self-determination. In Institutional Psychotherapy, there are not doctors in one corner who are authorities and patients in another corner in need of patronizing care. There are people who come together, prepared to be transformed through the work of living together. Meyer and Robcis (2014) write that La Borde deliberately functions as a place of "permanent revolution," in that singularities brought into a group produce the constant, on-going need for responsiveness, reevaluation, and change.[3]

Practices of Collectivist Integration at the A.P.A.T.E. Preschools

This brief foray into Institutional Psychotherapy provides insight into the philosophy that organizes practices of collectivist integration at the A.P.A.T.E. preschools. Herrou's husband, the psychiatrist and psychoanalyst Jean-Claude Pollack, began working at La Borde in the 1970s; in our 2013 interview, Herrou reported that the work at La Borde gave her a way of putting into words and practice ideas that she had already had. At the same time, she made clear to us that it would be silly to imagine that practices with adults at a psychiatric clinic are identical to practices with children at a preschool, if for no other reason than children's ways of communicating are often different from those of adults and require specific kinds of opportunities to develop and express their desires and beliefs about how best to live together. In what follows, we will take the three practices identified on the website (https://www.apate.fr/blank-cfvg)—decompartmentalization of functions, continual institutional analysis, and the relay—one at a time to highlight how each functions in relation to the emotional work of inclusion.

Decompartmentalization of Functions

Herrou and the director of Gulliver, Ghada Ouba, described to us that "compartmentalization" and "decompartmentalization" are central to Gulliver's daily functioning and to the accomplishment of collectivist integration. Ouba described *compartmentalization* as each child being assigned to a set classroom, teacher, and group of students and *decompartmentalization* as children moving freely among spaces, groups, activities, and teachers. Ouba described that neither the compartmentalization nor the decompartmentalization of the children creates the conditions for children and teachers to participate in the building of their shared life, but rather what happens when the two are brought together. Like La Borde, at Gulliver they use a grid—a kind of compartmentalization—that assigns and rotates the children among different teachers, classrooms, and activities throughout the day—a kind of decompartmentalization. The grid provides what Ouba described as a "skeleton" and a "puzzle," an organization of place, teacher, group, and materials in which both children and teachers are able to discover and exercise pleasures. The structure allows various kinds of focus; teachers can focus on passing down their pleasure in doing things they enjoy, and they can also focus on the responses of the children. The children can focus on the experience of doing a particular thing with particular materials, peers of different ages with and without identified disabilities, teachers, spaces, times, and types of activities, including a daily academic time focused on introducing children to the French national curriculum. Decompartmentalization occurs not only in constantly reconconstituting the groups and activities, but as the teachers are able to observe and learn from differences in the way a given child interacts, communicates, and behaves within a specific assemblage.

The staff meet every Tuesday to discuss their observations of particular children in a variety of settings with different people. In explaining how these meetings work, Ouba reminded us of the story of the three blind men and the elephant, wherein each man touching the elephant felt something different:

> So this renowned object was an elephant and all three of them were right because one touched the hoof of the elephant which was big and couldn't be circled; the other touched the tail which was short; and the other one touched the skin. The three of them were right but they touched the elephant on their own side. So to really know the object we need to turn around it like that; we have a global vision of that object and we see it from every angle. And our way of working … it's this.

Decompartmentalizations of functions is visible here in the way that no single teacher assumes authority to define a particular child. The multiple views provided through diverse experiences of the children shifts the participants' view from focusing on as the intrinsic character of a given child— "This child is difficult"—is repositioned as a quality that arises in a particular configuration, allowing for the more nuanced view that "In this setting, with this material or this peer or this teacher or at this time of day, this child has a hard time but, in this circumstance, the child flourishes." Or perhaps: "In this setting, with this material or this child or at this time of day, this teacher has a hard time but, in this circumstance, the teacher flourishes."

Further, the children's role as "the child," narrowly or rigidly defined within school settings in relation to compliance, is also decompartmentalized. Ouba explained:

> We are in a world that thinks about the adult first and the children are next. So the children, if they are not able to talk for themselves, nobody will talk for them, so we don't even give them the opportunity and occasion to give their opinion.

Sometimes the children can directly communicate their preferences, Ouba explained, but when they cannot, it is the responsibility of the staff to watch for signs of the child's desires. The grid system, she stated, is designed to allow for children to recognize their preferences and to provide for flexibility and change. If a child, in the many ways young children have for making their feelings and preferences known, communicates unhappiness about being scheduled to a particular activity, material, group, or teacher, it is easy to locate them elsewhere.

Continual Institutional Analysis

At La Borde, continual institutional analysis occurs formally in daily meetings as staff and boarders hash out policies and procedures that are and are not working. In the A.P.A.T.E structure, analysis occurs across the schools, as the similarities and differences across the sites provide a point of comparison that can call into question a policy or practice at any site. Another site for analysis occurs at The

Tavern of Ali Baba, a voluntary monthly meeting of the parents across the five schools in which they can gather to talk about their parenting experiences and about issues in the education of their children. Similarly, every morning at Gulliver, parents are offered a chance to gather around coffee and talk with Ouba and one another as they drop off their children. These gatherings bring together the parents of children at the schools with and without identified disabilities. Both Herrou and Ouba described these meetings as essential to combat the isolation felt particularly by parents of children with disabilities, and also to provide a normalizing sense that "many children, not just children with disabilities, are like that." They socialize the parents whose children do not have identified disabilities into more inclusive understandings of how they and their children are similar to and different from others in the school. One father with a child with a disability cried as he described to us his child being invited for the first time to a birthday party. In addition, these meetings are sites for feedback about their experiences with and concerns about their children's schooling. Herrou and the directors also welcome individual meetings with parents and as well, facilitate meetings with treatment teams related to the health and well-being of the children at the school. Again, these are sites for institutional analysis.

Within the school, the analysis also occurs in weekly meetings as staff come together to try to understand what things at the school work for whom. The teachers need to be willing to talk honestly about difficulties that arise in their daily practices, things that failed, and children or teachers who are struggling with an aspect of how things are done. The teachers we interviewed talked about the trust they built up over time through the leadership of Herrou and Ouba. One of the teachers, Aurélia, explained that understanding teaching as a collective effort facilitated the teachers' recognition that no one teacher or no one activity would meet the needs of every child: "Each of us leads our activities with our experiences, our personality, our personal or professional experiences. What the children are bringing will not reflect on us the same way." Recognizing that a group is more powerful and potentially inclusive than a team made it easier to acknowledge individual preferences and limits. Ouba elaborated on the importance of recognizing the limits:

> We are not almighty, we have our limits, and I think it requires a certain intellectual maturity to say that we don't have a magic wand and that we're not going to transform the children. And on top of that I think that there is something else. It's a—it's still a collective work that we're doing together regarding the, the team—the A.P.A.T.E. teams. I mean during meetings there is an authorization originating from the management allowing the colleagues to talk about their feelings and their frustration.

Two of the teachers, Aurélia and Mélanie, described their ability to speak honestly as "professionalism" and stated that Herrou made this possibility easier by expressing her own difficult feelings and behaviors in the meetings. They noted that the schedule rotations allow them to frequently see one another work, and they accept that it is professional to speak to one another about what they see:

Aurélia:	I mean, we're not in the judgment of—sometimes we can say, "Well, I would have done otherwise for this"; "Wait, you got angry a little today." We can say those things—
Mélanie:	Yes, we say it to each other—
Aurélia:	"You're yelling a lot today."
Mélanie:	Yes, that's right.
Aurélia:	I mean, we say the things face to face. Actually. I think that hearing colleagues' reflection impels us to be better, as if there are things a bit—like—some unpleasant things could have been [in the research film]; it might still have been constructive for our professional reflection.

In reflecting on the importance of decompartmentalization, Ouba described that to be stuck with a single teacher all day who finds a given child to be difficult would be unfair to the child and unprofessional. She described the team professionalism this way:

> During a meeting she can say, she can talk about her frustration and say, "Well I feel incompetent because I tried this, I tried that and it didn't work," so we can either give her ideas or tell her, "You need to stop now and someone else will take care of this child." Because children have affinities with the adults too, and we can't force a child to like a teacher; it's not possible. Hence the richness here, there are several profiles of people so the child can feel at ease with one person and not with another. It's completely normal.

A culture of talk about "what works" is, if not a formal practice in a given school, a common teacher practice. What stood out to us as unique and powerful at Gulliver is how this identification of what works functions deliberately as part of the decompartmentalization of functions. Recognizing that teaching and learning are best conceptualized as occurring "at the collective level of the team" and that people bring their singularities of experiences, preferences, limitations, biases, and skills to any given situation means that, as Mélanie pointed out, the focus can remain on the situation rather than the child.

Relay

Throughout the interviews with Ouba, Herrou, and the teachers, they referred to "the baton relay" or the "relay" as a central feature that made it possible for the teachers to acknowledge that their work was difficult and that sometimes they were not up to it. In short, the baton relay refers to developing a culture in which teachers are able to say to one another, "I'm not up to this today; can you take over?" The baton relay requires that Ouba schedule enough staff that they overlap and can step in if asked. Aurélia described the way the teachers bring this support to one another:

> We have a freedom of speech that we allow to ourselves precisely to ease off on the pressure. When it's hard, we tell each other. When we can't put up with a child, we also tell each other. We take over from each other. We try to listen, be attentive—I think that it's a state of mind to take over from one another and say to yourself, "I am also a good professional when I recognize that I reach saturation and I can't do anything any more with this child," and this doesn't mean that I'm failing.

Aurélia elaborated further, stating that the ability to serve the children well is a function of the team rather than an individual teacher: "I mean at some point it can look like a failure but we see that at the collective scale of the team and say, 'My colleague is going to take care of it. That's for the better if it works.'" Additionally, the teachers described having the comfort to say to one another, "Let me do that," when they saw another teacher struggling. About the baton relay, Herrou said that the baton relay requires the group to provide:

> common support even though there are singularities, particularities. It's only on this condition that we are a group, but we also are a group because there is something common, there's diversity, some of the same and some not, likewise together. And all of this work, so we are a made-up group and indeed there's something possible when together. We get discouraged when alone and if we're together we don't get discouraged or if we do, the baton is taken over by someone else, so we work a lot through baton passing.

Here, Herrou is using the image of the baton relay in the sense of actually taking over from one another. But she is also using it in the more figurative sense, describing the way that when a group deliberately agrees to function as a group, the passing of the baton participates in the creation of a team that is stronger and more capable of supporting difference than any one individual.

The Emotional Work of Difference

Across our talk with the teachers and administrators at Gulliver, we were struck with how readily they spoke of how challenging the emotional, intellectual, and physical labor of working across difference is. The Gulliver staff was not sentimental about the work, and they were not shy about the ways the differences impact them in challenging ways. They did not deny that particular disabilities are hard for a given child or those around the child, including themselves. In the films we made, we saw moments when teachers were not at their best. When we asked the teachers about these moments, they were matter of fact about the inevitability of anger, frustration, conflict, and disagreement. They were not surprised by their own or the children's' hard feelings or big emotions, stating simply, "We're human." Herrou said that because the French are "are very, very influenced by psychoanalysis," they would rather have someone "crying, expressing his anger rather than someone who—who—who doesn't express anything, doesn't bother anyone. We are scared of expressions—of—unexpressed emotions."

Herrou, drawing from what she characterized as a psychoanalytic perspective, communicated her belief that allowing her teachers to express their hard feelings and to explore them together meant that the teachers did not have to unconsciously act out those hard feelings and were able to make other choices. She described, for example, a meeting in which a teacher talked about being very angry with a parent:

> There was the case of a father who is very unpleasant, who doesn't say hello, etc. And one [teacher] was saying "I don't even want to talk to him anymore, I don't even look at him anymore." And there I said, "We understand, because it's really unpleasant. It's not about accepting it, but about trying to understand what's happening to handle the situation better," hoping that she also changes her own behavior but without telling her "It's not good. It's not the way to do it." No. So the person who said "He irritates me. He doesn't say hello." I know why it echoes with her. She says, "Oh no, I can't do that" and I say "It's okay," and there's another colleague who says, "You don't have to talk to him. We will do it." And I am convinced that she still will be the one to do it.

In this example, the described difference—a father acting differently than the teacher expected—is not related to anything described as "disability." Herrou was clear with us that disabilities are differences that are not the same as other differences, but that differences characterize all of us, that some differences are more difficult than others at a given time or in a given circumstance, but that a certain level of difficulty is not inherent to the difference. The grumpy, angry, or sad father and the people around him surely struggled in some ways and at some times and not at others, with the difficulties created by the difference—being or not being grumpy or angry or sad. Working with children with disabilities is difficult, but so is working with children in general, and so is working with people whose experiences, priorities, and temperaments are different from our own.

When we asked Ouba how she thinks about working with children with disabilities, she answered by telling us the story of her job interview with Herrou. She started out by describing how, as an immigrant, she had great difficulty contending with the prejudiced assumptions of prospective employers. She went on:

> So I get to Cécile's office and stand still saying, "Listen madam. I'm not here to make you lose time, so I'm Lebanese and don't have [French] nationality, so if you still want me like that I will sit. If not there's no need. I will leave." And there Cécile laughs and tell me "I like you already. Sit down. I think we'll get along well together." So after that, she speaks to me and says "I like you but I have a question to ask you. Can you work with disabled children?" Hmm—I mean, hmm—It's something I felt on the spot but I didn't tell it to Cécile because it was too strong a feeling. I told her afterwards; when our friendship set in I allowed myself to tell her. … My husband and I, we had chosen France to live in because we always used to hear "The country of Equality, Fraternity." And there when Cécile told me "Would you mind working with disabled children," I thought to myself "But what a question to ask!" I just left a country with—we had war, bombs, people I picked up off the street as I was first-aider for the Red Cross and so forth, and I am asked such a foolish question! But a disabled child and a non-disabled one, in what way is this different? It's still a child!

Ouba then told us: "I have spent 17 years of my life under the falling bombs, so I don't have the same vision anymore of the world, of children, families and even of problems. It's different afterwards."

What Ouba showed us in her story was a shift in perspective that we saw throughout our time at Gulliver; it is a way of seeing disability as only one among many labels, experiences, limitations, difficulties, and opportunities through which humans struggle and make meaning in life. These differences make life challenging, especially insofar as we are dependent upon others for connection, support, and love. They are also opportunities to live more expansive, creative, and surprising lives.

In any institution, as Guattari (2015) described, hierarchical structures and rigid roles defend its inhabitants from negative affective responses to differences they experience as challenging, frightening, confounding, or out of their control. As Herrou, Ouba, and the teachers made clear, having these responses is human. These responses are, for the most part, out of our control. We impose them on one another, confirming our worst tendencies in blaming and attempting to control the other.

What we see clearly at Gulliver is the need for institutional structures that allow us to actively think about and make a resource out of our responses to difference. We need to understand that inclusion as collectivist integration offer adults and children, families, teachers, siblings, and the larger community a chance for each of us to recognize our need for the life-giving potential of living in the presence of otherness.

Notes

1. For further reading, see WHO & World Bank, 2011; UNICEF, 2013: Children with disability, 2013; GCE 2014; UNESCO, 2016).
2. Nicolas Philibert made a 1997 documentary about one summer's play production, entitled *Every Little Thing (La Moindre des choses)*. The film is available on YouTube (https://www.youtube.com/watch?v=CKJp9JLqTkY) and provides a powerful look into parts of daily life at La Borde.
3. For more on La Borde, see Boldt and Valente, 2016.

References

Armstrong, F., Armstrong, D., & Barton, L. (2016). *Inclusive education: Policy, contexts and comparative perspectives*. New York, NY: Routledge.

Artiles, A. J., Kozleski, E. B., & Waitoller, F. R. (2011). *Inclusive education: Examining equity on five continents*. Cambridge, MA: Harvard Education Press.

Barral, C., & Velche, D. (2010). *ANED country report on equality of educational and training opportunities for young disabled people*. Utrecht, NL: Academic Network of European Disability Experts.

Birley, J. L. T. (2002). Famine: The distant shadow over French psychiatry. *The British Journal of Psychiatry, 180*(4), 298–299. doi: 10.1192/bjp.180.4.298

Boldt, G., & Valente, J. (2014). Bring back the asylum: Reimagining inclusion in the presence of others. In M. Bloch, B. B. Swadener, & G. S. Cannella (Eds.), *Reconceptualizing early childhood care and education: Critical questions, new imaginaries and social activism* (pp. 201–213). New York, NY: Peter Lang.

Boldt, G., & Valente, J. (2016). L'école Gulliver and La Borde: An ethnographic account of collectivist integration and institutional psychotherapy. *Curriculum Inquiry, 46*(3), 321–341.

Dosse, F. (2010). *Gilles Deleuze and Felix Guattari: Intersecting lives* (D. Glassman, Trans). New York, NY: Columbia University Press.

Ebersold, S. (2015). Accessibilité, politiques inclusives et droit à l'éducation: Considérations conceptuelles et méthodologiques. *ALTER-European Journal of Disability Research/Revue Européenne de Recherche sur le Handicap, 9*(1), 22–33.

Ebersold, S., Plaisance, E., & Zander, C. (2016). *Ecole inclusive pour les élèves en situation de handicap.* Accessibilité, réussite scolaire et parcours individuels. Conseil national d'évaluation du système scolaire-CNESCO, Conférence de comparaisons internationales.

European Agency for Special Needs and Inclusive Education. (2016). *Country policy review and analysis: France*. Odense, DK: Author.

Fage, C., Moullet, P., Consel, C., & Sauzeon, H. (2017). France. In M. L. Wehmeyer & J. R. Patton (Eds.), *The Praeger international handbook of special education [Vol. 2]*. Santa Barbara, CA: ABC-CLIO.

Global Campaign for Education, Handicap International. (2014). *GCE report: Equal right, equal opportunity: Education and disability*. Retrieved September 2, 2018 from http://www.right-to-education.org/resource/gce-report-equal-right-equal-opportunity-education-and-disability.

Guattari, F. (2015). *Psychoanalysis and transversality: Texts and interviews 1955–1971* (A. Hodges, Trans.). Cambridge, MA: MIT Press & Semiotext (e).

Haug, P. (2016). Understanding inclusive education: Ideals and reality. *Scandinavian Journal of Disability Research, 19*(3), 206–217. Retrieved February 10, 2019 from http://doi.org/10.1080/15017419.2016.1224778

James, A. (2014, June 4). *French psychiatry under occupation: Saint-Alban*. Retrieved September 2, 2018 from https://attemptsatliving.wordpress.com/2014/06/04/french-psychiatry-under-occupation-saint-alban/

Kanter, A. S., Damiani, M. L., & Ferri, B. A. (2014). The right to inclusive education under international law: Following Italy's lead. *Journal of International Special Needs Education, 17*(1), 21–32.

Lemoine, P. (1998). *Droits d'asiles*. Paris, FR: Editions Odile Jacob.

Meyers, T. (2014, June 3). *Jean Oury and clinique de La Borde: A conversation with Camille Robcis*. Retrieved September 2, 2018 from http://somatosphere.net/2014/06/jean-oury-and-clinique-de-la-borde-a-conversation-with-camille-robcis.html

Office for Civil Rights, U.S. Dept. of Education. (2012). *Civil rights data collection*. Washington, DC: Author. Retrieved September 4, 2018 from https://www2.ed.gov/about/offices/list/ocr/data.html

Philibert, N. (Director). (1996). *Every little thing (La moindre des choses)* [Video file]. Retrieved September 2, 2018 from https://www.youtube.com/watch?v=CKJp9JLqTkY

Plaisance, E. (2007). The integration of "disabled" children in ordinary schools in France: A new challenge. In L. Barton & F. Armstrong (Eds.), *Policy, experience and change: Cross-cultural reflections on inclusive education* (pp. 37–51). Dordrecht, NL: Springer.

Plaisance, E. (2009). *Autrement capables: Ecole emploi, société: Pour l'inclusion des personnes handicapées.* [*Otherwise able: School, employment, society: For the inclusion of people with disabilities.*] Paris, FR: Otherwise.

Polack, J-C. (2011). Analysis, between psycho and schizo (A. Goffey, Trans.). In E. Alliez & A. Goffey (Eds.), *The Guattari effect* (pp. 57–67). London, UK: Bloomsbury.

Senate Report (Sénat Rapport). (2012). Inspection générale de l'Éducation nationale, & Inspection générale de l'administration de l'éducation nationale et de la recherche. *La mise en oeuvre de la loi du 11 février 2005 dans l'éducation nationale* (No. 2012–100) (p. 165). Ministère de l'Éducation nationale. Consulté à l'address http://cache.media.education.gouv.fr/file/2012/95/7/2012-100_-_rapport_handicap_226957.pdf

Tobin, J., Wu, D. Y. H., & Davidson, D. (1989). *Preschool in three cultures: Japan, China and the United States*. New Haven, CT: Yale University Press.

United Nations. (2006). *Convention on the rights of persons with disabilities*. New York, NY: Author. Retrieved September 4, 2018 from https://www.un.org/development/desa/disabilities/convention-on-the-rights-of-persons-with-disabilities.html

United Nations Educational, Scientific and Cultural Organization. (2017). *School violence and bullying global status report*. Paris, FR: Author. Retrieved September 2, 2018 from http://unesdoc.unesco.org/images/0024/002469/246970e.pdf

UNICEF. (2013, May 13). *The state of the world's children 2013: Children with disabilities*. New York, NY: Author. Retrieved September 4, 2018 https://www.unicef.org/sowc2013/

Valente, J. M., & Danforth, S. (2016). *Life in inclusive classrooms: Storytelling with disability studies in education*. Occasional Paper Series 36. New York, NY: Bank Street College of Education.

Watermeyer, B., McKenzie, J., & Swartz, L. (Eds.). (2018). *The Palgrave handbook of disability and citizenship in the Global South*. New York, NY: Palgrave Macmillan.

World Health Organization. (2011). *World report on disability*. Geneva, CH: Author. Retrieved September 4, 2018 from http://www.who.int/disabilities/world_report/2011/report.pdf

Contributor Biographies

Gina Marie Applebee earned her BS in Geology from the College of Charleston, and MS in Marine Geophysics at the University of Missouri. After losing her retinal vision, Gina worked on implementing Inclusive Design for Learning at Missouri, where she helped raise access awareness and earned an Educational Specialist degree in Science Education. Gina developed non-optic sight, or pan-sensory synesthesia (PSS), that provides her with visualization based on other senses. Currently, she is pursuing a PhD in Integral and Transpersonal Psychology through the California Institute of Integral Studies.

Christopher Bass is a doctoral candidate in the Department of English at the University of Illinois at Chicago. He has more than a decade's experience teaching English Language Arts and executive functioning skills in both Chicago Public Schools and the Chicago suburbs. His research interests include Disability Studies, Literacy Studies, and English Education.

Usree Bhattacharya is Assistant Professor in the Department of Language and Literacy Education at The University of Georgia. Her research is inspired by questions of diversity, equity, and access in multilingual educational contexts, especially as they pertain to the circulation of English as a "global" language. Her work illuminates the role of discourses, ideologies, and everyday practices in the production and reproduction of hierarchical relations within educational systems. She has recently published in the *Journal of the Sociology of Language* and *Language Policy*.

Gail Boldt is Professor of Curriculum and Instruction at Penn State University. She is the program coordinator for Language, Culture, and Society graduate emphasis area. She is a practicing child psychotherapist and the Editor-in-Chief of the Bank Street Occasional Paper Series.

Dorothy Bossman spent a decade as a secondary language arts teacher, until she was sidelined by multiple sclerosis. After leaving the classroom full-time, she completed a PhD in Teaching, Learning, and Teacher Education at the University of Nebraska. Currently, she writes and engages in research related to disability studies and language arts pedagogy and teaches classes in composition at the University of Nebraska at Omaha.

Curt Dudley-Marling spent 33 years working at universities in the US and Canada before retiring from Boston College in 2014. He has published over 100 articles and book chapters and 14 books, much of this work focusing on literacy and Disability Studies. Taken as a whole his scholarship stands as a critique of deficit thinking that locates school failure in the minds and bodies of students with disabilities.

Patrick Graham is Assistant Professor at Western Oregon University, where he coordinates the Deaf and hard of hearing education program. He advocates tirelessly to ensure equity and excellence in deaf education, especially in the early grades. Dr Graham has provided many different presentations and collaborated with teachers of the deaf all over the world. His interests are in disability studies, multicultural education, and culturally sustaining pedagogy. In his little free time, he enjoys hiking and spending time with his family.

Jennifer Hensley earned undergraduate and master's degrees at Arizona State University and a doctorate at The University of Georgia, working with Dr. Joseph Tobin on the *Deaf Kindergartens in Three Countries* research team. Jennifer's research interests are bimodal-bilingual heritage language users, educational anthropology, culture and (dis)ability, and early childhood deaf education. She is the Director of Deaf Programs at the Arizona State Schools for the Deaf and the Blind, and Deaf Mentor Program serving families with deaf, hard of hearing, and deaf-blind infants and children.

Jaehee Kwon is Assistant Professor of Early Childhood Education in the Department of Curriculum and Instruction at The State University of New York at Fredonia. After working with immigrant families and their children in South Korea, she has studied the experiences of culturally and linguistically diverse families and their children in U.S. schools. Her research is also focused on instructional practices that support teachers in understanding diverse young learners and their families.

Kyunghwa Lee is Associate Professor of Early Childhood Education in the Department of Educational Theory and Practice at The University of Georgia.

A former kindergarten teacher from South Korea, Kyunghwa examines various sociocultural constraints, including taken-for-granted beliefs and practices that support and hinder teaching and learning in early schooling. Her recent research has focused on investigating early childhood teachers' beliefs about typical and atypical child development in general and their perspectives on and practices for young children with Attention Deficit/Hyperactivity Disorder (ADHD) in particular.

Sera Mathew is Assistant Professor in the Department of Community Engagement at Point Park University, Pittsburgh. She teaches Qualitative Methodology courses and researches educational inequalities and access in historically marginalized communities. She conducts research on women's education narratives with a specific focus on the Dalit community in Kerala, India.

Jooeun Oh is Assistant Professor of Early Childhood Education at Incheon National University in South Korea. She has explored young children's socialization and peer culture in preschool. In particular, her research focuses on the voice of children from diverse backgrounds by paying attention to their perspectives different from the teacher's. Her studies challenge the deficit views of children from marginalized groups in the United States and in South Korea and explore pedagogies for inclusive education.

Melissa Sherfinski is associate professor of early childhood and elementary education at West Virginia University in Morgantown, West Virginia. Prior to that, she has worked as both a general and special educator in inclusive public school classrooms in Wisconsin. Her work on homeschooling spaces stemming from her dissertation has been published in *Curriculum Inquiry* and *Gender, Place, and Culture*. Her most recent research on inclusive educational practices in pre-kindergarten settings has been published in the *International Journal of Inclusive Education* and the *Journal of Early Childhood Research*.

Peter Smagorinsky is Distinguished Research Professor in the Department of Language and Literacy Education in The University of Georgia's College of Education and Distinguished Visiting Scholar at the University of Guadalajara, Mexico. At UGA he is the faculty advisor to the *Journal of Language and Literacy Education*, edited by doctoral students in his department. His experiences with Asperger's syndrome, chronic anxiety, and obsessive-compulsiveness have led to explorations of how to develop supportive contexts for neurodiversity, conducted through the lens provided by Vygotsky's work in defectology.

Joseph Tobin is The Elizabeth Gerrard Hall Professor of Early Childhood Education at The University of Georgia. He was trained at the University of Chicago in anthropology and child development. His research centers on comparative studies of preschools in different cultures. Tobin's books include *Preschool in Three Cultures* (1989), *Preschool in Three Cultures Revisited*, and (with Akiko

Hayashi) *Teaching Embodied: Japanese Preschool Teaching as Cultural Practice* (2015). He recently led a research project on "Deaf Kindergarten's in Three Countries: France, Japan, and the United States."

Joseph Michael Valente is Associate Professor of Education at Penn State University. He is also the co-Director of the Center for Disability Studies and core faculty in the Comparative and International Education program. Dr Valente was the co-Principal Investigator of the video ethnographic study "Kindergartens for the Deaf in Three Countries: Japan, France, and the United States" funded by The Spencer Foundation and author of *d/Deaf and d/Dumb: A Portrait of a Deaf Kid as a Young Superhero* (Peter Lang).

Xiaoying Zhao recently completed her Ph.D. in the Department of Educational Theory & Practice at The University of Georgia and has accepted a position as an assistant professor of Early Childhood Education at Illinois State University. Her research interests include children's civic, political learning and agency in diverse spaces. She has published in *Teachers College Record, Theory & Research in Social Education, Citizenship Teaching & Learning*, and *Social Studies Education Review*.

Index

A

B

C

D

E

F

I

K

L

M

U

V

Disability Studies in Education

GENERAL EDITORS: SUSAN L. GABEL & SCOT DANFORTH

The book series Disability Studies in Education is dedicated to the publication of monographs and edited volumes that integrate the perspectives, methods, and theories of disability studies with the study of issues and problems of education. The series features books that further define, elaborate upon, and extend knowledge in the field of disability studies in education. Special emphasis is given to work that poses solutions to important problems facing contemporary educational theory, policy, and practice.